Wake Up Dead Man

TM

Wake Up Dead Man: Afro-American Worksongs

from Texas Prisons *Collected and Edited by Bruce Jackson*

Harvard University Press   Cambridge, Massachusetts   1972

First, for those who made the songs and lived that world that needed them: Chinaman and Alex and Ten-Four and Smitty and Bacon & Porkchop and Lightnin' and Cowboy and G.I. and Tippen and Tippett and Spring and C.B. and Matt Dillon and Filmore and all those others, named and unnamed.

And, second, for all my other friends in their own prisons, some public, as this one, and others terribly or beautifully private, just all over the place.

"Myth does not want to face the fact that violence is meaningless. That is my definition of myth—giving meaning to what has none."
—René Girard

Acknowledgments

Always there are so many people to thank.

I want to express gratitude here to the people who taught me what I needed to know to be able to do this work, friends who perceived informational deficiencies and politely tried to rectify them, and other friends who offered welcome and useful talk or havens from talk, and the many friends and colleagues who supplied advice and encouragement, offered respite from grimness, supplied vital information, warned me of specific pitfalls, or were just friendly when it was friendship I needed more than anything else. This book gestated a long time and a lot of people were involved.

In these days—with so much happening or being revealed in our exploding and littered world—it is hard to sit down and complete this sort of job, but three things helped it along: a promise I made Alex and Chinaman and a few other friends that I would finish this to document the dignity of their anguish, a debt to several friends and a few institutions who helped it along in various ways, and the scholar's peculiar demon of never being free of a body of data until he manages to give it away to others. So, here, I give it to you. And I thank the following people, whose contributions were in no regard identical or equal or similar, but without whom this wouldn't have happened or gotten finished:

Roger and Mary Abrahams, John Q. Anderson, George and Marilyn Beto, Benjamin A. Botkin, Billy Lee and Dorothy Brammer, David Freeman, John Gagnon, William F. Koock, Anne and John Kriken, Alan Lomax, Danny Lyon, Judy and Leon McCulloh, Mack McCormick, Tary Owen, Americo Paredes, Pete and Toshi Seeger, Alf Walle, and D. K. Wilgus.

This project was supported by a number of organizations and committees. I want to thank Harvard's Society of Fellows (especially the three men who were chairmen while I was a member: Harry T. Levin, Wassily Leontief, and the late Crane Brinton) and the Milton Fund (of

Harvard University); the University of Texas for a Ruby T. Lomax Fellowship (summer 1965); the Research Foundation of the State University of New York, the Graduate School of SUNY at Buffalo, and the Institutional Funds Committee of the Faculty of Arts and Letters of SUNY at Buffalo (for various grants, part of which supported fieldwork and manuscript preparation, 1967–1969).

I especially want to thank Dr. George Beto and his staff for innumerable courtesies, much kindness, and the present of friendship; Judith McCulloh and Norman Cazden for the splendid job they did with the difficult musical transcriptions and Diane Christian of the English Department of SUNY at Buffalo for her help with the indexing.

The comments preceding a few of the songs, part of the Introduction, and Appendix 1 have been published, in different form, as articles in folklore journals. I have corrected, revised, and updated most of these sections. I am grateful for permission to revise and use "Prison Folklore," *Journal of American Folklore*, 78 (October–December 1965), 316–329; "What Happened to Jody," *Journal of American Folklore*, 80 (October–December 1967), 387–396; and "Prison Nicknames," *Western Folklore*, 26 (January 1967), 48–54, and "Prison Worksongs: The Composer in Negatives," *Western Folklore*, 26 (October 1967), 245–268, both by permission of the Regents of the University of California.

I wish to acknowledge with thanks the following: The Texas Department of Corrections for permission to reprint its pamphlet, "A Brief History"; The University of North Carolina Press for permission to quote from Howard W. Odum and Guy B. Johnson, *The Negro and His Songs* and *Negro Workaday Songs* (Chapel Hill, 1925 and 1926 respectively); The President and Fellows of Harvard University Press for permission to quote from Newman I. White, *American Negro Folk-Songs* (Cambridge, Mass., 1928); and Mack McCormick for permission to quote his notes (in a private communication to me) on the Moore Brothers.

I would also like to thank Alan Lomax for permission to quote from his notes to *Negro Prison Songs from the Mississippi State Penitentiary* (Tradition TLP 1020); from the unpublished papers of his father, John A. Lomax, at the Archives of the University of Texas; and from John A. and Alan Lomax, *Our Singing Country* (1941), *Negro Folk Songs as Sung by Leadbelly* (1936), and *American Ballads and Folk Songs* (1936), all published by the Macmillan Company, New York; from "Governor Pat Neff," words and music by Huddie Ledbetter, collected and adapted by John A. Lomax and Alan Lomax, TRO- © copyright 1936 and renewed 1964, Folkways Music Publishers, Inc., New York, New York, and the Essex Music Group London, used by permission; from "Tie-Tamping Chant," collected, adapted, and arranged by John A. Lomax and Alan Lomax, TRO- © copyright 1941 and renewed 1969,

Ludlow Music, Inc., New York, New York, and The Essex Music Group, London, used by permission; and from "Mama, Mama," collected, adapted, and arranged by John A. Lomax and Alan Lomax, TRO- © 1941 and renewed 1969, Ludlow Music, Inc., New York, New York, and the Essex Music Group, London, used by permission.

I once regarded authors' notes about their editors in book prefaces as perfunctory exercises, but the gracious and skilled attention paid me and my manuscript by Denise L. Thompson of the Harvard University Press have convinced me of the foolishness of that assumption. She found and cleared away an embarrassing wealth of moments of textual opacity, factual inconsistency, and stylistic clumsiness, for which she has my honest thanks.

Some of the notions in this book were first worked through with students in my Afro-American Folklore seminars at Harvard and Buffalo, and in the course of talks and discussions at the Harvard Comparative Literature Conference, Simmons College, the 1965 American Folklore Society Meeting, the Smithsonian Institution, and the University of Montana.

Mrs. Rae Korson and Joseph Hickerson, of the Archive of American Folk Song at the Library of Congress, helped in many ways; I am especially grateful for the enormous amount of material they assembled in 1964 to prime me for my first Texas trip. The staff of the Texas Archives at the University of Texas graciously guided me through the enormous mass of material in their John A. Lomax collection.

I apologize to anyone I forgot above; I love you anyway.

Two more statements of gratitude, neither of them really expressible:

—to Sue, for everything,

—and to those to whom this book is dedicated. There have been friendships that have developed in these last several years I shall long treasure. There is no way I could briefly express my feelings toward and about those men and their situation, and I shall not dishonor them by trying.

Contents

Photographs

(*Following page 44*)

1. Squads and mounted guards on turnrows, returning to fields after lunch on the Johnny. Ellis. May 1967.
2. Benny Richardson (foreground, with axe). Ellis. March 1966.
3. Waterboy and treecutters. Ellis. August 1965.
4. Group crosscutting. Ellis. August 1965.
5. Group crosscutting. Cowboy is second from left with axe back; Chinaman is just in front of him, axe in. Ellis. March 1966.
6. Logging. Ellis. August 1966.
7. Chinaman. Ellis. August 1965.
8. W. D. Alexander and Chinaman. Ellis. August 1965.
9. Chinaman's admission mug photo. TDC 1942.
10. Mack Maze. Ellis. August 1965.
11. Guard watching cotton pickers. Ramsey 2. October 1968.
12. Cotton pickers. Ramsey 2. October 1968.
13. Cowboy at prison rodeo. Huntsville. October 1968.
14. Louis "Bacon and Porkchop" Houston. Ramsey 2. August 1965.
15. J. B. Smith. Ramsey 2. August 1965.
16. Flatweeding—Chinaman closest to camera. Ellis. March 1966.
17. Flatweeding—clodbusting. Ellis. March 1966.
18. Flatweeding. Ramsey 1. August 1965.
19. Logloading. Henry Petty, Francelle Norah, Joe Willie Austin. Ellis. March 1966.
20. Burning brush and logs. Ellis. August 1965.
21. Main hall and guard picket. Ellis. October 1966.
22. Looking out to front hallway. Ellis. October 1966.
23. Flatweeding squad heading in. Ellis. 1966.
24. Peckerwood Hill. Ramsey 2. July 10, 1965.

(All photographs, except no. 9, are by the author)

Introduction

The songs in this book are all used in connection with work activities by black inmates in the Texas Department of Corrections.

They are used so the singers can make it.

This is a book about worksongs and worksongs only. I have not included the many blues and spirituals and gospel songs recorded during the same field trips to the Texas prison farms. I have not excluded those songs because I have anything against them—but they do not belong here.

White and Latin-American inmates (about 70 percent of the convicts) do not sing these songs, nor do they have any body of metrically functional songs of their own used in similar fashion. The songs and the style of utilizing them are the property of black inmates exclusively, and they are clearly in a tradition going back beyond the importation of the first Negro slaves to the Virginia Colony in 1631. The tradition may have been influenced by other cultural streams, but it is still exclusively Negro, and closer in function to African than any other American genre.

The adjective in the subtitle of this book—*Afro-American*—refers to the music, not the musicians. The correct or acceptable term of referral for non-white Americans of partial African ancestry has varied so much in the last decade (colored, Negro, Afro-American, black) that I fear anything I use right now (when black is mandatory) will be dated by the time this book is actually printed. But for the *music* the adjective holds: the songs are sung by Americans, the style and function are African in origin. (For discussions of those African backgrounds, see Brandel, 1961, Merriam, 1962, Nketia, 1963, and Waterman, 1948).

With a few exceptions these songs do not exist in the outside world. Some of those few are outside songs temporarily residing in prison, others have been exported and settled in the repertory of popular performers like Paul Robeson or Harry Belafonte or Leon Bibb. The men who sing these songs in prison do not care to carry them outside when they are released.

The songs, sometimes, are compellingly beautiful; the subject, always, has to do with making it in Hell.

The songs are sung outdoors. They are sung in daylight only. They do not exist in the dark. But it is darkness or absence or lostness or vacancy or deprivation that they are about. This is not an easy thing (or group of things, if you think those words are different) to sing about. But neither is it an easy thing to experience and perceive, and the singing somehow makes it a little more bearable.

The constants of the songs and of the life are the most obvious: the guards, escape, sentence length, geographical places remembered or longed for or heard of, sickness, death, guns, the work itself. The songs concentrate on the devices and forms of control, and the manifestations of impotence. The language of the songs is highly concrete, but the themes are not; the themes are negatives: things like unlove and unfreedom and unimportance.

The songs are devices some of the men developed to keep their heads straight or busy enough to avoid giving in to that vacancy, that emptiness, that terror. They are a weapon against a kind of death not much appreciated by those of us lucky enough or clever enough to run free or to imprison ourselves by our own choice only.

What I want to do in this book is present some of these songs on a printed page (and suggest places one might hear them, which is always necessary), and offer some comments about how they are built and how they fit into the world. That means distancing ourselves for the sake of objectivity. I would rather not do that, but there is no other way for outsiders.* Abstracting or generalizing or distancing is necessary for outsiders just as it is necessary for someone who wants to make sense of what happened to him in the past; that is the way we grope toward a kind of sensibility—life has too much detail for that, it is too busy, really. The only other way of finding this particular sensibility is to be in the midst of the experience itself, which I urge upon and wish for no one.

There is an important difference in our approach to art song and folk

* The best way to appreciate these songs is to be in the place they are made; I realize that option is open to few people—fortunately. The third best way to appreciate them is to hear them on phonograph records; I have listed a number of these in the discography. The second best way to appreciate them is to see and hear them in a movie designed to permit such appreciation. There is one—*Afro-American Worksongs in a Texas Prison* (Folklore Research Films, 1966)—edited by Dan Seeger. The filming was done by Dan and Toshi Seeger, with audio and miscellaneous work by Pete Seeger and myself, during a March 1966 recording trip. It includes the versions of "Jody" and "Grizzly Bear" by Richardson in this book, as well as several other songs led by Chinaman, Cowboy, and others.

song. Art song requires that we perceive the nature of the art involved; folk song requires not only perception of the art but also the generating or supporting musical, social, and historical contexts. Folk song is not simply textual, but *contextual*: it does not exist—save for historians and scholars—on pages in books, or even on shiny black discs. It exists in a specific place at a specific time, it is sung by specific people for whom it has specific meanings and functions.

When we—outsiders all—look at printed versions of songs that have both physical and psychological functions, we have to know something about those specifics, otherwise we are looking at words and staves, nothing more.

It is not enough to look at words and staves only.

Which is to say: before you can make any sense of a body of folk songs, the world that made them must be sensible to you, the people who made them must seem as people to you. I considered beginning with a chapter about the convicts, their prison, and their songs, then decided that the men who made the songs tell that story very well themselves. The first chapter, for that reason, consists of pieces of conversations from tapes made during the years I did fieldwork in the Texas Department of Corrections.

THIS BOOK AND THESE SONGS

In 1962 and 1963, while a graduate student at Indiana University, I did some folklore and sociology research in prisons in Missouri and Indiana. I decided it might be interesting to visit a southern prison system to see what had happened to the various traditions documented by John A. and Alan Lomax and Herbert Halpert in the 1930's.

Once I decided that I wanted to observe in some detail the tradition of the convict worksong, it was necessary to make a decision: one prison culture with several visits or several prison cultures with one or two visits to each place. I decided against the sort of broad and fast sweep done by the Lomaxes in the South in the 1930's—they had done that already and I saw no need to do it again.

I wanted instead to spend a lot of time in one place to try to relate the songs to the culture in some detail, to get some idea of relevance and change—which required repeated visits and establishment of relationships with a group of performers. For background on Texas I first examined manuscripts in the Library of Congress Archive of American Folk Song (by John and Alan Lomax and Herbert Halpert), and later spent a week going through the John A. Lomax papers in the Texas Archives at the University of Texas in Austin.

The questions I had were these: What does the process of change (or for that matter, the concept of consistency) mean and how does it occur in a genre that is extraordinarily plastic? Where does change occur? What sorts are these and how much is idiosyncratic with individual performers and how much with all the performers in a given place at a given time? What are the differences in individual and cultural consistency? What is the meaning of the word *song* when it is so plastic a thing? What do these songs *do* for the people who sing them? Questions like that.

Some of the answers are in this introduction, some in the comments of the convicts on the songs, some in the introductory notes to the various songs. Some are still waiting for clarification.

In the spring of 1964 I told Crane Brinton, who was then chairman of the Society of Fellows at Harvard, that I would like to go on a long field trip through part of Appalachia, Missouri, Arkansas, and Texas. He approved of the idea, and he arranged a budget for the trip.

I wrote Dr. George Beto, Director of the Texas Department of Corrections (TDC), saying simply that I wanted to so some folklore recording in some units of the department. He invited me down.

We met for the first time the morning of July 1, 1964. We chatted awhile about prisons, about why Harvard was funding me, about academic places. I learned he had previously been president of Concordia Seminary and Concordia College, that he'd taken an M.A. in Classics and a Ph.D. in Education at the University of Texas—hardly the typical prison administrator.

Abruptly, he asked me how I wanted to work. I said I would prefer to wander about the prisons, find people to talk with, then record and talk without interference from guards or wardens or anybody.

He thought about that a moment, then said he thought that was a reasonable way to work. He picked up the phone and called Sidney Lanier, then warden at Ramsey Unit. Dr. Beto told Warden Lanier that I was coming down, that I might have some peculiar requests, but that I was to be granted every courtesy and not interfered with in any way.

Which is just how it went. In all the years I did research in the TDC, whether I was studying folklore or homosexual behavior or criminalization patterns, the same courtesy and freedom were there for me. No one ever questioned any request for access or information—I was permitted to examine any files I wanted to examine, I could wander in the fields or cellblocks without having guards fritting about.

(Some years later, I told Dr. Beto how surprised I had been that morning and how much greater my surprise was when I found out that it was true, for prison officials are usually secretive about their places and terribly suspicious and afraid of outsiders. His answer was characteristic of the man: "How can we find out what we're doing wrong if we don't let people like you in to tell us?")

My field notes from those first trips are full of amazed comments. Amazed at the richness of the folk traditions still there (hundreds of songs and stories and conversations with white and Latin and black convicts) and the insanity of the weather ("5 July: 105° in the shade yesterday before it rained. Cloudy for a while, then the sky broke open and it shot up again. Today on Retrieve at noon the temperature was a little over 100°. It is so humid that nothing dries. After a shower at 6:30 this morning I hung a towel on the foot of the bed—it is just as wet now, nine hours later . . . On the road from Ramsey 1 to Ramsey 2 I passed three black buzzards strutting around a runover skunk. When the car came near they waddled to the fence at the side of the road; when I was past, they waddled back to their feed. A fourth sat on a fence and then flew in a circle, then settled back on the fence again. He reminded me of a supervisor on a highway construction gang . . . Chiggers and ticks and it went up to 105° this afternoon. Blisters on the bottoms of my feet . . .").

On that first trip—in 1964—I had only a Tandberg 64, so I couldn't record outdoors. For all the later trips I had portable equipment, usually a Uher and later on a Tandberg 11, so I was able to record in the actual work areas.

The Texas Department of Corrections consists of 14 prisons (Central, Clemens, Coffield, Darrington, Diagnostic, Eastham, Ellis, Ferguson, Goree, Huntsville ["The Walls"], Jester [formerly Harlem: its name was changed in honor of Gov. Beauford Jester], Ramsey, Retrieve, and Wynne), about one hundred thousand acres of land (most of it along the Brazos and Trinity rivers), about two thousand employees, lots and lots of cattle and horses and hogs and dogs.

And a little over twelve thousand inmates.

Some of the units are specialized: Goree is the women's prison, Jester is where men are sent for pre-release counseling shortly before discharge, Ellis is for the more dangerous troublesome recidivists, Diagnostic is a processing unit for new arrivals, Ferguson is for young first offenders, Wynne is for physically and mentally disabled inmates (including geriatric cases).

I visited on at least one occasion every unit of the Texas Department of Corrections except the Coffield Unit up in Anderson County (which was still under construction during most of the times I worked there). For this study, however, most of the collecting was done at three institutions: Ramsey (Camp 1 and Camp 2), Ellis, and Wynne. It was obvious that there was no point in collecting worksongs among the first offenders at Ferguson, the women at Goree, or the men preparing to go home at Jester. But Ramsey and Ellis are both units for multiple recidivists, men who have been in and out for a long time (or highly troublesome for a short time), Wynne has some of the oldest inmates in the system and I was able to find there some versions of songs (though not at work) that were in all probability older than the versions I was able to record in work situations elsewhere; the Wynne population served as a kind of check when I tried to date some of the songs.

There is not a different song repertory on the different units; the active repertory seems always to have depended more on who were the competent song leaders around and what songs *they* liked to lead. Musically, Ellis and Ramsey represent the entire system—every inmate I recorded at either of them had spent time on at least one, and usually three or four, other units of the system.

There is enough population movement within the prison through transfers and reassignments and new locations on new sentences so that the repertory is metastasized throughout the recidivist units, so I felt it more useful to concentrate on a few places than to skip around.

I confess a certain ambivalence toward the songs and their contexts, and that ambivalence no doubt has had some effect on how I gathered the material and how I think about it and how I present it to you.

I experience an unmediated loathing for the context that made and makes these songs possible and necessary. I refer not only to the long tradition of slave labor in this country, but to the entire American correctional system, which to me is still based—in practice, if not in theory—on ancient sensibilities of revenge and punishment. I have written rationally in the past, and probably shall again in the future, about the American prison situation—what it is and what it does and what it means and what it needs (for example, Jackson 1966 and 1968)—but my inner sensibility tells me that I really shouldn't do that, because the institution itself is not rational and the social impulse that leads us to maintain such institutions is not rational. But so little in human behavior—individual or institutional—*is* rational that one can hardly point out the lack of it as the anomalous evil in any structure. But prisons are *bad*. They don't do what we tell ourselves they do. They do more harm than good. It is that simple.

I know about the internal problem with prisons—that they are populated on the whole by people who, on the outside, did not choose to behave in very nice ways. But that is no reason for us to maintain an institution that is neither nice nor fruitful. The arrogance we have in setting up and maintaining such institutions should demand at least that we do a decent job with them, that we are humane about what we do to people.

As prisons go, Texas has a good prison system now. It didn't always have one, a decade or two back it had one of the worst, but now it has a relatively good one.* Many sane and humane men work within that system and try to make it something good, but they always work uphill, and regressive forces ultimately bestow on their labors something of the sense Sisyphus must have had after one of his clumsier days.

So there is that.

But at the same time I am (obviously) drawn to the songs and the people who make them. On a cognitive level there is in them something significant of a world I hope will never be mine or be that of anyone I ever know (but there is that academic catholicism that tells me that any thing affecting so many people must be part of my world in some way), and that something is there in strikingly human terms (which has its appeal, in these days of rancor and murky rhetoric).

Our world is so dissonant, so incongruous, it is hard to make sense of things sometimes yet it is so tempting to try: Beauty must be kept, wherever it is found, however foul its genesis. Les Fleurs du Mal are still flowers.

There is a beauty in these songs, some hint of which one may get by being able to read music, some hint of which one may get by perceiving the poetry of the words, but it can be realized only by being there, by not only hearing the sounds of a few score axes cracking into green tree-trunks simultaneously, but feeling the vibration coming back through the ground, while the wind in the branches supplies a second meterless voice, with somewhere in the background the crackling of the big fire burning brush, the clanking of trucks and tractors, and the voices of the men rising out of there somewhere, out of all that movement, the sounds betraying the often simple or banal words.

The songs are dying and the reason they are dying is good: the world of the convict in a state like Texas is becoming one in which the songs are no longer *needed:* the big trees are not cut down very much anymore, much field work is done by machine, what is done by hand is done by groups who aren't interested in what seems to many oldtimeyniggerstuff, the guards' brutality has been cancelled.

But, as I said, there is also a beauty to them, the songs, and it is always sad to see things of beauty becoming anachronisms or curiosities. Given the choice, of course, I'd throw all the songs and all that art out for any improvements. But I'll also take this moment to document it so it isn't lost forever.

Since the Civil War, by the way, there have been predictions and observations about the moribundity of the worksongs, and some might

* For an informed essay on the situation of the black man in Southern prisons during the first half of this century, and for several excellent sources on the technique of paroling black convicts to wealthy landowners in a cruel parody of slavery, see Van Deusen, 1944, "The Negro Criminal," pp. 138–157.

claim my predications are no less premature than all those others. For a hundred years observers have smugly concluded they were the last to get to audit the functional group songs of the American black man (see Brown, in Jackson, 1967-B, pp. 110–119).

But I think such predictions now have a great deal more validity to them than ever before. Worksongs are related to a cultural nexus almost totally nonexistent in this country; only in artifically maintained anachronisms does it still exist; prison is one of these, and prison is changing.

Sung outside such a context, by singers white or black, there is an academic flavor—a sense of *performance* or a sense of doing a song-*with*-a-context, which is quite different from being in a context and singing a song. The difference may seem small; it is not. One is a historical operation, however aesthetic may be the motivation; the other, a life situation.

Wake Up Dead Man

"One Lost Valley": The Singers on Their Songs

These comments were taped in various Texas prisons during the period 1964–1966. Usually, a new heading indicates another speaker, another time, another place than the one just concluded.

I DONE SOME DAYS

Don't nobody know how much hell a man catch back in this lost valley. When I was leavin' the Walls a man shook hands with me. He said, "Well, friend, where you goin' I don't go much." That was Mr. Jesus Christ shook hands with me. This place was one lost valley. People with no understandin', don't know what understandin' is. They think a man is a mule, don't ever get tired. But I done some days I'd sooner been dead in hell with the wicked than hear that damned big bell ring. They'd make you go ahead on from sun to sun.

Until Mr. O. B. Ellis come along in the '40's and got trailers we walked all over these farms. Stand out in the field and eat your dinner. Be raining hard like it was before, raining hard like a cow pissing on a flint rock, wash the beans out a your plate. You got to keep on working. Rain didn't stop you, cold didn't stop you. There wasn't no sick. You don't have a fever of 202, then you ain't sick. Used to work people dead in the underworld down here. 'Cause one man couldn't keep up with it.

WE DIDN'T HAVE TVs

Take about twenty-five years ago; there's a lot of changes to today in this institution. Most anyone can make it here now. You take twenty or twenty-five years ago, anyone couldn't make it. It was hard days. I been here now ten years and a few days and I been here before. I started out workin' [here] in 1938. That was my first time. I'm a fourth-time loser and I been here ten years on this sentence already.

1

I've saw a lot of radical changes made in this institution. There's a lot of differences from those times and these times.

We used to couldn't get a drink a ice water here. They didn't have water coolers in the building. Another thing they didn't have in the building: they didn't have fans. We didn't have TVs in the building.

And we didn't ride to work. We walked or ran. Slowly trot. Mostly run. Have shotguns on the horses as well as pistols. You get worked to death or beat to death. That's why we sang so many of these songs. We would work together and help ourselves as well as help out our fellow man. Try to keep the officials we was workin' under pacified and we'd make it possible to make a day. Be tired sometimes, be nearly too tired to eat sometimes, but we would make a day like that.

RESTING MULES

During that time we walked everywhere we went. Seemed to be that as fast as you could walk you still wasn't walking fast enough. Men would be hollering, "Get out from under my horse's feet." And the old horses, sometimes, the horses dropped on their feet from exhaustion. The horse fall down; but the man still going on. That was, of course, years back. All that's changed now.

It's funny to me, though: I would see them rest a mule, I'd see a man get whupped because he didn't rest a mule—but *we* couldn't rest. I couldn't figure that out. We just had to go ahead. One of those things.

THAT HOE!

Take work where now they put ten tractors in a field. They didn't have those years ago. We went in there and did what they doing with tractors now with a hoe then. That hoe! I never seen so much work with a hoe, so many things did with a hoe, in all my life till I come in prison. Man, we'd even build roads with hoes, just hoes alone and we'd build a road. A big old wooden tamper made out of a stump with a two-by-four nailed onto it, two men use it to tamp the road down and make a road.

The way we had to walk and work then, these young men here couldn't take it. Too soft. They ride to work now, they ride right up to the woods and get off. We had to walk seven or eight miles to work, seven or eight miles back in to dinner, same thing after dinner, same thing at quitting time. That was from sunup to sundown. Wasn't no letup. And we worked Saturdays. They just stopped working Saturdays I think in '52. Used to work a half a day on Saturdays.

A HEAP SEE

(in the narrow area of shade alongside a brick boilerhouse one outrageously hot September afternoon, a little while before the sun dips low enough to develop the shadows the enormous fall mosquitoes wait for, and everyone without an outside job is driven inside the cellhouses)

I tell you.

> A heap see and a few know
> A heap start and a damn few go.

It's just like that. It goes down the road like this here, that's just the way it start out. You see and don't see, *yeah* and don't *yeah*. 'Cause if you want to live a long time and stay healthy that's what you do, 'cause another dead man can't help you. You actually can't tell how nothing happened. You got to go on the side with them if you want to live a long time. But if you just don't care nothin' about your life and throw it away, that's just the way it happen.

You may be cuttin' wood and they say, "He was cuttin' wood and a tree fell on him." All the rest of the guys say, "How did he get killed?" Say, "He was cuttin' and got trapped by a tree."

You can't never tell. Things I actually seen here and things that actually happened—you got to lie, you got to lie. You tell just how it happened, a dark cloud will go over you, and nobody never know what became of you. You runned away. "Did he get away?" "Yeah, he got away."

He got away in a shallow pit grave somewhere, in the woods somewhere. Ain't nobody can come back and tell a report but *them*. So that's the way that goes.

When I first came here I was in A-number-one shape, A-number-one shape.

"What you doin'?" a passing guard says.

Ah, yessuh, boss, I'm just gonna make a few old crazy sounds for Mister Bruce. A little later on when the sun gets low and we get all them other guys together.

"You goin' home this weekend?"

No suh, I don't think I'm goin' home this weekend. The warden told me I had to work, boss, I can't make it.

The guard walks on.

See, that's what I tell you. When you been in this joint a long time you know how to address all the officers and bosses like that. That boss, he asked me was I goin' home this weekend. He know I can't go home. So

I told him, "No, boss, I can't go. I got to work this weekend." That's the way things go like that. You get smart with 'em or something like that—

Another inmate passes by and slows his pace to hear what we're talking about.

—man, where you goin'? Man, didn't nobody send for you and I can't write for you. I can't write. Now what you want?

"I want one of your cigarettes," the inmate says.

I ain't got 'em. I left 'em in the shop.

The inmate leaves.

Boy, that guy, he somethin' else. He outer space, man. He outer space. Have to play with different inmates like that with things like that. We trade the dozens, talk about one anothers' people. Different things we be playin'. The dozens like that just to pass away the time. There's nothin' else to do. That's how you have to do it to make time. Some of it is happy and some of it is miserable, all like that. That's the way to make time in the penitentiary.

BOSS SUCH

I eventually got where I could handle a axe with the pros, with the next man. I could handle a axe as good as the next one once I got started on it.

Cane was something I had never been in. The man wouldn't let me cut wood or pile brush, but soon as we got in the cane and started cuttin' down the cane I went to work. Cane was lots bigger than what we got here. This is sorghum, that was pure ribbon cane down there because at the time they had a big syrup mill and a sugar mill down in Sugarland.

They had windstorm and rain just before we went in to cut and it had the big cane twisted every way. I'm the first man he calls. "Old Big Four, you get your cane knife and go yonder way. I want to see some daylight up through that cane. I want low stubbles and high tops."

I said, "Well, you asked me about the wood, and I hadn't never cut no wood. I haven't never cut no cane."

He said, "Shut up, you born in the canepatch. Go on and cut me some cane."

And that was the only time I ever thought about leaving.

I had promised my mother, who was living at that time, that I wouldn't run off. It was the first time I'd been in prison. I'd said, "I won't try to run off." Well, I was dead set on running off because the man rode me all that morning. I didn't know nothin' about cuttin' no cane. I was cuttin' it too high, supposed to cut it low. Because they didn't dig that cane up, they dug it out and shook the stubbles around it after the cane was cut and covered it over so it would grow out next year thicker. By me not knowing how to cut cane I had them long blisters in my hand and they burst and was bleeding. My hand was bloody. I couldn't hardly hold that cane knife in my hand. And I was set to go. I said, "I'm gonna try it."

He called me, said, "Old Big Nigger." I wouldn't say nothing—I was dead set on leaving.

Right on the edge of the woods and the temptation from this man riding my back. I says, "I'm gonna hafta go."

And he rode up there and said, "When I calls you, you tells me to go to hell or something."

I said, "I'm goin' on, boss."

"All right. Tell me somthin'."

Sergeant rode over and told him, "You quit foolin' with that man. You been ridin' that man all the mornin'. That man been workin' and you been ridin' him all the morning."

He said, "I know. I just like to fool with a big nigger." Well that *did* burn me up. And I'm all set to go. As soon as the sergeant rode off he called me over and he said, "Mister Big Nigger, would you please come over here, please, sir." He said, "How come somebody didn't tell me about you? You come here heavy. First time the sergeant ever got on me about eatin' out a convict." And I didn't understand the man and he said, "You haven't got the cut." Said, "Now you get back over there and you can straighten up the cane. If you want to, that is. I'm not tellin' you, just *if* you want to."

And I didn't know all the time that this man, you have to argue with him just like you argue with a inmate. That's the way he carried his squad. That's the only way you could stay in this squad, you had to joke and argue and squabble with him like you do another inmate. I didn't take no chances on that because you know, at that time the punishment was a little cruel.

Soon as the captain rode over, he said, "Captain, I want to show you my number one lead row," says, "I'm gonna make him my number one lead row." Says, "Mister Big Nigger, would you please come over here, please sir." He say, "You see him there, Cap. He look too big now," say "I don't know what I'm gonna do with him till I get that weight off a him." Say, "He's too small for a mule and he's too big for a nigger."

I looked at the man and I got tickled. You know, snuff runnin' all down out a both sides of his mouth. And the boys say, "He gonna ride you till you squabble back with him."

And I say, "Well he got the wrong partner. I'm not gonna squabble back with him—he got a shotgun and a .38 on his hip."

He say, "Oh, that's Boss Such. He'll carry you like that all day from now on."

And he did until I caught on to him. See, everybody was squabblin' with him, you know, and he'd just fuss and squabble. "What's the matter with you? You all crazy? You all go over and work. Soon as that captain come over here I'm gonna loudtalk him." Then soon as the captain come over he say, "Well, how's everything in your squad Mr. Such?" He tells him, "Captain, I wish you'd help the rest of us farm this land." Say, "My squad about to do all this work." Soon as the captain would ride off he'd get on us. "I thought you was gonna eat cheese." He says, "Captain ain't gone too far, I'll call him back."

And I watched the man, you know. I caught on to him. I said, This man, he never bust nobody, he never give nobody to the captain, nobody never got busted in his squad. Everybody worked. Now he never ride nobody, but he just steady meddle and agitate all day long. He just steady pick a lot of squabble. He liable to see one lookin' out there and he call, "Go on to Dallas, I ain't lookin'. Go on." Tryin' to encourage him. Even on Saturday mornin', we'd have to work half a day, they count his squad out to him and he'd say, "Twenty seven of 'em. Hold it up there. Captain, can I have three more, please, sir?"

"What for, Boss Such?"

"I figured if I had thirty I could find one dissatisfied in the bunch and I'd get a chance to bust me a cap at a runnin' target. Well, maybe I can get one out of this 27." Then he'd holler 'em off, he'd encourage one: "Go on to Dallas, I ain't lookin'."

The man was real comical but everybody loved him after they got on to him. And when they changed wardens he quit because I think he had some difference with the warden over the years and when the warden changed he said, "Well, you men do the best"—only time I heard him stop and talk sensible without a lot of foolishness—"you men do the best you can. You've all made me a good hand and I'm proud I got a chance to carry you. And I want you to try to straighten up and get out of here. Do the best you can under this man. I'm quittin' because I don't like him. That don't meant that you don't like him." He said, "I don't like him because we've had our differences, but he's a fair man. You all do the best you can."

I think that's one boss from the Red Heifer days that I don't think there's an inmate in the system could say a hard word against him, and that's rare up against the bosses that carried squads in the Red Heifer days. 'Cause back in that time a man's life wasn't worth no more than a cigarette. When he'd go out he didn't know if he was comin' back in or not. He's liable to get shot down on the turnrow 'cause he left a patch of grass.

Durin' that time the bosses couldn't buy his squad anything, but all of 'em did. A lot of times if a man didn't have smokin's, just about every man that caried a squad would buy his squad tobacco and put it on their water wagon. Buy 'em maybe a carton a Bull Durham or something to dish out to the squad. So they would have something to smoke. And he'd always tell his squad when he had some, "Go on over to the water wagon. The water boy liable to have a barrel a chock over there, you don't know."

Somebody say, "I don't want water, I want eats."

"You go on to that water wagon. I think he got some chock in that middle barrel." And they dish out the Bull Durham to the whole squad, you know. Durin' that time just about every boss that carried a squad would buy the squad tobacco because so many of us didn't have anything.

When he come in the building he had to come right by the wings. The picket sets right in the middle of the building—the old type building with the tanks. He'd come in there and they'd say, "Here comes Boss Such." He'd hide his pocketbook and say, "I ain't got nothin'." He'd come in the door saying, "I ain't got a nickel, I ain't got nothin'." He'd slip his money out 'fore he come in, buy his snuff and ease back out. That's the only way he could get out 'cause they'd catch him when he come in. That was back before things got modern. See, they didn't have any young men in the system then, all was old men.

THE MAJOR

You know the old major on this camp, don't you? They call him the Sidewinder, they call him Mr. Matt Dillon, they call him Mr. Blockbuster, Niggersplitter. They call him all them names. He got more names than anybody. He's been here about eleven or twelve years. Me and him came in about the same time. He's a terrible guy. He's a good man, you know, but he don't take too much puttin' on. *Nobody* puts him on. 'Cause he don't just go behind a pistol: he'll throw that pistol away and get with you. He's what you call a roughneck. I've seen him do it. Terrible. And he'll come and go off with you.

He'll carry you off and say, "Don't you think I'm hiding behind that damned pistol. I'll go with your damned ass anywhere. Just me and you." He say, "If you whip me you can go home." He's there!

He's gotten up in age, he's in his forties. I knew him when he was in his early thirties. He was a warhorse, a wildcat. Not only niggers. Mexicans, whites, anybody else.

Some sonofabitch say, "If I had a pistol I could be like that." But he ain't like that.

Now some have been like that just because they got a pistol and they're up there on that horse. But he's different. He'll tell you, "Do you think I'm doin' this or do you think I'm sayin' this because I got a pistol or because I'm a major?" If you tell him "yeah," he'll carry your ass twenty miles away from here. He's a fierce man, just like that wood or concrete out there. And he'll go a while.

BLACK ANNIE

The truck that Bud Russel drove or carried was called Black Annie. I remember when I was a kid we used to go up to Fort Worth, we lived nearby, and a lot of times my mother would carry me up there. Everybody knew when they was gonna pick up the chains. The news was spread that Bud Russel was pickin' up the chains, because it was somethin' to see. During that time they had a old outdated thing. I couldn't describe it now because that's been almost forty years ago. He would have the guards lined up with machine guns. The convicts would come out chained by the ankles and by the necks and by the hands. Come out in what we call a "Chinese shuffle." Everybody would be there to watch Bud Russel take the men to prison. And it used to be like that for years. After I'd been in my early teens, we used to see it when he pick up his chains. I never knew I'd be a victim of the same circumstances. The truck that goes to the farms from the Walls is called Black Betty.

BLACK BETTY

Instead a having the bus like they have now, they had just a barred truck. A bed on it with a cage like a bear is in it. They called that Black Betty. It'd go to the county jail and get you and bring you to Huntsville. They had one that'd bring you out here on the farm. They called that Black Betty. It'd *bring* you but it wouldn't *take* you like it do now. It'd bring you here but it was up to you to try to get away from here. If they turned you loose, if you lived to get loose, it was up to you to walk up to the highway and try to catch that bus.

THE BAT

They used to had to get a order to whip you, you know. The doctor'd come down to check your heart to see whether you could stand the whipping or not. And then if you could stand it, he'd okay it. And if you couldn't, he wouldn't. A whole lots a times the captain just didn't pay no attention to whether he'd say you could or not. He didn't care whether you lived or died no way. So they'd spread you down. Man would stack up five a them red bricks like them there up on somethin' solid and haul off and hit it with that bat and bust a brick at the bottom. Well, you know about how it'd take a man's skin. He hit the top brick and bust the one at the bottom. A man had to take all that kind a stuff. Whole lots of them had the whole back of their britches cut out.

You could tell all them guys what got whipped. They couldn't set down, had to lay on their stomach and other than that he couldn't lay no other way. All the back part back there would be just raw blood.

But a man went to work after the whippin' was over with.

Some would run off. They'd know what day the whippin' was coming up and they'd run off to keep from meeting that day set for the whipping.

One time Captain Powell was whipping a boy with that bat and he kept a hollerin', "Oh lordy, oh lordy!" And then finally he bust him again and he say, "Oh lordy, Captain!" And captain said, "I thought you'd get around to me directly." Cause he wanted him to know that Jesus wasn't whippin' him, it was *him* whippin' him. And Jesus couldn't help him neither.

Old days. The man would step down out a his saddle and reach and get that bat, pull it across under his boot and step back over you, your britches down, then he'd rare back and bust you one.

As the leather'd leave, the hide 'd leave with it.

THE UNNECESSARY KILLING

You walked everywhere you went. Food was bad, livin' conditions was bad. But the restrictions was lots easier than they are now, which led to a lot of killing. Now gambling is eliminated. And during that time there was a lot of cash, everything was cash money. They didn't have scrip like they have now. There was a lot of killing. A lot of killing over little petty debts, petty thefts, money, hustling money to gamble. Then you could buy whiskey from the trusties traveling back and forth outside. Used to be whiskey hid all in the fields, buried in the fields. Stash it out where you could go get a pint when you needed it. Send a trusty to get it. But when they eliminated gambling they eliminated a lot of this killing. In fact, it eliminated just about all the unnecessary killing they had in the system then.

JESSE JAMES SEEFUS

Jesse James Seefus and Johnny Thomas: they'd pick nine, sometimes a thousand pounds a cotton a day. *Apiece.* Two men, they used to put those two men in a patch and let 'em pick against each other and they'd pick eight or nine hundred pounds. That's before four o'clock. That's been ten or twelve years ago. Old Jesse James Seefus still here. I think he's on Retrieve.

The average man back in those days, generally, he'd pick around five or six hundred. That was steppin' it. On the average he'd pick three-fifty, four hundred. And he have trouble there if he didn't get up there and give a bit more weight. Things have changed now. They've got a little modern. But back in those years a man would pick three or five hundred pounds for himself and he'd pick four or five hundred pounds for his sissy, so you wouldn't tell how much he was picking. Every time he goes to the scales the captain would holler, "Ring that bell!" What he meant was ring that bell when you weigh up over a hundred. Wasn't nothin' for a man to go up to the scale and weigh up a hundred and sixty, a hundred and eighty pounds.

The man who picked the most cotton in a week would get a carton of cigarettes. The way it turned out there wasn't but two men gettin' it: Johnny Thomas and Jesse Seefus. They'd break the cotton wagon down with their cotton. They'd look in their sack to see if they was weighin' up a log in there. 'Course a couple of incidents did happen of weighing up a dog. Had a dog follow the boys, they weighed up that dog in the cotton, tryin' to get that weight.

THE COTTONPICKING PRIZE

They used to give prizes here in the penitentiary for picking cotton. What broke me up from pickin' for a prize was Captain Stewart, O. O. Stewart. He had me and a old boy named Willie Lawrence and another boy out of Fort Worth called Foots. He had us pickin' for a prize. I came out of Five Hoe and got in One Hoe with him. We picked. First round, Willie come up with one hundred and five and I had one hundred, Foots had ninety. I seed how he was getting it and I said, "I'll go and get me some too." Next round I had a hundred and ten and Willie had ninety. So he said, "How you getting it?" I said, "Just like you all is." Boss ain't said nothing about how is we picking. So that night I think we wound up with Will, he picked four-something, I just did get five, and Foots was back behind there. The captain called us up to the picket. He said, "Give me my three best cotton pickers here." Me and Willie Lawrence and old Foots, we all went up there. "Seein' the way you picked, I'm gonna give you all the prize." He say, "You all split this." He gave us a quarter.

After that I never picked for no prize, that broke it up.

COTTON PICKING WITH A CADDY

My favorite song was the woodchopping song, "Let the Hammer Ring." I used to watch one old boy. That's when I first come to the penitentiary. I had my mind set on running off. Everytime that we'd get in the bottoms and get to cutting wood and he'd get up in them tall trees, in them bushes, he'd get to singing that song. Watching for the man, naturally, I wasn't going to run off. I'd say, "As soon as he leave and get on the high and going in, I'm going." Well, I never *did* run off, but I guess that's what struck me on that song so much. Well, he just sung it beautiful. An old boy named—what was the boy's name? He was a cottonpicking man, he'd pick seven or eight hundred pounds of cotton. What was his name now? Kind of funny name. I forget his name now, it's been so long. But only two of them could be picking a bale of cotton, used to pick them together. One of them's still in the system, old Jesse James Seefus. Jesse *picked!* I believe that boy is named Tony. They picked them together. Tony's out now. They put them in together and Jesse James made him quit the field. Because he picked about nine hundred pounds of cotton. He had a caddy, you know. (Cotton picking with a caddy, that's what he had, man. He had them packing the sack and packing his cotton. And he'd be clean. It wouldn't be like when some of them weighed up. That's how some of them got their nicknames: they'd weigh up rocks and this and that, they'd weigh up dogs. They'd have an old pet hound out there and they'd weigh that hound up in the sack. They had that old hound out there that they weigh forty or fifty times a week. They'd put him in there to make their weight and that old hound would never say a word until they dumped him out of the sack.

WEIGHING UP

I weighed up a jackrabbit one day. Happened to catch him sittin' down in the middle and I picked him up and put him right in my sack.

BEARTRACKS I

Of course any name that's given to anybody, eventually it'll wind up that everybody knows it, including officers and the inmates. The same as our warden right now: the inmates refer to him as "The Track" or "Beartrack," even officers refer to him as Beartrack or the Track—but only when they're *not* around him. You couldn't pay one to say, "How are you Captain Beartrack," when they're around him. Man, that would be detrimental.

In one instance they did. A new one came on the farm on Ramsey and the warden told him to stand in the hall. All he heard in the Walls before they sent him down on the farm was, "You goin' down to Captain Beartrack on the Ramsey. He'll hold you." When the major came through and asked him, "What're you doin' out here?" he says, "Captain Beartrack got me waitin' down here."

He says, *"Who?"*

"Captain Beartracks."

Well, he went and got the warden. Warden said, "Who did you say had you waiting out here?"

"Captain Beartracks."

Man, the warden blew his top. If anybody had any thoughts of callin' him Beartracks they lost it after that session.

BEARTRACKS II

I seen a guy call him Beartracks and that like to been the end a him. He knows they call him that but nobody ever call him it.

Because that name rings all over America I guess. I guess there's people everywhere done heard talk about Track. He walks like this here, and that's the way a bear do. When he jumps on somebody—that's the reason they call him the Bear. He's got big feet like a bear. That's why they put in that song: "He make tracks in the bottom like a grizzly bear." I don't know how big he is now. I hear he done lose weight. I haven't seen him in about four years. I know he used to be real big.

He asked me one time on this farm—I was arrested—he said, "What do they call me?"

I said, "I don't know, sir."

He said, "You lyin'! You know what they call me."

I said, "Some of them say—"

"What do you mean *some* of them say?" He made me tell him.

I told him, I said, "Somebody called you Beartracks."

"Where you hear it?"

I said, "Some a them guys what's gone home."

'Cause if I told him it was somebody here it might a got somebody in trouble.

THE ORIGINAL JACK O DIAMONDS

Back in years back there used to be a lot of gambling in the system. And cooncan—mostly a Negro game, played with ten cards, you make eleven—he always called "Jack O Diamonds is a mighty man." That was his song. They even made up a worksong from the Jack O Diamonds. And everybody knew him as Jack O Diamonds because he's a pretty shrewd card player. Playin' monte, which is another Negro game in gambling, and you can lose a fortune on it if you don't know what you're doing, cooncan, cotch. Diamonds being the high suit in cotch, same as in poker. That's how this man got his name of Jack O Diamonds. He was a big powerful man, a hard worker. Could outwork just about anybody in the field that stand up under him. And back in those days the work was hard.

That was the *inmate* Jack O Diamonds. Now the *captain* Jack O Diamonds, he got that name when he killed Jack O Diamonds in a fight. Jack O Diamonds jumped on the warden and he was forced to kill him and they give him that name of Jack O Diamonds. Two of the inmates give him that name and eventually it grew on him.

THAT WAS A KILLER (two inmates rapping)

—You talkin' about coldblooded. Now if Bart Rader catch you first, he'd bring you back, but if Jack O Diamond catch you he'd say, "You'd better pray, son, 'cause this is your last time." He'd want to beat you to that Brazos, him and his German Luger.

—That's right.

—If he catch you, boy, a dark cloud would go over.

—That was a killer.

—That's the onliest bully in Darrington. On Darrington State Farm. He's dead now. That's a old captain. He told the Devil, said, "If you stick me with that pitchfork I'm gonna shoot you with this smokin' forty-four." He runs Hell now, don't he?

—That's right. They chained him down to die 'way over at Central Unit. Central One, that's where he died at. Chained down in bed.

JACK O DIAMONDS

Jack O Diamonds. His name was Powell, Jack Powell, and they named him Jack O Diamonds. That's all of the names they got was what the inmates give to them.

Jack O Diamonds carried a German Luger automatic. If a inmate run off, he'd tell the boss, "Don't hurt him, bring him back just like you find him." But if he run up on you he'll kill you and he ain't gonna shoot nowhere but right between the eyes. "Ohhh," that's the way he talked, "ohh, you won't see your mama no more."

"Oh Lord, captain, don't kill me!"

"You won't see your mama no more." And would kill him, shoot him right between the eyes. Most of Peckerwood Hill on Darrington was Jack O Diamond's men. He killed every one of them. He didn't allow no boss to kill no one that run off. Whenever they kill them they had to do some tall explaining, say they tried to mug 'em or do like that. But if *he* run up on you, he's gonna kill you. And he carried that German Luger automatic. And he say, "Huhhh, you won't see your mama no more, I'm gonna shoot you right between your eyes with my Luger." A black German Luger automatic. He was a great big man. I seen him take and unhitch a mule and take the singletree and whip a man down to the ground if he plowed a crooked row.

SAID HE HAD A GRAVEYARD OF HIS OWN

Jack O Diamonds was the man that was on the Central farm back in '47, '46, '45. And was coldblooded. He killed, you know. Said he had a graveyard of his own. I think he did because he killed about six whiles I was there. And he could a got a lot more than that killed 'cause he used to try to make building tenders kill them. And they called him Jack O Diamonds and he talked real funny: "Uhh. Killll, killl!" That's all he knew, you know. And he died there. One day while we were getting ready to go to work when he was sitting out there and he turned as white as the snow. Something wrong with him. I was on my way out to work and I was looking right at him. Trembling with his hands up in the air. "I hate for all these niggers to see me die. Well, I don't give a damn: I seen a many a them die."

And many of them was hollerin', "You got *that* right."

That was in '48.

HOW JACK O DIAMONDS DIED

He turned white, you know, real white. White as a sheet. And he set there on the bench. A bunch them old niggers was going by, you know, and one said, "Captain Jack, you feel all right?" Everybody know he's about to die.

He says, "I don't need nobody to ask me how I'm doing. Especially you niggers. I know you want me to die. Well I'm gonna live 414 years and a quarter!"

He died right then. The line was going out to work and he sit right there. But didn't nobody know he was *really* dying, they know he was changing colors.

About ten minutes after we went out in the field the waterboy came out there and said, "Captain said Jack O Diamonds died." Man, a bunch a them was glad.

"Jack O Diamonds is dead! Hooray!" He was so cold, you know, he was a field captain, then he was made a picket boss. He was made picket boss because he got old and sick.

I went there in '46. All I would hear was Jack O Diamonds this and Jack O Diamonds that. I was stuck out going to chow and he was up there in the picket and I had heard all that talk but never seen him. One day I told the building tenders, "Can I go eat?" The line was going in. Building tender said, "Have one here, Boss Jack." He said, "Kill him, kill him. Get the blood from him. All I want to see is that red blood coming from his black ass." I broke and run.

He made them building tenders beat them guys. One day he said, "I want you to ride him." That was his word, "Ride him." Building tender say, "So-and-so doing this," and he say, "Well get you something and *ride* him." And everytime he see you up there he just jump up and pat his hand. He want to see some blood, you know. And one day they had this building tender hooked up over there, them guys were sticking him, killing him, you know. He called the building tender: "Ride him, old Fork!"

Somebody hollered up there, said, "Boss, it's the other way around the way they see it. They is riding old Fork."

"I don't give a damn who is riding who, all I want you to do is ride. Just to see somebody ride him, just so it be some riding."

JACK O DIAMONDS AND BIG RED

Captain Powell was knowed everywhere. They called him Jack O Diamonds. They had to hold him in his bed when he died.

Why?

The men he killed. He said, "Big Red!" Said the Devil was on his bed. They had to hold him down.

RAP (two oldtimers, talking about things then and now)

—You ain't supposed to cop out to nothin'. If the judge catch you flyin' a kite you supposed to plead not guilty.

—That's right. The facts of the business: you ain't *never* guilty.

—That's right. Let 'em *find* you guilty. Sometimes a lie help you and sometimes a lie stick you. You know how it go.

—Ol' buddy, you never tell the truth. You never do tell the truth.

—You think everything they say I steal, you think I be doin' all a that?

—You probably not stole, but you misplaced it, so they had to give it some kind a name.

—I guess you right about that. Well, you know, if there's something layin' around, like you go into the kitchen and catch the boss away, now ain't it better gettin' a nice big porkchop and stickin' it in your pocket and some light bread and goin' on outside way around the corner and eatin' it? Anything you steal. Don't you know it's better than to eat it at that old table. You know how that go. What you think about the old time and the new time.

—I'd rather wished it so I could call back the old time 'stead a this new time. The way it is now.

—Why would you want to call back the old time?

—It was easier for a man to make it if he wanted to make it.

—Was it easier on stealin'?

—It was easier both ways. Now they got night watchmens and day watchmens and everything else. A man can't get away with nothin'.

—On top a that, they got walkie-talkie. What you think about that?

—A walkie-talkie: you just can't beat that.

—You can't beat a walkie-talkie. Anywhere you go: walkie-talkie, walkie-talkie.

—Man already got it. Whenever it happen, he's already listening.

—He may be right around the bend with the walkie-talkie. You could beat 'em when they would have to come five miles back after you. Now they's just got a walkie-talkie. They tell 'em: "Be on the lookout." You may be cuttin' right into 'em then. And what to you think of them old halicrafters, them planes that lit down anywhere?

—Helicopters they call 'em.

—Yeah, you know what I'm talkin' about.

—Helicopters. They just light down on you anywhere.

—Anywhere, anywhere. I always run the dogs and I could always know whichaway I could beat 'em because of that. Can you beat the dogs?

—Yeah, the dogs can be beat. But you can't beat them walkie-talkies.

CHANGES

You know how Col. Lee Simmons do? You know what his orders was? "Bring 'em back on the water wagon." That was his orders: to bring 'em back on the water wagon. But that Mr. O. B. Ellis, a long man come from Tennessee, a man that looked under-eyeded at you and say he will lead better than he will drive. And then come the high-powered Dr. Beto, a man with the wide wings. You know how he brought out this system, a man with few words, a man that's always glad to shake hands with a convict.

Mr. Beto, he stopped these longtimers working on these turnrows. Many a man with broken veins in his legs like a woman that had a kid—

"Many men has lost their lives," another inmate sitting nearby said.

Couldn't keep up on the turn rows. Shot down. But Dr. Beto stopped that. He stopped 'em from huggin' the shotguns. The shotgun don't go off no more on the accident. You know how that was. An accident.

RAIN

It's comin' down pretty fast now. It was beautiful here this morning, early this morning. It started raining about shortly after noon. That's something kind of unusual for June in this part of the country. Usually we get our rain around April and May. Plenty of April and May showers. In June it's usually hot and dry. July and August—the hottest months here. Dry months, usually. And practically right up to the harvest. You might get a rain every once in a while, a little cloudburst. Sun dry it out or the earth drink it up and it just don't last long. Kind of unusual to rain like this in June.

It may be too wet to get in the field to chop tomorrow, they may have to cut turnrows or flatweed or something like that. It depends on if the water's standing in the middles or not. Sometimes, if it's standing in the middles, to save the cotton, pulling it up by the root and mudballs on your shoes, you stay out of it till it dries some.

THE SONGS

When those old worksongs came out, that would relieve the tension. Sometimes a man get to singing something that's an old one, sometimes a song never was in pattern. It was made up for words as it went along. Sometimes they would touch so close that everybody would take a liking to them and then repeat them. That's how they became popular. No song was set in patterns: the guys would just make up the words when they go along, just the first thing that would come to his mind to relieve that tension as he worked. That's how these songs came about. There was no set pattern.

But sometimes a guy be burdened down and doesn't want to pass his burden on to nobody. That's because he don't want nobody feeling sorry for him or thinking he's feeling sorry for hisself. So he'd do it in a song, and he'd make it real sad:

> My baby come down to see the wall
> My baby will let me go

Well, he's thinking about his family and doesn't want other people to know it so he makes it into a joke song, a work song. Right along with the working rhythm. That's how all those come about.

What makes one song better than others?

Sometimes it's the beat, because you can either slow it up or make it fast and that's why a lot of the old songs are sung over and over again, because it serves its purpose for a man's feeling, or it serves its purpose for timing work because sometimes he can't hold a slow beat. He's got to go ahead so he can tighten up the song a little bit faster. He can either sing it fast or sing it slow.

THE VERSES

These are mostly just made-up verses by the inmates. I don't know whether there ever be a song writer or another, but you can stay here so long, you have so much time to think, and you spend it in so many different ways. That's one way we used to get those river songs made up and help us do our time, help us work together and harmonize squads. The day wouldn't seem so hard. Even if we did have to stay here so long we would soon forget about it and time just pass on by like that. That's one way of doin' time.

YOU TELL THE TRUTH ABOUT HOW YOU FEEL

In the river songs you tell the truth about how you feel, you know, but you can't express it, see, to the boss.

They really be singing about the way they feel inside. Since they can't say it to nobody they sing a song about it. I mean, you know, long time ago when the penitentiary was kind of rough they used to sing songs about the bosses, captains, sergeants, lieutenants, whatever they think about them, that's what they'd sing about them.

ROCKIN' DEAD EASY

They call it "rockin'," "rockin' dead easy." That's what they call it when they start singin' the river songs.

Did you ever notice that when they really doin' it white guys never did do it?

Why didn't they?

The way they work, they works a lot different. The way we do it, we do it by time. We have a steady rock. Everybody raise their axe up and come down at the same time, just rock. I guess that might a came from many a year ago. We see in the picture show the way Africans beat and paddle boats together, just work together. I guess work by time. I can do a whole lot more work workin' by time than I can workin' loose.

Why?

Well, it looks like it's more fun. Even picking cotton, I likes to sing. When I sing, picking cotton, before I know anything I be three blocks ahead of the squad. Just picking along.

But if there's nobody saying nothing, then everybody look like they mad or crazy or something, and I'll get stuck and forget what I'm doing.

THAT'S THE WAY THEY FOOL THE BOSS

When you're working the convicts get tired and they say, "Come on, you all, let's rock a while," and they get together, you know, and that's the way they fool the boss. They come down with their axe and then they work it like it's stuck, they be resting, see. Then they take it, carry it out, hang it, carry it over their head real high: they resting. And they drop. But they ain't hitting as hard as they would if they's working. See, if they was working they'd be chopping fast like this—bam . . . bam . . . bam—but if they rocking they got their time and they going slower, they draw it way back and just drop it. They ain't doin' much. They rocking. That's called "Rocking along easy." And it's a lot different than just a steady hack. We're the only ones that ever rock, you know. Mexicans, white guys, I don't think they know nothing about it 'cause I think it originated from us.

SINGING LEAD

At times just about everybody would take the lead according to the mood the guys was in. They didn't just pick a man to take the lead. If he's working, maybe a guy didn't feel like singing and if he thought that I sung this song better he'd tell me so. "Why don't you get so and so and make our work a little easier. Let's rock a little." So it wasn't in any particular pattern, anybody was liable to take off.

What makes a good leader?

A man with a lot of drive and a good voice, where he can give out plenty of power. The more, the stronger a man sings, it seems like he's pushing a man along, working a little bit easier. And when a man get to singing he doesn't got time to think about his problems or the work. He can even be tired 'cause it's all over with.

Is it easier backgrounding or leading?

I believe it's easier being a leader because the group is pushing you and you're pushing the group. And it urges you to go just a little bit strong with the group pushing you. You got to go.

A LOT OF FELLOWS CAN CALL THEM

How does somebody get to be the songleader in a squad?

He's the one that has the clearest voice and can holler better with more time, you know, just harmony like. I mean, keep the time for the work going. You see, a lot of fellows can call them, but they don't be calling them with the time.

How long were you down here before you got to be a songleader?

I was in the squad I'd say about three months. I knew this old boy cutting down a tree and I was pulling brush down there at the time. So one fellow there asked me could I sing a song, so I said, "Yeah, I can sing just like he can. I can sing the same song *he* sing." He said, "Come on over here and cut in my place." And I took it up. And then from there on as we drove logs I'd lead the songs' time and then another fellow would lead just like that. Cutting down the tree that time, the song was "Black Betty."

I'd been in before that. I knew that song. I learnt that back on Clemens in the '30's.

Did you sing lead then?

Sometimes I'd sing lead.

Now the guy who sings lead isn't always the lead row man. Anybody can sing lead no matter where he's working at. A lot of times if you're singing they wants you to get right into the center of the squad where everybody can hear on each end. And all of them ask it when you're calling like that.

GUYS LIKE TO HEAR YOU SING

Guys like to hear you sing and when they get to the bottom they holler, "Come on, get on a tree with me." A whole lot of times I'd be out there calling, wouldn't even have no ax, just be hitting on the tree.

Just standing there?

Just standing there hitting on a tree.

What would the boss say?

Nothing. Wouldn't say nothing. He liked to see it done. Two or three bosses just sit there and I'd just be standing up there leaning on the tree and the rest of the guys would be cutting.

SONG LEADERS

The best song leader that I've heard, out of all the singing I heard, is an old boy called Highpockets—Robert Coop—out of Houston. We all called him Highpockets, a lot of them call him Jazz Baby. He was down on Clemens. That was back in the 30's. He got out. He took 25 years and got out. I saw him in '44 last time I saw him. He was out, in Houston.

What made him so much better than the others?

Well, it seems like to me he just had more harmony and seemed like to me like it just got good to him and he *got* there.

Did you try to copy his way of singing?

I sure did. I tried to copy some of his style. I like his style, the way he lead.

Anyone else you try to copy from?

There was another old boy called Ginny Bird. Ginny Bird, he had a pretty fair song I liked. He had one song I liked to hear him sing and that is a song about "Don't you hear me keep a calling?":

> Don't you hear the people call?
> Oh Lordy
> Don't you hear the people calling?
> Godamighty knows

That was his song. He liked that. And he sang that song. I used to be on squad with him and I'd sing with him.

CHINAMAN

Chinaman. 'Course he wore down now after 35 years in prison, but I've known him to cut in the woods when the boss would holler, "Ole Chinaman, sing, son."

I remember when I first came in the prison, the boss wouldn't let me cut no wood. He asked me, "You ever cut any wood?"

I said, "I've never cut no wood in my life."

"You put that axe down." Said, "They *cuts* wood here. You set right there and I'll show you how they cut wood down." He hollered over to old Chinaman, said "Ol' Chinaman," said, "sing, son!"

Chinaman said, "I ain't got no snuff."

Boss was a chronic snuff-dipper and he generally carried six or seven boxes of snuff in a big jar, a big brown jar. He said that's his social security. Now he knows those six or seven cans, he was gonna give them to different inmates. He says, "I don't care if you don't sing, I ain't gonna give you my snuff." About five or ten minutes later he says, "Here, Chinaman, here's you a firebox."

Well, in that time cigarette lighters wasn't known in the prison system and everybody made their own cigarette lighters. You made one out of a burnt cotton and a flint rock and a little old piece a file. And that would never miss, you could light that in any kind of wind. And he'd tell Chinaman he's throwin' him a firebox and he'd throw him a box a snuff.

And Chinaman would sing in them bottoms and there'd be three hundred axes droppin' with him. When they cut, everybody be cutting. Same thing when they be cutting down: he'd be singing lead on "Let the Hammer Ring." Everybody be in chorus with him on "Let your hammer ring." All the axes be dropping. When the timber's on the ground there'd be three hundred axes dropping with him. All in harmony. That's something to hear. I'd never seen nothing like that in my life.

COWBOY

Old Cowboy's voice done got hoarse now. He used to be one of them oldtimers. A lot of them oldtimers used to work them bottoms for years. Any of them could pick up a lead and push them as they go.

They had one they called old Greyhound. They called him Greyhound because he was running so fast. Everytime you turn around he was running off. And there was this old boy they used to call old Eagle, Red Eagle. They called him that because he was a traveling man. He could tear up squads. He could walk a horse to death, horse would still be trotting.

All them guys was good songleaders.

BACKGROUNDERS

When you have a good background that gives them more spirit, more courage to lead a song.

What do you mean by a good background?

The fellows that are backgrounding, whatever the background might be—just like we're singing "Here Rattler Here," if they all say that together that makes good background and the leader wants to sing sort of.

For a leader to be good it takes a good group behind him?

Right.

How is it if they're not good?

Well, the leader can go ahead on and do his part, but it would be better if he had a good backing group.

THE GROUP

When you're swinging that diamond you got to have somebody who knows how to handle a diamond and knows the song where he can push for it. When you're working with that diamond you got eight or twelve men on a tree with the axes and all of them swinging in union, in rhythm. They got to have rhythm and everybody got to know what they're doing. So generally, when a good group works together, maybe seven or eight or ten, they work together all the time. And they keep singing together. So it's just regular harmony. Something like the Ink-spots: got it down perfect.

When you got axemen that close, when they're working twelve around a tree or eight around a tree, they're back to back. When the axe hits left, everybody's got to be left. If one man's off he's liable to chop a man in the hand. So generally they don't put no greenhorn on one of them trees. They won't even work with one until they learn them how to use the axe. You ain't going to worry about no mistake. You've seen how they swing them diamonds, heave them axes. They got regular time on it. The song gives them a regular beat.

PULL-DOS

If everybody come up together and come down together, there's much more safety. Especially when the men are standing side by side up on the log. They stand up on the log and cut between their feet.

Anybody ever cut toes off?

Very seldom that. Usually a guy that cuts his toe, what we call a pull-do, he'll hit one of those glancing licks and cut his shoe or something like that. But you take a good woodchopper with a good sharp axe, he'll cut straight down. You don't swing with the axe, you cut straight down. Raise up high and hit hard and straight. That way it don't do no glancing licks.

The pull-dos, well, a number one man is scared to work with them because they chop them up. They cut themselves sometimes. And sometimes they throw trees on one another. You have to watch that, where the tree's falling. Guys don't know when they're going to fall sometime. Unless he's a old woodcutter—he know. He can tell where it's going to fall because the way he cut it, it fall in a certain direction. But a pull-do that don't know how or is just learning, a beginner, we call them pull-dos, we watch them to keep them from hurting us, tell them how to keep from hurting themselves while they learning.

SONG TIME I

When you time yourself with the song, see, you're chopping with a axe. Well when you sing like "Here Rattler Here," then you cut your song off as the axes hit the tree and that makes the song. Same thing when you bring your axe out. You got four axes coming in and four axes going out. You can time yourself like that. Other than that you cannot time yourself with a song. That's just like using a hoe in the field. If you using a hoe in the field you can't time yourself 'cause the guys can't time themself if they talk. And the song has got to be timed to it to sound right. If you don't have it timed right it wouldn't do no good cause it's not going to sound right. When you got the hoes you can time yourself right. Because when you hit the ground you cut off the song with your hoe where that hoe makes a sound because when you pick it up off the ground you back in time again. You cannot time yourself other than that.

SONG TIME II

Some of them is a faster beat and some of them is slower, depending what you're doing. You take your chopping with aggies that got a long handle, a hoe, longer than an axe handle of course, you raise it way up, the time you raise it way up and get it back down gives you time to catch your wind. We call that "rockin" here, call that "makin' it," and you don't just run out of wind. In fact, you can do it all day. If you take those long strokes and time it like that and everybody hit together.

With an axe it's a little faster, because the handle is shorter and you're bent over and you got to go get it down.

Choppin', like flatweedin' or something, the boss he so hard sometimes, you can kinda take your time as long as you continue a steady movement.

You take cutting up a tree. After you get it on the ground you got a little more time to cut it up than you had to cut it down. You can stand straight up, you're a little more at ease, you can raise your axe high in the air and drop 'em down a little slower. Get a little more rest in that. That's the difference in cutting down or cutting it up or chopping.

A butt cut is the first cut off a the tree, close to the stump. When it hit the ground somebody, a good woodcutter usually, gets on the buttcut with a sharp axe and he usually gets his off just about the time somebody gets the second or third one off. If he's a good woodcutter. It'll always be good woodcutters get them big cuts like that. 'Cause the tree's larger there and gets slimmer as it goes up. And the wind, that's up in the top of the tree, and the guy's just cutting the top out of it. Got a man come along and trim it up, and everybody line up on it and drop 'em down together, call out those river songs and rock. 'Stead of just hackin' and beatin' in and out of time.

TREECUTTING

I like cutting trees, cutting them down.
Why?
It just feels like to me I can do that kind of work better on account

of when you get to singing good you can do good work. Whenever we're cutting trees down all the guys get together and sing songs and so I guess we pass off the time more better. Looks like you do your work more better and you keep steady working and it don't seem like the work is hard.

FLATWEEDING AND WOODCUTTING

Flatweeding and woodcutting are the two best songs you use. That's what most of them are used for, flatweeding and woodcutting. 'Cause if you're flatweeding you're liable to flatweed from here to yonder—all day long. That's just pretty tiresome when you start weeding with that hoe and you got to go all day long. During that old time you work ten to twelve hours, as long as there was sun. Eight hours—I didn't know what eight hours was then, you heard about it on the radio or something.

Nowadays, eight hours and you ride to work. Eight hours they spend in the field and they ride to work. We walked it when *we* went. Sometimes we didn't walk, we practically trotted. Seven, eight, and ten miles to work. A lot of times we had to come back in to the building for dinner and jump right back out there and run back our seven or eight miles to work. And you hit that road, boy, you're on the way: you don't tarry, and that was all day. You didn't let up. The weak fell out, they'd haul them back. If one was just too weak to make it walking, he'd just hang on to his buddy's shirttails or belt loop. Sometimes they'd hang onto the horse's tail. Man, I seen as many as six or seven of them hanging onto the horse's tail. One of them hanging onto the horse's tail, one hanging onto his shirt, hanging on the boss's stirrup and he says, "Latch onto that stirrup and hang on," and all of them would practically be dragging along through they were still on their feet. They could barely even fall down.

WHAT HAPPENED TO THE SONGS

Very seldom do they use the worksongs now. They don't use the worksongs in the fields chopping because they don't chop, they don't work the fields now like they used to work. They have tractors now to do the work we did with hoes. And the tractors plow up close and eliminate a lot of our work. The turnrows, they don't have to clean them no more because they got graders that grade off the turnrows.

Back then, you had to chop a row and back up, the squad would line up and clean off the turnrow, that called for a lot of chopping that high grass on the back of the turnrow. Probably clear across to the next ditch. Well, everybody would get together in union, in harmony. It made the work seem easy even when it's hard if you singing. Everybody chop together and pullin' together. It would be a lots easier now with the little choppin' they do if they did sing and work more closely together, 'cause now when they're not singing every man has probably got his lip stuck out 'cause he's got time to think. All you got to do is concentrate on your song and your rhythm and the time goes by.

But now everybody works individually in most cases. He won't even carry his part. When you working together in union in a line everybody carries his part. Now you liable to be in a line with nobody singing, maybe two or three squabbling about "Move over, don't come hit me!" or "Get your part!" That's all you hear all day. And it makes the work a little bit harder. Even though they're not working as hard as they did in the past.

Same thing applies in the woods. Now every now and then you get some of it. Some a the old convicts will get together, they'll work in the woods, mostly in that heavy timber. They'll call the old convicts to cut it down because the young ones can't handle it. They can't handle a axe like a old convict can. You take four or six around a tree and they'll sing it down, they'll sing it down in harmony, they'll sing and cut, and they'll have it down an hour quicker than those that's actually just runnin' their head and talkin' when they workin'. In union, when you workin' in union and singin' in union, it makes it a lot easier all around.

The oldtimers still sometimes sing. That is, if whoever is carrying the squad will let them. In some cases the boss won't let them sing.

Why?

You take in the system now, there's more educated men. Back in those days we was referrin' to when they did all the singing while they worked, the system couldn't hire educated men, they hired who they could, and they thought it was a big thing to let 'em sing. Which it was, it was helpin' the inmate. But now we have mostly college men, young college men, men that's finished college, still taking some classes in college, just carryin' squads, they never experienced that. And in most cases they don't know whether they can or whether they can't. They don't know whether they can permit 'em to sing or not and rather than step out of bounds and be wrong they say: "Don't. Just knock off the singing and work." Actually, we get more work done when there's singing then when we're silent. Because that leads into arguments and confusion if a man hasn't anything to occupy his mind. If his mind is occupied he's steady working in union.

The young mens don't get a chance to work with the older mens and they haven't experienced working with the older mens before. A lot of them have never been in the system before. And they crews they work with don't even know the songs, the worksongs that they work by. In most cases their world is so modernaire, they all daydreamin': they drivin' the Cadillacs and sleepin' on the silk sheets, you know. Living a fictitious life and daydreaming. But once they get to working with the older men, they learn the songs, and they try to carry them on when they can.

The Texas Convict Worksong Tradition

The worksong—the song used to pace work, not a song that happened to be sung while someone was working—has a long and venerable history. Like many other cultural devices, it is being made obsolete by machinery.

In ancient Greece there were songs for pulling ropes and drawing water and stamping barley and treading grapes; in West Africa there were songs for almost every kind of work; in the Georgia Sea Islands there were songs for mashing grain and shucking corn and rowing boats; in the Hebrides there were songs for pulling wool to make tweed. Some gave directions (the railroad section leader calling pulls and pushes while his men lined track), some timed the work (the sea chanteys for pulling lines or turning winches), some controlled body movements (the roustabouts in the Mississippi River and Chesapeake Bay used songs to time their steps on swaying gangplanks to avoid being swung right off into the water). (See Brakeley, 1950.)

The aesthetic has always been one of *participation,* not performance; what has always mattered first with the worksong is the ability to keep the time going and to be heard, not a pretty voice or wide range. The songs differ from all other folksongs in one regard: they do not posit an audience.

The worksong is gradually dying as mechanization fulfills the functions mentioned above. Totally gone are the seafaring and dockside songs: ships are loaded by crane operators a block away; ships are not sailed, they are operated. The only place in this country where a viable worksong tradition now exists is the southern prison, and that is because the southern prison maintained a social institution long dead outside its fences: the culture of the nineteenth-century plantation.

The worksongs serve at least three functions:

1. They help supply a rhythm for work. This is useful for survival in the dangerous work of cutting down trees, efficient in the other kinds of

work, and in general an aesthetically pleasing way of working. This rhythm, in addition, once served another survival function. In the old days men who worked too slowly were singled out and not infrequently summarily punished by strokes of the bat. By singing together and keeping the strokes together while cutting logs or working with hoes, none could be singled out for being too slow, so no one could be punished simply because he was weaker than his fellows.

2. They help pass the time, which is nice, because prison work is usually rather boring.

3. They offer a partial outlet for the inmates' tensions and frustrations and angers. There is a long tradition in the South of the black man being permitted to sing things he is not permitted to say (note all the insulting lines about captains in the songs); it is as if sung words were not real.

The most poetic of the prison worksongs are those used for untimed work, such as picking cotton or cutting sugar cane, which are often sung alone or by small groups (songs like "Go Down Old Hannah," "No More Cane on the Brazos," or the songs of J. B. Smith). The worksongs that accompany axes and hoes must be simple and straightforward because the pace is rapid and there are often many men involved. Because the cotton and cane songs are often sung alone, they tend to have not only the most complex lyrics but also the most complex melodies—the singer does not have to worry about confusing other people and he is free to experiment and develop.

In all the songs, textual complexity and metric complexity are inversely proportional to the involvement of others in the work and the speed of the work being done. The *simplest* songs, treecutting songs, usually do not even rhyme; they have a short line and often automatic repetition, which gives the lead singer time to think up another line. The songs used for timed work patterns are regulated by the exigencies of simple predictable metric patterns, and all musical qualities—melody, text, harmony—are subsidiary to that need. For these songs—used with an axe and hoe—it is meter that is more important than anything else. In the songs used primarily for diversion, those for cane and cotton, there is opportunity for experimentation, and as a result those songs tend to be more complex in text, melody, and ornamentation.

The songs have one other function. I am not so sure of it that I can list it with the clear and definite group of functions above, but I am interested enough in it to offer it here as a suggestion: The songs change the nature of the work by putting the work into the worker's framework rather than the guards'. By incorporating the work with their song, by, in effect, co-opting something they are forced to do anyway, they make it *theirs* in a way it otherwise is not.

It is important to note that, except for the leader, the singing is completely noncompetitive: it is a voluntary association. Few things in prison are like that; the rest of the time you are housed in cellblocks or tanks with people assigned by someone else, you are marched into a chowhall and told when to sit and when to get up. There are dangers everywhere: a man smiles at you in the hallway and you think "What does he want?" or "What does he know that I don't?" With the songs there is no threat, no hidden agenda, no plot. It is just everyone trying to make it together.

Worksongs are not songs about work, and they are not songs one happens to sing while work is going on. Worksongs are songs that help a person do work.

There are two groups of worksongs in prison: those used for metrical stabilization of large groups of persons in metered work (crosscutting, logging, flatweeding), and those used for pacing one's own motions or the motions of a small group in nonmetered work (cane-cutting, cotton-picking). Both groups of songs supply diversion; the first group supplies metrical stabilization for everyone singing, the second group supplies a metrical pattern for each person singing.

Crosscutting is the name given to the way trees are cut down when there are two men hitting in each cut (it is also called *double-cutting*). When the convicts cut down large trees, they often work with several men around one trunk—I have seen as many as eight on a tree, and some convicts have told me that when a really thick trunk is being chopped there may be even more than that. If there are four men working on a tree, two will work on a cut on one side, two will work on a cut on the other. One of the cuts will be closer to the ground than the other cut (the older woodcutters can just about aim where the tree will fall). Consider the four men as primary compass points. East and West swing in as North and South draw their axes *back;* then as East and West draw their axes *back,* North and South swing *in;* the process repeats until the tree is down. East and West swing from their *right* to the tree trunk; North and South swing from their *left* to the tree trunk (the better workers swing equally well left or right). There is a cut between North and East in which they alternate stokes, and there is a cut between West and South in which they alternate strokes. Ideally, if the axes are sharp and strokes well-placed, a chip pops out every other stroke or so.

So one always swings *in* phase with the person 180° around the tree; one is always one half-cycle *out* of phase with the persons on either side of oneself. If there are more than two pair of men on a tree, then every other man swings from the left and the other men swing from the right, and all men swinging left swing at the same time and all men swinging right swing at the same time.

Timing is critical in this work: if one is too far forward or too far back at the wrong time, there is danger of lopping off the fingers of another man's hand or having one's own fingers severed; there is danger of having the axe of the man behind you imbed itself in your skull. The song keeps the workers in time, and the timing keeps the axe strokes regular and thereby supplies the metric frame for the body movements of all persons in any one work group.

Not all convicts do this (nor did they all even in the days when the worksongs were sung much more than they are now). White and Latin-American convicts, and new convicts of any ethnic background, tend to work with just two men on a tree, one on each side. It is too dangerous to let them double up on a cut, to let their axes cross. With eight or ten men around a tree there is a lot of sharp steel in the air and a lot of flesh moving around the same place. Only the older black convicts work in larger groups around trees—because they are the only ones who have the necessary safety device.

The songs used for this kind of work have two characteristics: they are metrically fast, and they are lyrically simple. They are fast because an axe is in the air all the time, and because the loud punctuation of the axes striking the tree occurs twice each work cycle (because there are two alternating groups—if there are ten men working on a tree, each strike will consist of five axes hitting at once). They are simple because the fast pace does not give the lead singer time to think up nicely-rhymed couplets or long, complex lines. The song structure is often one line sung twice, with a regular burden at the end of each line by the rest of the group. Sometimes the group sings the repeat line as well as the burden. Only rarely is the group's involvement any more complex. Melodies tend to be unornamented—the lead singer does not have time to play with melody or wind to spare for ornamentation.

With the crosscutting songs I have grouped three songs which were recorded while men were working with spades: 37-C. "Grizzly Bear," 39-A. "Crooked-Foot John," and 40-A. and 40-B. "I'm in the Bottom." They are all in the meter of the crosscutting songs, because the workers slapped the backs of the spades on the ground on the return strokes, mimicking the axe meter. The first two are usually sung as crosscutting songs, and the men said the spade songs were simply crosscutting songs adapted for the spade work.

Logging is the name the men give to the job of cutting felled trees into small sections. In the old days the trees were used to fire water boilers, heat stoves in the barracks, fire the boilers in the cane-processing unit, and for lumber. The wood is still used for lumber (in which case the top branches are trimmed off but the trunks are not cut up) and some for the cane plant, but the other uses are mostly gone. The various sections of the tree have names: the thickest part is called the *butt cut*, second cut is next to that, and so on up the trunk to where the branches start, a section called the *wing*. The best chopper gets the butt cut, for it is preferable that everyone finish about the same time; a loser, a pull-do if there happens to be one in the squad, gets the wing, for he has to mess around in all those branches and can not work with the others but must hack and chop away.

When the log is on the ground the men line up along its length and chop down, so that it is cut into sections about four feet long. If it is a very thick log, they may stand on top of it and let the axes fall between their feet. The work is slower than cutting trees down because there are two points in the cycle where the axes can pause—at the top and bottom of the arc.

Because there is no physical danger from bad timing, the strokes are not timed together so carefully. They are together most of the time, but not all, and often you hear a brief ripple as the axes hit within a second or so of each other; with crosscutting there is just one crack as they all hit at once.

Flatweeding is any kind of work done with a hoe: building roads, busting clods after a tractor has gone through and turned up dry ground, turning turf, cleaning ditches, chopping cotton. As the prison system acquires more and more heavy machinery, less and less work is done with hoes, but they are still necessary for chopping cotton and getting into places too tight for the machines. The cotton work tends to use short arcs, but other work gets a long stroke with the hoe. Because of the length of the hoe and the long arc of travel, these songs are the slowest of the songs used to meter work, and of the three kinds these tend to be the most complex lyrically and melodically.

Unmetered group work, such as cotton picking or sugarcane cutting, is associated with the songs which are most complex melodically and lyrically, with the most intricate vocal ornamentation on the part of the lead singer, and with the most likelihood of harmonization by other participants. It also produces the largest group of solo songs. This work does not time the group, but it does time the individual worker—that is, he can work at several different paces, depending upon how he chooses to read and relate to the meter of the song, but a half-dozen men singing will not be moving the same way at the same time. Metric control, the relation of rhythm to body movements, is least present in these songs of all the kinds of convict worksongs.

In crosscutting, logging, and flatweeding—and to a significantly slighter extent in unmetered group work—what matters to the singers is keeping in time; they are concerned with physical fulfilment of function more than verbal articulation of problems. That does not mean they are *not* concerned with the verbal part, just that the physical part matters more. The lead singers like followers who can sing well together, but a group that can work well together is more important.

THE SONG LEADER

Two qualities are prized in a song leader: the ability to keep a steady meter going (one paced so that the men can work to it without being overworked, yet fast enough so that the bosses won't get upset that everyone isn't doing enough), and the ability to be heard over the noise of brushfires, movement, wind in the branches, and other miscellaneous sounds that one almost never notices but which really exist as a curtain or wall of sound in a forest. The song leader must be steady and he must be loud.

For the critically timed songs—those used for cutting trees down—the leader can get by for a long time with very few lines. Many of these songs are such that one can interject names in formulaic lines—names of guards, fellow-workers, people one has known or heard of, and so forth—and there are chorus lines and repeats that give the singer time to think up another verse. He may rhyme, but that is neither expected nor required by the group; many would not notice if he did. The lead singers who *do* rhyme in these songs do so because of their own personal aesthetic, not because the group's aesthetic demands it.

Some of the very good leaders are quite incapable of altering a line. They may be very adaptable in the way they use lines that are obviously formulaic (for example, the lines with slots for varying nouns), but they will not change the line structure and they will not generate new lines. This is true of someone like David Tippen. Some singers have an enormous repertory of stanzas and verses, so large they are almost creative in the way they assemble songs—Chinaman, for example. A few others are highly creative; they sing not only the well known lines and stanzas, but they add many of their own or vary the existing ones. J. B. Smith is such a song leader.

The group itself, however, is not concerned whether the leader is creative, or his voice "nice," or his melodies interesting; they may appreciate such qualities, but only as embellishments if the two required qualities—regularity and volume—are there first. Without these two qualities the others do not matter at all, and the group will not permit a man to sing lead. One inmate said, "You got to have a good leader in order to make the feeling come out in the rest of them. If you don't have a good leader, they don't get the feeling out of it. Now Chinaman could make 'em sing. He could do it; he knew enough of them river songs he could carry right on—whether somebody back him up or not, he could carry right on."

Nevertheless, the leader does not function alone. In order to be most efficient, he needs a group behind him (called *backgrounders* by some) that can sing together and work together almost as well as he can lead. The backgrounders and leaders seem to pick their group members with care.

Most leaders are tenors. I remember being surprised the first time I heard a Leadbelly recording—I had not expected his voice to be so high. I realize now that my image of the prison song leader had been formed by listening to Paul Robeson when I was very young. A moment's reflection reveals why a deep baritone or bass is not good for this sort of leading: it takes a great deal of air to produce those low notes, and they are not very loud. If one is swinging an axe and wants one's voice to penetrate a lot of background noise, one must sing fairly high in the male range. Tenor range requires far less wind than bass range, and it projects better.

The good leaders tend to be good workers. They are usually lead hoe in Number One Hoe Squad—the first man in the first squad. It isn't that the best singer is given that work position, but usually it is only the man who is the strongest worker who has the energy to spare that is required for lead singing.

There is, by the way, a kind of pride to being in One Hoe, even though that group does more work than the others. When I heard that good song leaders often made it possible for the men to work along at a good pace, I asked if the inmates wouldn't want to kill a leader who pushed them too fast. One inmate said that some might want to, but usually wouldn't because they were afraid of reprisals. But another inmate argued with him: "After a while it becomes a challenge. You kind a get a little team spirit more or less, you like to be in One Hoe. I mean, you work harder and faster, but you're better than those pull-dos. You know. Just like a guy that can drink more whiskey than somebody else. It's ridiculous, but it's that way. And after you get broke in, it still can wear you down, but it's not the same. It's not impossible any more. And something else: the higher squads that these guys are in, they get other breaks. Like maybe they got some trucks to load or something while the rest of them are working, well they go unload the trucks. You get some compensations." The first inmate listened to this, and said, "Yeah, that's right. That's the life here. A guy says, 'Well, I can do it a little better than Bill, and it makes me feel that's the only consolation I can get.'"

I would have thought, once, that inmates would prefer to be in the slower squads where they wouldn't have to work so hard. But people are adaptable—they survive so much insanity—and what happens is, given a situation in which one is required to do the work, one co-opts it partially and finds the urge to be as good as one can; there is pride in being the best, as there is always such pride in human affairs, and there is competition for being recognized as the best cotton picker or tree cutter. It isn't so much the urge to please the guards, but rather the natural movement among Americans for stratification even within a rigidly defined stratum.

Although there is no sense of ownership of any of the songs, some become identified with certain leaders simply because the specific leader enjoys that specific song so much that he does an especially good job with it. He has more stanzas for that than other songs in his repertory, perhaps, or he will sing it more often than anything else. Chinaman always sings "Yellow Gal" when flatweeding; he always sings "Hamin' on a Live Oak Log" when logging; and one expects to hear those songs in any work session when he is around. The only time that someone else leads "Pick a Bale of Cotton" when Houston is present is when Houston doesn't feel like singing lead.

In solo songs a singer will sometimes become attached to a single melody and use that melody in a highly personal way with a variety of verses (see Maze's 10. "Mack's Blues," 9. "If You See My Mother," and J. B. Smith's long group of songs). Other inmates would not think of joining in on these songs or picking them up. Although they are sung publicly, there is something peculiarly private about them, and that privateness is not so much respected as observed.

There is one other qualification for a good song leader: he must know enough songs to lead; he has to have been around for a while. Almost all the well-known leaders I recorded had been in prison several times, usually for long sentences. G.I. was on his fourth sentence when I met him in 1963, serving, according to his record, "a forty-five year sentence from Lamar County for the offense of Burglary. In 1929, he served a five year sentence in the Texas Prison System for Theft. In 1934, he served a ten year sentence in the TPS for burglary. In 1945, he served a five year sentence in the TPS for robbery. He has been arrested about thirty other times." Alexander is doing forty years on eight charges; he has been in before. Maze is doing life for murder. Tippen is doing life as a habitual; this is his seventh incarceration—the first was in 1918 (he was born in 1895).

Chinaman's rap sheet (the list of arrests and convictions and sentences sent out by the FBI in response to official queries) indicates that he has been arrested as Buck Jones, Jess Brown, James Mitchell, and J. C. Fields. He was first admitted in 1935 with a five year sentence for assault with intent to murder (he served two years of that sentence); there were a number of minor arrests during the next year; then in 1938 he was returned on a three year sentence for another charge of assault with intent to murder. In 1942 he got life for yet another assault with intent to murder charge (he shot a deputy sheriff who was questioning him about a stolen car he happened to be driving while coming back from a hunting trip); that is the sentence he is now serving. In the years following 1942 there were many entries on his inmate rap sheet for escape, fighting, possessing prohibited knives, destroying state property, assaulting other inmates, and so forth. The last charge of any seriousness was in 1958; since then he has had most of his lost good time restored. Warden C. L. MacAdams considered him one of the most dangerous people he had ever known; the inmates considered him the best song leader they had ever heard.

The song repertory of any culture always has *some* cultural relevance. Even when words deal with anachronistic or abstracted topics (such as many ballads, and many "art" songs) the choice of anachronism or abstraction has meaning for the audiences hearing the songs. Sometimes there is a sentimental involvement with the words—as with much folk music performed in urban situations; sometimes the words are nothing more than syllabic vehicles upon which the musical instrument of the voice can operate—as for an American audience listening to a *lieder* concert.

For the group generating folk songs there is a part of the content and context that is obvious, but to limit our understanding of the songs' content to the surface material is to ignore much of what we have learned in social science in the last half-century: men sing about what they know, of course, but there are many things to sing about; what they *select* tells us more than the lyrics would seem to indicate. Many psychological defense mechanisms—denial, repression, transference, reaction formation, and so forth—are present as much in song lyrics as they are in conversation.

J. B. Smith said to me once, "Guy down here, if he's thinkin' about anything at all, he's thinking about his freedom and his woman." That is only partially true; a man also thinks a great deal about the things that keep him *from* his woman, the things that restrict his freedom. And those restrictions are far more concrete, more corporeal, than a distant female or an abstract concept that can be identified only by its absence. It is imprisonment that pains, not lack of freedom.

The songs themselves reflect these concerns. In Smith's songs, for example, there are eighteen stanzas about the *length of his sentence* (1, 3, 5, 8, 16, 18, 19, 20, 26, 27, 28, 29, 30, 31, 38, 59, 76, 108) and eighteen stanzas about *his woman* (5, 9, 14, 15, 16, 24, 25, 46, 47, 64, 82, 83, 87, 91, 92, 119). Of slightly greater concern is the possibility of *escape*, which occurs nineteen times (8, 10, 17, 24, 26, 36, 37, 39, 40, 45, 67, 68, 91, 92, 105, 106, 120, 124). Closely linked with this is concern with *geographical locations;* there are in Smith's songs twenty-three mentions of places outside the prison: Mobile Bay (24), Hot Springs (25, 117), Boot Hill (42), Abilene (47), Texas (47, 81), Illinois (57), Pocatello, Idaho (65), Louisiana (79, 118), Butte, Montana (80), Big Muddy (86), Des Moines (103), Brazos (3, 7, 67), and unspecified rivers (15, 30, 32, 73, 106).

The *guards, riders, major,* and so on are mentioned thirty-one times
(8, 10, 12, 13, 14, 31, 36, 43, 44, 67, 68, 69, 71, 77, 88, 98, 100, 104–
108, 110, 111, 113, 116, 117, 121, 126, 127). The two other important
themes are *sickness and death,* cited twenty-four times (2, 13, 14, 22,
31, 33, 39, 40, 41, 42, 46, 48, 50, 51, 72, 78, 85, 95, 96, 97, 98, 115, 117,
118), and *firearms,* cited twenty-two times: pistol (12, 39), thirty-two-
twenty (13), fire iron (27), German Luger (35), two-barreled derringer
(36), horse pistol (69, 70), shotgun (86, 122), Winchester (120), men
shot at (39, 86, 120, 122, 124), firearm as equalizer (12, 13, 35, 69, 70),
and chancing gunfire (124).

I made the content list from Smith's songs because they form a coherent unit in other ways, but one could do the same sort of theme
cataloguing with the rest of the songs and come out with the same sort
of distribution.

These lists tell us something about an interesting problem of composition, one that is thematically central to the entire song sequence performed by Smith and all the other songs generated within the prison
context. The singer is concerned with his relationships to certain institutions of the state, certain legal situations, certain interpersonal relationships, and he must somehow express these in his songs. Because of
the rhythmic demands of the singing style, the songs are frequently
a-syntactic: words are dropped and slurred; pronouns, conjunctions,
and particles are frequently omitted; so it remains for nouns and verbs
to bear the burden of the thoughts and to imply the relationships. The
metaphors and analogies in almost all the songs are highly concrete.

Kenneth Burke (1966, p. 375) has said, "Socio-political institutions,
with the personal and social relations involved in them, and the vast
terminology of attitudes, acts, and motives that goes with them do not
enjoy exactly the kind of extraverbal reality we find in the commonsense
vocabulary of the natural realm; yet they are not identical with the
verbal order as such (the order of words-about-words)." But the language of work songs is not abstract; it is highly imagistic, highly concrete. The themes are almost entirely negative or institutional: non-
freedom, nonlove, nonvolition, nonimportance. The natural world itself,
the world from which the images derive, has no negatives: man makes
those things in his head.*

"The essential distinction between the verbal and the non-verbal,"
Burke writes, "is in the fact that language adds the peculiar possibility
of the Negative" (1966, p. 420). *"For the negative is an idea;* there can
be no image of it. *But in imagery there is no negative."* "The negative is
properly shown by a *sign,* not by an *image.* For a 'negative image' would

* For this I am indebted to a discussion with John Gagnon and a reading
of Burke's essay, "A Dramatic View of the Origins of Language and Post-
scripts on the Negative," in Burke, 1966, pp. 419–479.

be a contradiction in terms" (1966, p. 430). In this concept we even find the dramatic necessity for the theme of Hell (Smith mentions it four times, in stanzas 7, 21, and 32) which, Burke says, "is, to perfection, a function of the negative . . . The notion of Hell involves a scenic reinforcement of the negative as a principle, the total ultimate thou-shalt-not" (pp. 474–475).

The reason Smith (he is the most creative song leader I met; the statements here apply even more to the others) cannot dwell at any length on his woman or his freedom is that he does not really think of *them* so much as of their *absence;* he perceives the negative, and in his imagistic song-world there are no terms to present these feelings (for they are not *things*) directly. All he can do is deal with the *devices* of control: the number of years he has to do, the weapons of the guards, the presence of the guards, the existence of other places to which he has no access. To express both hope and longing, both his sense of self and his lack of control over that self's movements, the singer is forced to document the concreteness of the enemy, the prison itself, because that is all that *is* concrete, and depend on rhetoric to return to his real themes. The singer needs the ugly, the abhorred.

The dependence of expression on the loathed and ugly is not so frustrating as one might suspect. According to Hazlitt:

> Not that we like what we loathe; but we like to indulge our hatred and scorn of it; to dwell upon it, to exasperate our idea of it by every refinement of ingenuity and extravagance of illustration; to make it a bugbear to ourselves, to point it out to others in all the splendour of deformity, to embody it to the senses, to stigmatize it by name, to grapple with it in thought, in action, to sharpen our intellect, to arm our will against it, to know the worst we have to contend with, and to contend with it to the utmost. Poetry is only the highest eloquence of passion, the most vivid form of expression that can be given to our conception of anything, whether pleasurable or painful, mean or dignified, delightful or distressing. It is the perfect coincidence of the image and the words with the feeling we have, and of which we cannot get rid in any other way, that gives an instant "satisfaction to the thought." This is equally the origin of wit and fancy, of comedy and tragedy, of the sublime and pathetic.
>
> (From "On Poetry in General," Bate, 1952, p. 306)

PRISONS IN THE STATE OF TEXAS

One of the reasons I decided to visit Texas prisons was that I wanted to see what conditions were like in a truly awful place. For years the prisons of the South have been known as the worst prisons in America, and in the 1940's Texas's prisons were among the worst in the South.

I was surprised to find that most of my assumptions were based on history, not present fact. It is true that Texas prisons for a long time were awful places, but it is also true that *now* Texas has one of the two or three most humane prison systems in the country. (I think prison itself is usually inhumane, but within that context, as prison systems go, Texas has a good one.) I find the following in my notes from the first trip:

> The food surprises me: most of the inmates eat better here than they ever did outside. There are plenty of fresh vegetables, what seems to be a lot of meat, milk, etc. It all comes from their own crops. (Someone tells me an inmate here is supported for about an eighth of what it costs to support an inmate at San Quentin.) I thought, while checking the inmate chowlines here these last few days, of the food at Indiana State Prison: the inmates complained about it so much I asked to see it, but the officials refused to let me into the messhall. And I remember the food at the *guards'* mess at Pendleton Reformatory, which was so foul I could hardly imagine what the inmates had to eat.
>
> The old brutality seems to be gone. The men work hard and there isn't much time or facilities for education or avocation [I found out later this wasn't true: TDC has more educational opportunities than almost any other state], but they seem to be treated fairly. So hard to tell: in prisons they don't do the bad things when people like me are walking around. (But how many prison systems are just willing to *let* someone like me walk around? New York wouldn't and Massachusetts wouldn't.) And inmates are sometimes afraid to talk to someone like me until they get to know me well enough to know it's safe. But one indication of the change in the system is that the old river songs are not sung very much any more. The reason, Johnny Jackson told me, is that the men are now allowed to work at their own pace and they don't need the extra drive and pacing the old songs gave them.

Since then I have written elsewhere about American prisons and how I think Texas rates among them (Jackson, 1968). It is not necessary to go into much detail here, except to say that Texas has made more progress in the area of correctional administration since 1948 than any other state. I pick the year 1948 because in that year Gov. Beauford Jester appointed O. B. Ellis as administrator of the system and massive reforms began.* One gets an idea of the administration of the system in earlier days from the autobiography of Lee Simmons, who was general manager of the system from 1930 to 1935.

* For a good history of the system, the convict lease problems, and the beginnings of the changes, see Webb, 1942, pp. 411–414.

I opposed the legislators who sought to forbid the "bat," the twenty-four-inch leather strap, four inches wide, used in prison discipline. I told my friends on the legislative committee: "Gentlemen, it's just like using spurs. You get an old cow horse without spurs—and you can't head even a milking-pen cow; but when you've got your spurs on, the old horse will do the job. And you don't have to use the spurs, because all he needs to know is that the spurs are there. It's the same with us and the 'bat.' The record shows we seldom have to use it. But the boys all know that it is there."

Committeemen smiled and failed to recommend abolition of the "bat." But after my resignation as general manager, the next legislature forbade the use of corporal punishment—in response to the urgings of misguided and ill-informed humanitarians" (Simmons, p. x).

I do not belittle the methods of correction advocated by the modern sciences, and I have made use of them, but I am a firm believer nonetheless in corporal punishment—in the home, in the schoolroom, in the reformatory, in the penitentiary. I know my notions about that are diametrically opposed to the notions of almost all present-day psychologists, psychiatrists, and penologists. I have most of the wardens and prison board members against me on that. But I came to my belief from experience, and experience is what I base my conclusions upon. Whatever else I may lack, I had had, I think, plenty of experience.

Of course I do not claim to have all the answers to these prison mutinies and outbreaks which continue to plague our penitentiaries. But, right or wrong, in the Texas Prison System, we whipped our hardened criminals, when other means of persuasion failed" (Simmons, p. viii).

Simmons, and people like him, could never connect prison riots, convict self-mutilation, and high escape rates with the conditions they themselves created. They saw the world in terms of a spiral of action and punishment, counter-action and counter-punishment. Because of an inability to question their own modes of response they were never capable of breaking that spiral. In Texas it was not until the appointment of Ellis, and the subsequent appointment of George Beto, that the pattern was broken (and the basic indicator of some success is there: escape attempts are slight, self-mutilation almost nonexistent); in some other states too many things have not changed at all.

In 1968 the Texas Department of Corrections published a small booklet, "A Brief History," which I quote here in its entirety:

The Texas Legislature in 1846 passed an act directing the appointment of three commissioners to select a site for a penitentiary. The act also appropriated $10,000 annually for the operation of the penitentiary but this was reduced to $5,000. The commissioners selected Huntsville as the site for the penitentiary and five cleared acres and 98 acres of timber were purchased from Grace McGary, Robert Smither, and Pleasant Gray for $493.

The Governor appointed James Gillespie as the first superintendent of the penitentiary at a salary of $800 per year.

The prison began operation in 1849 in a wooden building. The first convict, received October 1, 1849, was William G. Sansom, who was convicted by the court of Fayette County and sentenced to three years for cattle theft. The second was Stephen P. Terry who was sentenced to ten years for murder, and the third was Thomas Short, sentenced to two years for stealing a horse. Sansom was pardoned by Governor Bell, Terry died of gunshot wounds while in prison, and Short served his full term.

In 1868 the Texas Legislature had no money to appropriate to run the prison and decided to lease the entire system to a private operator. After numerous delays, the penitentiary was leased in 1871 to Ward, Dewey, and Company for 15 years for $5,000 a year for the first five years, $10,000 a year for the second five years, and $20,000 a year for the last five years.

Abuses of every sort occurred under the lease system. No underclothing or socks were furnished and no additional clothing was provided in winter. Men were forced to work on farms late in fall barefooted. Conditions were so intolerable there were 382 escapes in 1876. The lease system was discontinued in 1883.

Until 1927, the prison's function lay in punishing convicts for their transgressions against society and preventing them from escaping. In that year a Board of Prison Commissioners was replaced by a board of nine members which formulated plans for inmate rehabilitation but little was done to put the plans into operation. These were hard and brutal years. Many men severed their Achilles tendons in order to avoid the backbreaking labor in the cane and cotton fields. The dormitories became jungles, where the strong preyed upon the weak.

In 1948, Governor Beauford Jester effected the first real reforms in the penal system of Texas by appointing a strong Prison Board composed of outstanding business and professional leaders who labored diligently to achieve goals. The Board appointed O. B. Ellis, a career penologist, to administer the system. Whereas, emphasis to this time was almost entirely upon security and agriculture, the base was now broadened to include construction, industry, and treatment.

Following the death of Mr. Ellis in 1962, George H. Beto, Ph.D., assumed duties as director. The momentum gained in the Ellis era increased. Using any measuring stick, the Texas Department of Corrections is now among the best penal systems of the nation and is unequaled in work programs, agricultural production, economy of construction, and feeding program.

In 1957, by act of the 55th Legislature, the name of the Texas

Prison System was changed to the Texas Department of Corrections, and the name of the chief administrative officer was changed from general manager to director.

Over the years, many notorious criminals have been imprisoned in Texas. In the 1870's, two famous Indian chiefs, Santanta and Big Tree, were incarcerated for inciting a massacre. John Wesley Hardin, who is reputed to have murdered 20 people, also served time in Huntsville. The first woman convict was Elizabeth Huffman who was convicted in 1854 for infanticide. The most unusual sentence was for "worthlessness." The shortest sentence on record was given to William Saunders for one hour in 1870. The youngest convict was a nine-year-old Negro boy sentenced in 1887 for robbery.

The most dramatic incident in Texas prison history occurred in 1934 when Bonnie Parker and Clyde Barrow liberated four prisoners from Eastham Farm. Bonnie and Clyde were killed by Texas Rangers and other law enforcement officers a few months later.

Given that Texas prisons are better than most and far better than they themselves were not long ago, it is necessary—for an understanding of the songs—to sense something of that prison world now. For it is still prison, after all.

If one responds to the poetry of the songs and to what the inmates had to say in the first chapter, one might sense some of the feelings associated with being a convict.

The role of convict is marked not only by the white suits the men wear and the little cells they sleep in at night, but even the physical positions of everyone else during the day: the men are on the ground, the guards are up on horses. That difference is not simply one of comfort.

I remember one day on Ramsey when I wanted to go out and take some photographs of the men picking cotton. It was a pleasant day, and, since I would be moving around in the middles to reach the workers, I decided to take a horse. Warden Terill Hutto kindly lent me a horse and one of the majors lent me a saddle. Two dog boys were riding out at that time, so we rode out the two miles or so together and chatted about things, until they decided to give their horses some exercise and it turned out that their horses were much faster than mine, which they of course knew when they took off. I turned off the road and followed a turnrow near where the men were working, then followed a middle over to their area.

Before this I had always been on foot when I was in the bottoms. I had always walked around with the inmates, while around us or off in the distance the guards would be on their horses. I felt an identification with the inmates, but thought it was just because they were friendly and we were doing things that were interesting.

This time, however, from atop the horse, I found myself looking *down* on the cottonpickers, looking directly *at* the other people on horses. There is no way to chat casually with someone when you are on a horse and he is on the ground; those two or three feet of height make all the difference in the world. (In *Anna and the King of Siam* the king would not permit anyone's head to be higher than his; he understood that symbolism quite well.) I thought of the last time I had driven a large truck and how I had related to the little people in their Buicks and Oldsmobiles and whatnot, little bugs so far below, with so much less vision on the world than I commanded; I had felt the same arrogance of mere physical position.

The guards experience this; the convicts sense this. They sense it all the time. That is a major part of what prison is about.

Photographs

1   *Squads and mounted guards on turnrows, returning to fields after lunch on the Johnny. Ellis. May 1967.*

2　*Benny Richardson (foreground, with axe). Ellis. March 1966.*

3   *Waterboy and treecutters. Ellis. August 1965.*

4   *Group crosscutting. Ellis. August 1965.*

5   *Group crosscutting. Cowboy is second from left with axe back;*
    Chinaman is just in front of him, axe in. Ellis. March 1966.

7   *Chinaman. Ellis. August 1965.*

8 *W. D. Alexander and Chinaman. Ellis. August 1965.*

9   *Chinaman's admission mug photo. TDC 1942.*

10   *Mack Maze. Ellis. August 1965.*

11　Guard overseeing cottonpickers. Ramsey 2. October 1968.

12   *Cotton pickers. Ramsey 2. October 1968.*

13   Cowboy at annual prison rodeo. Huntsville. October 1968.

14   Louis "Bacon and Porkchop" Houston. Ramsey 2. August 1965.

15　*J. B. Smith. Ramsey 2. August 1965.*

16   Flatweeding. Chinaman is closest to camera. Ellis. March 1966.

17   *Flatweeding. Workers are clodbusting with the hoes. Ellis. March 1966.*

18   *Flatweeding. Ramsey 1. August 1965.*

19   *Logloading. Henry Petty, Francelle Norah, Joe Willie Austin. Ellis.*
       March 1966.

20   *Burning brush and logs. Ellis. August 1965.*

21   *Main hall and guard picket. Ellis. October 1966.*

22 *Looking out to front hallway. Ellis. October 1966.*

23   *Flatweeding squad heading in. Ellis. 1966.*

24   *Peckerwood Hill. Ramsey 2. July 1965.*

The Songs

About the Format

Each song is listed by the title most often given for it or the title given by the singer who performed the text chosen for publication here. When there are other titles given by singers of the variants, they are listed in the variant list at the beginning of each note before the performer's name. A note might read,

57 Raise 'em Up Higher

A. Johnny Jackson and group, *flatweeding,* Ramsey 1, 22 August 1965, 400.4, N.C.

B. Johnny Jackson and group, Ramsey 1, 1 July 1964, 23.2

C. "Twenty-One Hammers," David Tippett and Johnny Jackson, Ramsey 1, 2 July 1964, 26.4

D. "Forty-Four Hammers," Virgil Asbury and group, Retrieve, 5 July 1964, 46.2

E. "Alberta," Joseph "Chinaman" Johnson and group, *flatweeding,* Ellis, 21 August 1965, 398.3, N.C.

Fifty-seven is the number of the song in this collection, and it is followed by the song title most frequently used. The texts listed without titles (A and B) had the chosen title. C, D, and E had the variant titles listed.

After the name of the performer is an entry for the kind of work being done at the time of recording. For the A and E texts here, the groups were flatweeding, and that is indicated in italics. When the group was not at work, that slot is empty and the note proceeds directly to the prison unit (Ellis, Ramsey, Retrieve, and so on) and the date of recording.

The number following the date (for example, 400.4) is my original tape number. I list these numbers for the convenience of scholars who might want to check the music or word transcriptions, or who need those originals for some research purpose of their own when the materials here or the portions available on LP records are not adequate. Tapes of all songs included in this book will be available at the African and Afro-American Research Institute at the University of Texas and the Archive of American Folk Song of the Library of Congress.

The initials N.C. or J.M. appear with versions of songs whose music has been transcribed and printed here. The initials identify the tune transcriber—Mrs. Judith McCulloh or Mr. Norman Cazden.

The list of songs at the opening of the headnote refers only to those texts published here; I do not list all variants of a song. Only a few songs were recorded on less than three occasions, and I attempted to pick the versions that were most typical. When a text is atypical, I point out how it varies from the norm.

The rest of the note attempts to identify special points of interest about the song or to supply background information that clarifies it. When argot words are used idiosyncratically, I define them in the immediate context; all other argot words and the names of some important people who appear in the songs are defined or identified in the glossary. Some of the well-known wardens and inmates are discussed in the inmate remarks in the first section of this book.

The headnote refers the reader to various recordings and printed versions of the song. These references are meant to be illustrative, not comprehensive. They are meant to explore one particular aspect of the song or to give some idea of the song's provenience, not to document its life history. References to books and articles are by author's name and, if there is more than one entry by him, by the date of publication (for example, Lomax, 1942, p. 42).

All items so referenced are in Works Cited, section A. References to LP records give the full title of the LP and the manufacturers jacket number; full citations for these are in section B. References to single recordings *without* a manufacturer's code (214B1, 205A1) all refer to field recordings in the collection of the Archive of American Folk Song (AAFS) of the Library of Congress; these numbers are taken from the two-volume *Check-list of Recorded Songs in the English Language in the Archive of American Folk Song to July, 1940,* published by the Archive in 1942. I relied on that list because, until my own deposits in 1965, there were no other accessions of Texas prison material in that Archive.

TEXT AND TUNE TRANSCRIPTIONS

With rare exceptions, tunes used with the axe and flatweeding songs are taken from recordings made while the men were actually at work. The note to each text indicates what the men were doing at the time.

None of the cotton and cane songs were recorded at work; they were all recorded sitting or standing around somewhere inside or outside the building—but not in the fields. I thought it necessary to record the songs in which meter was vital to the work being done while the men were at work; the whole style of the song, the phrasing, everything changes when the singers are sedentary. This was not critical with the cotton and cane songs, which are not work-controlling and can be sung anywhere. Even if I had tried to record them in the field, it probably would not have been possible. These days the cotton and cane songs are sung in the fields very rarely, if at all. There are two reasons for this: they have none of the physical functions the other songs do (there is not even the convenience of working as a group, since the men never work in unison anyway at cotton chopping and cane cutting); and the psychological necessity is not what it once was. In addition—unlike woodcutting, where the older convicts tend to work together simply because they work better and more safely—work in the cane and cotton fields is undifferentiated: everyone does the same job, but by himself.

The musical notations are from Mr. Cazden's holograph copies of his and Mrs. McCulloh's original transcriptions. Where the music is notated, for convenience in reading, at a pitch level different from that of the recording, the first note of the original pitch level is given as a point of comparison. Arrows indicate intonation slightly higher or lower than the pitch indicated. Mrs. McCulloh noted, in addition, "Except for 'Midnight Special,' I have tried to pick representative or typical stanzas. Metronome markings are given for the particular stanza being transcribed; at best they are approximate. 'Blue notes' are indicated by accidentals within parentheses, in the key signature if they occur consistently throughout the song, within the transcription of they seem to be a sporadic phenomenon. Everything is an octave lower than written, except the whistling in 'Three Moore Brothers.'" Mr. Cazden usually transcribed the *first* stanza of each song, then indicated with additional measures what seemed the normal variations for specific measures; the number over those additional bars indicates what measures they are variants of. (There is no point in saying just when in the performance they occur, for they can occur at any time and within any stanza; they simply indicate that such variation *did* occur.) One can identify the stanza transcribed by comparing the text printed with the music to the text of the song itself.

It is important to keep in mind that a transcription of any specific stanza of a folk song is a transcription of that verse as it was performed at that moment, nothing more. If the transcriber is attuned to the general musical sense of the song, he can either indicate the general range of variation for specific sections (as Cazden did) or he can select a stanza that has in it the most representative characteristics of the range of variations (as Mrs. McCulloh did). All transcriptions of folk tunes are in a way approximations of an archetype that exists in the mind of the singer and another archetype that exists in the mind of the transcriber; one hopes that the perception of a good transcriber will be close to that of the singer, that he not only will accurately transcribe the individual notes in a specific stanza, but also that he will have a sense of the general form adequate enough to permit him to hear the significant variations.

The musical transcriptions should be considered samples of what the song might be like; the complete song cannot be reconstructed from the partial transcriptions because of the continuing variation common in folk song. Transcription of a fluid form is always a matter of taste and judgment; no two people do it in quite the same way. There is a particular problem with the perception of ornamentation. The usual notion of ornamentation has to do with "little extras" added to the basic tune; that involves deciding what is tune and what is extra. Mrs. McCulloh wrote, "If Smitty sings the 'same' tune a hundred times, and in ninety verses uses similar patterns of 'ornamentation' (say what would be indicated by grace notes, clusters of short duration notes all sung to one syllable, flips, slides, 'feathering,' and so forth), why shouldn't they be considered essential to the tune, if it is exceptional when he doesn't use them?"

In the texts of the songs I have used quotation marks to try to indicate logical changes of speakers (dramatic speakers, not song leaders), for some of the stanzas are dramatic monologues, and without those quotation marks much of the sense is lost. In 15. "Midnight Special," for example, it is obvious that the third stanza consists of a reported dialogue between two people (the first line) and the singer's comment on that dialogue (the second line); the difference in person is made clear by the singer's use of the third person "he" in the second line. So I used two sets of quotation marks for the first line of the stanza, none for the second. Later in the song there is no introduction of another voice for the "Rosie" stanza, so I left that in the singer's voice and used quotation marks for the interjected questions only.

When the lead singers made a comment about the song immediately before or after performance, I sometimes printed those comments along with the text in the form of statements within quotation marks.

In many transcriptions I have, for clarity, indicated the group's part by printing their lines in capitals and the lead singer's lines in lower case. The music transcriptions indicate most clearly where the group comes in and where the lead singer sings alone.

I have not attempted representative orthography. Unless one uses phonetic spelling such attempts are not usually very helpful, and phonetic spelling would not be familiar to all readers. I reject dialect-style writing because I find it almost impossible to read. If one has ever heard Southwestern Negroes speak, one has as good a sense of how these songs are articulated as one would get with spellings that would make the thing clumsy to read and silly to look at. If one has never heard any Southwestern Negroes, the queer spellings would only reinforce an invalid caricature. (I suggest listening to some of the generally available LPs listed in the discography.) I have occasionally dropped a terminal consonant where it was very obvious in the singing or important for rhyme or consonance, and on very rare occasions I have dropped a medial consonant when the singer's elision was such that printing the word with the consonant included would have made scanning impossible.

Although the lead singers are good at isochronic manipulation—that is, they can usually manage a wide range of syllables within a line of set beats—there are some occasions when an extra stress is needed, or the line is drifting to the trochaic, so an extra syllable is put in to realign the iamb. This is usually in the form of an *uh* sound (written "a") between two words or attached to the end or beginning of a word. When such an "a" does occur, I try in the transcription to indicate, by a hyphen, what word it seems to be attached to; if the "a" seems neutrally stressed between two words it is unhyphenated.

The expressions "you know," "oh well," "I say," and so forth are often used for metric expansion. If I followed standard punctuation, by placing commas after and in the middle of such terms, some lines would sink under a plethora of commas. Most of the time I try to follow the sense of the *singing*. Those introductory expressions are often sung without pause, so I have not usually used commas with them. There is often a heavy caesura in the middle of a line even when there is no break in the sense of the line, and I *have* used commas to indicate those caesuras. The music transcriptions, which have the benefit of having the musical phrasing to indicate sung phrasing, usually follow standard usage.

There is a general tendency to drop final consonants, especially within a line where there are elisions; I have usually *not* written the words this way because the mess of apostrophes is annoying to read. Consonants are dropped far more often in polysyllabic words than monosyllabic words, and the consonant dropped most often is the present participle's terminal "g"; for example, they might sing *ring* and sound the "g," but only rarely will the final "g" in *ringing* or *hammering* be sung.

Certain words are consistently elided or expanded. *Hammering* is two syllables: *hamm'rin'*. *Louisiana* is four syllables, not five, with the second sung syllable quite weak: *Loos-y-an-a*. *Grizzly* is three syllables rather than two: *grizz-a-ly*. *Believe* is almost always elided as *b'lieve*.

Cotton and Cane: Solo Songs (1–13)

---

1 Three Moore Brothers

A. Joseph "Chinaman" Johnson, Ellis, 11 July 1964, 64.4, J.M.
B. "Mr. Tom Moore," Johnny Jackson, Ramsey 1, 16 August 1965, 369.1, N.C.

The Moore Farm stretches along the Navasota River near where it joins the Brazos. The family is well known in the Brazos bottom country, an area more cotton-South than cattle-West. This is big-plantation territory where, until not very many years ago, the landowners exercised an authority that was almost feudal in dimension and style. William F. Koock and John Q. Anderson, both of Texas A & M, have looked into the background of this cante-fable and tell me that there is an extensive folktale repertory pertaining to the brothers' adventures with their employees and the law. Mr. Koock noted, in a paper sent me by Professor Anderson, that "there were apparently three brothers, Mr. Steve, Mr. Tom, and Mr. Henry Moore. Their father's name was Mr. Tom Moore," and that there are stories involving all of them.

The Moores are well known within the units of the Texas Department of Corrections. Some of the inmates are from the Brazos valley, others remember the days when the older Moores would have inmates paroled in their custody and would set them to work on the plantation. Descriptions of conditions on the Moore property range from the fabulous to the hellish, often within the same statement. For example:

> This fella told me Moore would buy you automobiles and say you could ride about in the plantation in the car but you couldn't leave. He said you could ride around, he would buy you any kind of car you said. But you couldn't go nowhere. You had to just drive around on the plantation. Had that little commissary store there. I guess they'd run up to that commissary and gamble. That's mostly what

them fellas did out there—gamble. You earned the money and you owe him so much for the car, which cost so much. You just tied down when you get there. That's the way I heard it, now. I never been out there. I just figured plantations are as bad as the penitentiary from the way I heard guys talk about it.

I remember a boy named Jesse in 1946. I came to Two Camp on a one-year [sentence]. Jesse ran off from this Mr. Tom Moore in Navasota and went to Mexico. The man went and got in the car over there and got him. Went into Mexico when he found out where he was. His sister was living on Mr. Moore's farm. He wrote his sister a letter, and Mr. Moore got ahold of the letter and went to Mexico and brought him back. Jesse told me about this after we got to this camp together. Told him on the way back, "Don't you know better than to run off from Mr. Moore, nigger? I come and get you anywhere you go. Why did you leave? Wasn't you eating good? Wasn't you doin' all right, doin' better than you was in the penitentiary?" See, Mr. Moore had paroled him out.

He says, "Well, I was doing all right in that respect." But they gamble there on Saturday night and they get drunk; you know how them old plantations and country places are. He says, "Too much fightin' out there and I was ascared I'm gonna get killed and I just left."

He says, "Would you rather be there or be in the penitentiary?"

"Man, I don't know. Ain't quite as much fightin' in the penitentiary, but I'd rather be free."

The man said, "Well, you can't have both of them. You either stay with me till your parole is up or you go back to the penitentiary."

Jesse said, "Well, I'll try to stick it out because my sister's there."

That was facts, he told me that. I did time with him. Got him and brought him back.

Mr. Tom Moore. I heard that he's a man to get you out of the penitentiary. He get you out through the governor, some kinda way there. After he get you out he put you out there on the plantation and you had to work. There wasn't no leavin'. Whenever you go to town you had to see him. And he had his own town. They say he had something like a commissary, you know. A canteen or something like that. You go up there and just buy so much merchandise. You never did get out of debt, though, you was always in debt. And I heard they had riders out there. When you tried to leave they'd ride you down and catch you and bring you back. Then they'd put you in some kind a little old house out there, something like a jail. That's what they tell me. And then work you with chains on. They say when you come out they'd have you hobbled down so you couldn't run no more, not with that ball and chain.

The first time I heard that song was back when I first came in the penitentiary in 1954. Chinaman was the one I heard singin' it. We was working out in the squads. That's the first time I heard it, but I didn't learn too much of it then.

Said they was all right and they had a big farm and had a bunch a niggers workin' for them. They was good, you know, but if you did something wrong they was mean. Said their farm was something like a plantation. Said they had a bunch a womens workin' for them and a bunch a mens, say a lot of them was ex-convicts that had put a lot of time in the penitentiary. Said they got 'em out of the penitentiary, had 'em paroled and things, had 'em work for them and let them have their womens, give 'em money. Tom Moore said, "If you keep yourself out of the graveyard, I'll keep you out of the penitentiary." No matter what you do, say, just work. All they had to do was do their work for them and they could go to town, raise hell, fight, pick up other men's women, anything they wanted to do. Said, Tom Moore said he'd see to them not coming to the penitentiary long as they wasn't in town.

That's what they all say.

The boy that composed that song was a great friend of mine. He was a hand out there about eight years. Everytime something would happen to those people they would criticize him in their way so Mr. Tom wouldn't hear it or know it. They'd get out in the field and he's way over yonder there. He couldn't hear what they was talking about and they'd just say things about him to one another, and when he come they'd hush up. And this boy, he was out there working, and saw him and he made up all these verses about the way Mr. Tom would treat them and how he would do the hands. You never will get to the end of that song: you will find more and more to put to it. You can sing it all day and then wake up in the morning and add some more to it. You can't get that thing all finished up because they add to it every day. They making up more verses to it.

I met one old man, not an inmate of the prison, who had lived in the area of the Moore property some years before. He had spent a considerable amount of time in and around the farm when he was younger. He remembered it this way:

They started gambling there about one o'clock. They had a great big store. Clothes, groceries, call it a commissary. All the hands would go there to get paid off on Saturday noon. The first ones he paid off would go right outside the store and go to gambling. Just as he'd pay them off, them that did gamble they'd go right out there and gamble. Start gambling at one o'clock and it'd be Monday when he ring that bell to go into the field when it was over. Them gambling games would last just that long. And if they got broke, according to who he liked or how much they owed him, he'd keep them going with that money to gamble on. So they'd be satisfied there on the place.

This was on Allen Farm. And where Curry was you could gamble, too. He had a store there at the river bridge. It's seven miles back up from that river bridge back up to Allen farm. That farm's so large till he can't put all of his people right together. It runs from the Brazos River right up to the Allen Farm. Now it done spreaded from Allen Farm into Clay Station about eight more miles.

Their daddy was an old man, I didn't get to know him. But I knowed pretty well all his boys: Tom, Clarence, Steve, Harry, and Walker. Walkamo. He died before any of them. Then Clarence was next on the list. When the daddy died those kids was kids, just Walker and Clarence was grown. And they seed after those boy's interests until they got grown and then divided it up, quartered the land off into sections, so each one of them would know where their land was. I think they didn't part that land up until about four years ago. Before then it was just Moore Brothers, the Four Moore Brothers. If you workin' for one you workin' for all of them. And they was brought up in that old slaverytime way that their daddy did over in Washington county. He was a slaverytime man. He raised colored peoples and Mexicans and everybody else over there. Just told them, "Well you go yonder but you better hurry up back before night." They were grown but they had to come back, else he'd whip 'em. Well, those kids come up looking at that and they knowed it and they wanted to get right in their daddy's foot-tracks. And they kept it up for thirty or forty years too, until they whipped John Row and beat him up and that broke up the bad part of the Moores . . . The song was written I'd say back in the twenties. I heard it about in '28.

Mack McCormick wrote me a long note about the song, part of which I quote here:

> The song originated in the 30s, had only one obscure appearance on record (Gold Star, a Houston firm) until the two versions which I included in Vol. II of *Treasury of Field Recordings*. These two versions are quite different but they compliment one another . . .
>
> I've collected 23 versions of the "Tom Moore's Farm" item and regard it as one of the few genuine examples of protest in traditional song uncovered in recent years—but note it is not a social protest, it does not condemn a system or take any such lofty position, it simply describes the literal actions of one farmer named Tom Moore.
>
> . . . Your version is one of those which presents a fair picture of life on the Moore property—with both the pros and the cons. It is quite true that the food was excellent, the women were supplied, and the man who did his work could engage in a little Saturday night cutting and never worry about going to the penitentiary. In short, Tom Moore and the brothers take good care of good workers. The work they expect is, however, excessive.

I was sufficiently interested when I first learned of the song to confirm each of these points by extensive interviews with various people in the area. I developed an understanding of all that went into the song's origin but at the same time found that I had best delay my plans for writing anything using this material since it would cause further misery. It is quite a thorn in Moore's side— knowing the Negroes are singing this, which in some versions is quite humiliating—and he is in a power position where he could easily take out his feelings on Negroes who work for him, live in the area and are in various ways affected by his actions. On the record I mentioned, one of the singers says that Moore would burn him out if word reached him that this man was singing this song. It is frankly hard to predict actions of this kind in view of present changes. Local rumors do not ascribe any such violence to the family since about 1957—but since it is liable to be him, not me, who gets burnt out, I've always been careful about distributing word of the song's existence . . . Actually he doesn't seem to mind the local Negroes singing the song, but it upsets him to know that people in Houston have heard of Tom Moore not because he is an important farmer (he is, too; quite progressive in agricultural methods) but because of a little Negro-made song.

Mrs. McCulloh wrote about her transcription of Chinaman's version that "Without a doubt this is one of the absolute peskiest things I've ever tried to transcribe. It is quite free, and so the time values of the notes in the transcription are to be taken more as ratios than as God's truth. Fortunately, this is on the LP, so anyone who wants to check or improve or modify can do it . . . I've just done the first two song/whistle sections, not much in terms of elapsed time, but sufficient to show certain favorite patterns (of, for example, ornamentation) which recur."

The whistling in Chinaman's version is curious; I've never heard anything quite like it. The structure and ornamentation reminded me of the kind of break a very good guitar player might make, but Chinaman insists he never heard anyone sing the song to any kind of instrumental accompaniment, and that the person he first learned the song from had that sort of whistled break at the end of each line.

Chinaman's version appears on *Negro Folklore from Texas Prisons,* Electra EKS–7296. Lightnin' Hopkins sings a "Tim Moore's Farm" on *Fast Life Woman,* Verve 8453, that shares some lines with the prison version; it was also released as a single by Gold Star. The Texas *Lomax MS* (144) has a three stanza "Blues" in the AAB form about Tom Moore; one of those verses is the Rice Hotel/food verse sung by Chinaman and Jackson. Two versions of the song can be heard on *Treasury of Field Recordings, II,* 77 Records 77LA-12/3. The "Meet me in the bottom" stanza of the A-text appears in a different song, "Meet Me in the Bottom" sung by David Lee on *Negro Folk Music of Alabama,* vol. 6, Folkways FE-4474; that song is printed in Courlander, 1963-B, pp. 97 and 274.

1-A   Three Moore Brothers

(♩ = 60)

Well, who is that I see come rid-in', boy, Down on the low turn row?

(whistle)

No-bo-dy but Tom Dev-il,   That's the man they call Tom Moore.

(whistle)

(whistle)

Well,   as I went walk-in' down, A-cross Mis-ter Tom Moore's field,

(whistle)

I was gon-na steal a lit-tle corn, man, Just to make some bol-ted meal.

(whistle)

Spoken:
I was down on the Moore Brother farm. I seen a rider down on the low turn row. I ask one a the workers, "Who is the fella I see ridin' on the low turn row?" This is what he told me:

Sung:
"Well who is that I see come ridin', boy, down on the low turn row?"
"Nobody but Tom Devil, that's the man they call Tom Moore."

Spoken:
   Now I was goin' down across Mr. Tom Moore's field. I was goin' to steal a little corn to make me some bolted meal. Now this is when the man caught me.

Sung:
Well as I went walkin' down, across Mr. Tom Moore's field,
I was gonna steal a little corn, man, just to make some bolted meal.

Well I cried, "Please, Mr. Tom, man, please don't you murder me!"
Well he laid down his pistol and he picked up a singletree.

Well Mr. Tom got land, boys, from the river bridge plumb up to the Allen Farm.
Well he stands down on the levee, watch his eight grey mules move along.

Spoken:
   Now Mr. Curry, he went to Mr. Tom, he told Mr. Tom, said, "Mr. Tom," said, "I don't think I'm gettin' enough wages for the work that I'm doin'. I would like for you to raise my wages." Well this is what Mr. Tom told Mr. Curry:

Sung:
Well Mr. Tom told Mr. Curry, he said, "Man, you oughta be satisfied,
I give you big black woman, saddle and horse to ride."

Well the reason I like to work for the three Moore Brothers so well,
Well they feed at their table like they do at the Rice Hotel.

Well Mr. Harry told me, boys, without a smile or grin,
Said, "You keep yourself out the graveyard, boy, I keep you out the pen."

Wo, wake up, wake up, Lucile, put on your mornin' gown,
Babe, I don't want no loving, I just want to feel around.

Wo, meet me down in the bottom, babe, and bring me my boots and
   shoes,
Says, "I'm leaving the three Moore brothers, I don't have no time to lose."

Additional stanza:
Earlier in the same recording session (64.2), Chinaman sang:

There's one thing 'bout the three Moore brothers, boys, I sure do like
That is when your wife or woman quit you, they'll go and bring her back.

1-B   Mr. Tom Moore

(♩=63)

1. This is why we love the Moore broth-ers so well:
They feed us on the farm like they do in the Rice Hotel.   3. Well,   Mis-ter Tom Moore,   you know, I
shined   his shoes,   He gave   me   a
nick-el and a bot-tle of wine   to get the blues.

This is why we love the Moore brothers so well:
They feed us on the farm like they do in the Rice Hotel.

Tom Moore told me, "Boy, where you been?
It's all right, just keep yourself out a the graveyard, I'll keep you out a the
   pen."

Well, Mr. Tom Moore, you know I shined his shoes,
He gave me a nickle and a bottle of wine to get the blues.

I was down in the penitentiary doin' natural life,
I heard about Mr. Tom Moore and I gave him a wire.

He wrote me back and told me, "I will set you free,
But nigger I want to tell you, you got to slave for me."

Woooo, that is why we love Mr. Tom Moore so well—
They feed on their farm like they do in the Rice Hotel.

2   Poor Boy

A. J. B. Smith, Ramsey 2, 17 August 1965, 374.5, J.M.
B. "Cold Penitentiary Blues," Joseph "Chinaman" Johnson, Ellis, 11 July 1964, 65.2
C. "Poor Boy Number Two," J. B. Smith, Ramsey 2, 12 June 1966, 463.1

Professor D. K. Wilgus of the Center for the Study of Comparative Folklore and Mythology, UCLA, has written me that there are at least twenty-two, white, country recordings of this ballad. It seems to be known throughout the South, usually with the title "Poor Boy" or "Coon Can Game." David Freeman of New York City sent me a tape of B. F. Shelton's "Cold Penitentiary Blues" (Victor 40107), recorded in 1928 and released in 1930; Shelton's record was clearly the source of Chinaman's version. Smith's A-text seems to be an amalgam of several sources, but the final stanza is probably his own. His C-text is a different song, but it shares title, melody, and emotional impetus with the standard version; Smith translates the song into the prison context and manages, while keeping the mood of the traditional song going, to create something quite splendid.

For a bibliographical note on the song, see Laws' entry I-4 (p. 248). Two of the many other texts in print are Lomax, 1941, pp. 308–310 ("As I Set Down to Play Tin-Can," from Kentucky), and Scarborough, pp. 87–89.

2-A   Poor Boy

($\bullet$ = 40)

As I walked in-to the de – pot, boy, a train come a-

roll – in' by, Well, I looked out the win-dow, I saw the

girl I love, hung down my head and cried. I hung down my

head and I cried, poor boy, hung down my head and

cried. Well, I peeped out the win-dow, I saw the girl I

love, hung down my head and cried. Well, the judge say, "Boy, are you

guilt - y, now?" "No, judge, not guilt-y, you see." "Well,

if we find you guilt-y, poor boy, gon-na

send you to pen-i - ten-tia – ry. Yeah, I'll send you to the

pen - i - ten-tia-ry, poor boy, I'll send you to the pen-i-ten-tia-

ry." Says, "If I find you guilt - y, poor

boy,   gon - na   send you   to the pen - i -   ten - tia - ry."   Well, the

ju - ry found   me   guilt - y, poor   boy,   and the clerks,   they

wrote   it   down.   So they turned me   in the hands   of the

trans - fer man,   till   I   was   Hunts - ville bound.   Yeah,

I   was a - Hunts - ville   bound,   poor   boy,   yeah,   I   was a-

Hunts - ville bound.   Well, they turned me   in the hands   of the

trans - fer man,   till   I   was   Hunts - ville   bound.

(opening)

My   moth - er   called me   to   her   bed - side

(basic pattern)

"I learned this from a bunch a people I was workin' with. Some old inmates like myself. We sing those songs in the field to pass away the time. And there's so much truth in some of them. Some of them is true songs. This is practically a true song. I mean either direct or indirect for me or some other guy. But there's a lot of true meanings to it."

My mother called me to her bedside and these is the words she say:
"Son, if you don't stop your rowdy ways, you be in trouble all a your days.
Be in trouble all your days, poor boy, in trouble all a your days,
If you don't stop your rowdy ways, in trouble all a your days."

As I walked into the depot, boy, a train come a rollin' by,
Well, I looked out the window, I saw the girl I love, hung down my head
and cried.
I hung down my head and I cried, poor boy, hung down my head and
cried.
Well, I peeped out the window, I saw the girl I love, hung down my head
and cried.

Well the judge say, "Boy, are you guilty now?" "No, judge, not guilty,
you see."
"Well, if we find you guilty, poor boy, gonna send you to the penitentiary.
Yeah, I'll send you to the penitentiary, poor boy, I'll send you to the
penitentiary."
Says, "If I find you guilty, poor boy, gonna send you to the penitentiary."

Well, the jury found me guilty, poor boy, and the clerks, they wrote it
down,
So they turned me in the hands of the transfer man, till I was Huntsville
bound.
Yeah, I was a-Huntsville bound, poor boy, yeah, I was a-Huntsville
bound,
Well they turned me in the hands of the transfer man, till I was Huntsville bound.

Till they give me two sixes upside down, now they call me Ninety-nine,
Yeah they give me two sixes upside down, now they call me Ninety-nine.

When we enter the penitentiary, my number was twenty-three,
All I could hear those poor boys say, "Someday we'll all go free.
Someday we'll all go free, poor boy, someday we'll all go free."
All I could hear those poor boys say, "Someday we'll all go free."

2-B   Cold Penitentiary Blues

I got the cold penitentiary blues, poor boys, I got the cold penitentiary
blues,
Just thinkin' of the girl I love, I got the cold penitentiary blues.

As I set down to play cooncan, I couldn't hardly play my hand,
Just thinkin' of the girl I love, she run away with another man.
She run away with another man, poor boys, she run away with another
man,
She run away with another man, poor boys, run away with another man.

My mother called me up to her bedside, and this is the word she said:
"Son, if you don't quit your rowdy ways, you be in trouble all your days.
You be in trouble all your days, poor boy, you be in trouble all your days,
You be in trouble all your days, poor boy, you be in trouble all your days."

I got the cold penitentiary blues, poor boys, I got the cold penitentiary
    blues,
Just thinkin' of the girl I love, I got the cold penitentiary blues.

As I went down to the old depot, the train was rollin' by,
I saw the woman that I love, I hung down my head and cried.
I hung down my ole head and I cried, poor boys, I hung down my head
    and cried,
I hung down my head and I cried, poor boys, I hung down my head and
    cried.

2-C   Poor Boy Number Two

Very first day on the Brazos line, poor boy, on the Brazos line,
Number One was a buckin', Number Two was flyin', wo boy, Number
    Two was flyin',
Number Three was a hurryin', the pull-dos cryin', poor boy, the pull-dos
    cryin',
Number Three was a hurryin', the pull-dos cryin', poor boy, the pull dos
    cryin'.

Next day, poor boy, on the old turn row, you know the sun was a hunderd
    degrees.
All I could hear was a poor boy say, "Some day we'll all go free.
Some day we'll all go free, poor boy, some day we'll all go free.
All I could hear was a poor boy say, "Some day we'll all go free."

Hot scalding water rollin' down my eyes, [so] busy I can't hardly see,
Can't keep up with the other boys, won't you please have mercy on me.
Won't you please have mercy on me, poor boy, Captain, have mercy,
    please.
Now I can't keep up with the other boys, please have mercy on me.

Just one more chance in a-life, poor boy, to do the right or wrong,
This hell wouldn't be my potion, boy, this hell wouldn't be my home.
This hell wouldn't be my home, poor boy, no boy, wouldn't be my home,
Just one more chance in life, poor boy, to do the right or wrong.

I'd go someplace and settle down, contented with well-doin',
Tell all the people on the street I meet what a lesson I have learned.
What a lesson I have learned, poor boy, lesson I have learned,
Go somewhere and settle down, with the lesson I have learned.

To be a disobedient child you often pay full fair,
You boarded your train 'way down the line, to finally pay off here.
You finally pay off here, poor boy, you finally pay off here,
You boarded your train 'way down the line, you finally pay off here.

The sun's goin' down and so am I, wonder who will be the first.
Of all the things ever happened to me, tell me what could be the worst.
Oh tell me what could be the worst, poor boy, tell me what could be the
    worst,
Out a all the things ever happened to me, tell me what could be the worst.

Go down sunshine, go down sunshine, oh hurry, please go down,
This aggie hoe, this grassy row, won't let me see sundown.
Won't let me see sundown, poor boy, it won't let me see sundown,
This aggie hoe, this grassy row, won't let me see sundown.

Don't want no supper, just want my bed, get all the rest I can,
Be morning again before you know, I'll be in another strain.
Oh I'll be in another strain, poor boy, I'll be in another strain,
Be morning again before you know, I'll be in another strain.

Wish I had-a listened to mom and dad, they knew the best for me,
I'd never had this bridge to cross, never had this misery.
Never had this misery, poor boy, this misery,
I'd never had this bridge to cross, never had this misery.

Here's to the boys in my home town, Highway Six at Hearn,
Gamin' and chancin' with the law, don't worth the time I'm doin'.
It don't worth the time I'm doin', don't worth the time I'm doin',
Gamin' and chancin' with the law, don't worth the time I'm doin'.

Chancin' with the long-armed law, you seldom win or draw,
Gamin' and chancin' with the law, you seldom win or draw.

"That's 'Poor Boy Number Two! The day then was so hard, hard that
I couldn't hardly make it, and it was a strain for me to make it through.
And I was so tired I wanted to go to bed. Didn't even want my supper,
too tired to eat. And wanted to get all the rest I could 'cause I knew
I'd have to go the next day and I'd be in another strain. So I wanted
every minute I could possibly get of rest."

3 I Can Buckle a Wheeler

A. Joseph "Chinaman" Johnson, Ellis, 19 August 1965, 388.1, N.C.
B. "I Worked Old Moll," M. Filmore, Ellis, 22 March 1966, 448.4, J.M.

This sort of levee camp song about mule skinning seems to exist in many versions throughout the South. Individual stanzas are highly migratory. Lomax, 1936-A, pp. 50–52, prints a "Levee Camp 'Holler'" which is a composite from several Southern states.

The song survived in prison because differences between the conditions of work in the early twentieth century levee camps and in prisons were not that great. See stanzas 44, 49–54, 71, 83, 115–116 in the songs of J. B. Smith (songs 28 through 34 in this collection).

3-A I Can Buckle a Wheeler

"Good mornin', Captain." "Good mornin', Shine.
Shine, I want another skinner for to roll my line."

"I can buckle your wheeler, Captain, man, I can roll your line,
Whoa, I can press my initials on a mule's behind, mmmm."

Well when you wake up in the morning, bring me my old forty-five,
Whoa, I'll knock down skinners for a solid mile, mmmm, Lord, Lord,
   Lord, mmmm.

Whoa, come on Tippy, come on Tippy-do,
Oh the Captain call me and I got to go, Lord, Lord, Lord.

Well I went all around, this whole corral
Lord, I couldn't find a mule with his shoulder well, mmmm.

Well I worked old Moll and I worked old Belle,
Lord, I couldn't find a mule with his shoulder well, Lord, Lord, Lord.

Out in the rain, all out in the cold,
That old Captain called me and I got to go, mmmm.

Well I went to the commissary laughin', oh Lord, I come back cryin',
Lord, I couldn't pay for the Bear brand peaches my old gal been buyin'.

Well I'm goin' down yonder, tell that old commissary man,
Don't let my woman have no Bear brand peaches, cub on the can.

If I should die on the levee, Captain, I ain't got no home,
Take the buckle off my wheeler for my own tombstone, hmmm, let the
   levee roll on.

3-B   I Worked Old Moll

I worked old Moll and I worked old Belle,
I couldn't find a mule, oh, with her shoulder well.

I say, I looked all over this whole corral,
And I couldn't find a mule, oh, with her shoulder well.

You know, I rode so long, oh Lord, till they call me Mr. Rollin' Stone,
Oh boy, I say, call me "Mr. Rollin' Stone."

"Oh Captain, Captain, what time a day?"
I say he looked at me, oh man, and he walked away.

"Captain, Captain, what's the matter with you?"
I say, "If you got any plugs, please give me a chew, hmmmmm."

I say, I work so long, so they call me Rollin' Stone.

4   Yon' Come Roberta

W. Mitchell, Wynne, 20 August 1965, 390.1, N.C.

Although the tune is completely different, the text of this blues is
obviously derived from the well-known field song "Midnight Special"
(15).

Yon' come Roberta, got a hundred all in her hand,
Yon' come Roberta, got a hundred all in her hand,
She said, "Good mornin', judge, you know I come to get my man."

Well he just turned around, boys, and he commenced to chewin' his cud,
    (2x)
He said, "A hundred, Roberta, won't do your man no good."

Well they brought me coffee, oh man, they brought me tea, (2x)
Well they brought me everything, Lord, but that jailhouse key.

Well I left Roberta, well she laid and cried all night, (2x)
Well she just a good little girl, but you know I didn't treat her right.

---

5   Butt-Cut Ruler
C. B. Kimble, Ramsey 2, 4 July 1964, 37.8, N.C.

6   Should A Been on the River in 1910
Arthur "Lightnin' " Sherrod, Ellis, 19 August 1965, 387.2, N.C.

7   Roberta
C. B. Kimble, Ramsey 2, 17 August 1965, 379.5, N.C.

These three songs are about as loose as single musical events can get and
still be called "songs." They begin in nearly strophic form, then shift to
rambling and barely structured sequences of lines and images in which
the musical lines vary as much as the metrical length; this is especially
true in songs 5 and 6. "Butt-cut ruler" is an ironic brag—the term simply
means someone who chops well enough to get assigned the largest part
of the felled tree to cut for sectioning; the irony is clear when one hears
the tune and meter along with the words—the song is slow and dragging
and the *sound* belies the brag of power in the words. The second song
begins with a stanza from "Go Down Old Hannah," then shifts to a grim
sequence of negative images: the lost partner, the unfaithful woman,
the two-timing buddy, the woman who doesn't appear. "Roberta" is
fairly regular in its verse form, but the song is nearly as much a moan
as the other two. Chinaman and Mack Maze sang similar versions of this
song for me (11 July 1964, 62.4, and 22 March 1966, 444.5). Recorded
versions of "Roberta" in the AAFS include those by Leadbelly, recorded
by John A. Lomax in 1935 (51B), and Richard Amerson, in Livingston,
Alabama, recorded by John A. and Ruby Lomax in 1940 (4048 A1).

5   Butt-Cut Ruler

(♩=92, freely)

Don't you walk on down,   I'll drive you in the tim - ber,

If you dare to walk in the tim - ber,   I'm a butt - cut

rul - er,   Oh my   Lord - y,   Won't you help me to call   'em,

Good God - a - might - y,   Won't you drop 'em down to - geth - er,

Good God - a - might - y,   I'm call - in' lit - tle Car - rie,

Wo my   Lord - y,   Well, I'm turn - in' just to fool   you,

I'm a butt - cut   rul - er,   In the tim - ber,   Good God - a -

might - y,   Let's drop 'em down to - geth - er, bull - ies, and make 'em

sound like one,   Good God - a - might - y,   Let's go to dog - gin',

God - a - might - y,   Got a red - eyed ser - geant,   Red - eyed ser - geant.

Don't you walk on down
I'll drive you in the timber
If you dare to walk in the timber
I'm a butt-cut ruler
Oh my Lordy
Won't you help me to call 'em
Good God amighty
Won't you drop 'em down together
Good God amighty
I'm callin' little Carrie
Wo my Lordy
Well I'm turnin' just to fool you
I'm a butt-cut ruler
In the timber
Good God amighty
Let's drop 'em down together bullies
And make 'em sound like one
Good God amighty
Let's go to doggin'
God amighty
Got a red-eyed sergeant
Red-eyed sergeant

---

6   Should A Been on the River in 1910

(♩=63)

Well, you should a been on the riv-er   in nine-teen ten,

Yeah, when they was driv-in' the wom-en   like they drove those

men.   Well, when I first came down   on the Bra-zos line,

Yeah, they was driv-in' those wom-en   like they drove those men.

Yeah, you can talk to the Cap-tain; Cap-tain, he will see you in.

let-ter from my ba-by, she say she'll be down, Know the day pass,

she not a-round. That's all right, I'll be 'round

some day, When I get luck-y, I'll be home some day.

Well, you should a been on the river in nineteen-ten,
Yeah, when they was drivin' the women like they drive those men.

Well, when I first came down on the Brazos line,
Yeah, they was drivin' those women like they drove those men.
Yeah, you can talk to the Captain, Captain, he will see you in.

Say, when he give me my evenin' bread,
He say, "Son, let me tell you, don't you never go away."
Says, "You know I gotta go someday, Captain, and I never know."

Say, you know my buddy, he gone on home,
Wonder where did he leave me alone.

I got a partner on Ramsey doin' ninety-nine.
Say someday, someday, someday, baby, I'll be home,
Someday you'll see me around.
When you hear me, when I call you to me, baby,
Don't you run and hide.
Oh, but I be back home on the fourth of July.
See my buddy, whoa man, he goin' down,
Well, he had so much time, they done drove him down.
Well, when he first come to the river
He had 'em down,
Now he gone on home with this girl a mine.
Got a letter from my baby,
She say she'll be down,
[You] know the day pass, she not around.
That's all right, I'll be 'round some day.
When I get lucky, I'll be home some day.

7   Roberta

(♩=54)

Lit-tle Ro - ber-ta,   let your hair   grow long,

I'll be home   next   sum-mer,   Oh, Lord, Lord,

If I don't   stay long.   Lit-tle Ro -

ber-ta,   will you let your   hair grow   so

long,   Till it drag   on the ground?

Lit-tle Ro - ber-ta,   Lord, Lord, Lord,   I got all   these

years.   One day   'fore long,   lit-tle Ro-ber-ta,   at the

riv-er   I'm gone.   Just meet me   at the

banks   a big Bra-zos,   lit-tle Ro-ber-ta,   Be-

cause   I'll be on my   way.   Ser-geant,

Ser-geant,   you can blow your horn,   I'll be

long gone   to the pro-mised   land.

Little Roberta, let your hair grow long,
I'll be home next summer, oh, Lord, Lord,
If I don't stay long.

Little Roberta, will you let your hair grow so long,
Till it drag on the ground?

Little Roberta, Lord, Lord, Lord, I got all these years.
One day 'fore long, little Roberta, at the river I'm gone.

Just meet me at the banks a big Brazos, little Roberta,
Because I'll be on my way.

Sergeant, Sergeant, you can blow your horn,
I'll be long gone to the promised land.

8   Make a Longtime Man Feel Bad

A. Mack Maze, Ellis, 19 August 1965, 387.9, N.C.
B. Mack Maze, Ellis, 11 July 1964, 63.5

The mood of this song is as anguished as the words are simple. It describes—with the "don't hear" image—one of the most painful aspects of the life of the long time convict: the gradual erosion of all ties and connections with the outside world. Versions of this song have been recorded in several states: one version by a group on Cummins Farm, Gould, Arkansas, recorded by John A. Lomax in 1934, appears on *Anglo-American Ballads,* Archive of American Folk Song (AAFS) L-1; Johnny Smith and group, Parchman, Mississippi were recorded by John A. and Ruby Lomax, 1939 (2679 B1); see also, "22" and group on *Negro Prison Songs from the Mississippi State Penitentiary,* recorded by Alan Lomax, Tradition TLP-1020, and published by him in Lomax, 1960, pp. 541–543; and James Russel and gang, "I Had Five Long Years," on *Angola Prison Worksongs,* Folk Lyric LFS A-5, recorded by Harry Oster in Louisiana.

8-A   Make a Longtime Man Feel Bad

Roberta, let your hair grow long,
Let it grow so long till it drags the floor,
Make a longtime man feel good.

She won't write no letter,
I don't hear from home,
Make a longtime man feel bad.

8-B   Make a Longtime Man Feel Bad

Roberta, let your hair grow long,
Let it grow so long till it drags the ground.
Make a longtime man feel bad.

Make a longtime man feel bad,
I don't get no letter, I don't hear from home,
Make a longtime man feel bad.

Long time, 'Berta, for to hear, waitin' on,
She don't write no letter, I don't hear from home,
Make a longtime man feel bad.

9 If You See My Mother

Mack Maze, Ellis, 11 July 1964, 65.3, J.M.

This is another of those songs that are too anguished to come through on a printed page. The words are simple, the tune sometimes becomes no more than a moan, then the moan becomes words again. This performance appears on *Negro Folklore from Texas State Prisons*, Electra EKS 7296. Some of the stanzas have appeared in other songs. Texas Alexander's "Levee Camp Moan," on *The Country Blues* 2 RBF-9, originally recorded in New York in 1927, has, "Lord, they accuse me a murder / I haven't harmed a man." A sequence of "got me accused of . . ." with the appropriate crimes is the structure of Eddie Boyd's "Third Degree," recorded in 1950, Chess U-4374. Lomax, 1941, p. 355, prints "Mama, Mama," from the singing of Augustus Haggerty, recorded in Huntsville, Texas, in 1934: "Little boy if you see my Mammy will you please tell her for me / Lawd, to see the governor, tell him to set me free?" In the *Lomax MS* (144) there is a song by "Track Horse" at Huntsville (numbered 210A2) which seems to be the same performance, though there are some differences in the transcription. Alan Lomax included a song callèd "The Murder's Home" in *Negro Prison Songs from the Mississippi State Penitentiary*, Tradition TLP 1020, with the stanza: "Pray for me—o mamma, pray for me, pray for me, / Lord, I got a long holdover and I can't go free . . ." (the word Lomax transcribes as *holdover* is probably *detainer*.) That stanza seems to be much older, however. The opening stanza of "Ride on Conquering King," a religious song in Parrish (p. 182) begins in much the same way.

About the tune Mrs. McCulloh notes: "I've transcribed the first three lines. As is often the case, the first stanza of a song is not typical of what follows; thus here the tune used with 'tell her pray for me' does not recur. Subsequent lines follow the tune of 'I got life . . .' and 'They 'cuse me . . .' This is a curious thing—it also exists in white tradition; you will get a two-part melody used for the first stanza or two, then just the second half used for the rest of the song."

9   If You See My Mother

If you see my mother, partner, tell her pray for me,
I got life on the river, yeah, never will go free, never will go free.

They 'cuse me a murder,
Never harmed a man, never harmed a man.

I say wake up ol' dead man,
Help me carry my row, help me carry my row.

Well the row so grassy,
I can hardly go, I can hardly go.

10   Mack's Blues

A. Mack Maze, Ellis, 21 August 1965, 399.3, N.C.
B. "Easy Rider," Mack Maze, Ellis, 19 August 1965, 386.7

This is a personalized version of the "mule skinner" songs (for example, song 3 in this collection). The penultimate stanza in the A-text is common, appearing for example in White, p. 264, as reported from a Mississippi construction gang in 1906; the third stanza of the A-text is found in Lomax, 1936-A, pp. 50–52, in "Levee Camp Holler," a composite text.

Mack's texts are obviously conflations of prison and levee or railroad camp versions. The first and third stanza of the A-text and the last two stanzas of the B-text are clearly prison in origin; most of the other stanzas originated in the free world.

10-A   Mack's Blues

Say, I told the Captain, he don't worry me,
Got a hundred and twenty-nine summers, partner, never will go free.

Hate to get up in the morning, so doggone soon,
I can't see nothin' shinin', but the stars and moon.

The boss packs a big horse pistol, and he think he bad,
I take it in the mornin', if he make me mad.

I don't mind rollin', from sun to sun,
But I want my supper, partner, when suppertime come.

Waterboy, bring water 'round,
If you don't like your job, buddy, set your bucket down.

I worked a mule called Emma, and one called Belle,
I never seen a mule, work like Ada and Elle.

10-B   Easy Rider

Oh, easy rider, what make you so mean,
You not the meanest man in the world, but the meanest one I've seen.

Say, oh, easy rider, what make you so mean,
I yell for water, partner, give me gasoline.

Waterboy, won't you bring the water 'round,
If you don't like your job, boy, set your bucket down.

I hate to see the rider, when he rides so near,
He so cruel and cold-hearted, boy, these twenty year.

I ask him for mercy, he don't give me none,
He ask me my trouble, and I didn't have none.

---

11   I'm So Glad My Time Have Come
J. B. Smith, Ramsey 2, 18 November 1965, 420.7, J.M.

12   Ration Blues
Jesse "G.I. Jazz" Hendricks, Ramsey 2, 4 July 1964, 47.2, N.C.

13   Been on the Chain Gang
Jesse "G.I. Jazz" Hendricks, Ramsey 2, 4 July 1964, 37.9, N.C.

I haven't found "I'm So Glad My Time Have Come" anywhere else, but it I have a feeling that Smith learned the first stanza and chorus somewhere, then added the other two stanzas himself later on; he said he first heard the song in a county jail "a long time ago" and doesn't remember if the singer was white or black. (I asked about that because of the anomalous chorus.) Though G.I.'s "Ration Blues" uses an amorphous popular blues tune, the lyrics obviously originated in the TDC ("Captain Mac" in the first line is Carl Luther McAdams who was Ramsey warden before he went to Ellis Unit); even so, I can't help but wonder if this song hasn't existed somewhere outside with different words—"ration blues" is a strange complaint to have in the only Southern prison system that really does feed well, a place where *ration* is not argot for "food." "Been on the Chain Gang" seems to derive from a popular blues recording of some time back, but I have not found the specific disc. Odum and Johnson, 1926, pp. 78–79, print a song called "Chain Gang Blues"; two of that song's nine stanzas are similar to stanzas in G.I.'s song:

> The judge he give me sentence
> 'Cause I wouldn' go to work.
> From sunrise to sunset
> I have no other clean shirt.

> All I got is lovin',
> Lovin' and a-sluggin',
> Say I feels just like a stepchild,
> Just gi' me the chain gang blues.

They note "The first four stanzas of this song, except for some slight variations, are also found in Chain Gang Blues, a popular phonograph piece" (p. 78 n), but they don't say by whom or when it was recorded. Earlier in the same book Odum and Johnson have the first stanza above, which they say was sung by a convict in a chain gang, and also a stanza from the record (p. 28); the stanza from the record is almost exactly the same as G.I.'s first stanza. G.I. doesn't remember where he learned the song, but said it might have been from a record.

I group these three songs together here because I think they all derive from commercial recordings, but each is a different distance from the original version, and each has been modified differently. The usual pattern is for commercial songs to develop from traditional songs and for the commercial disc either to reinforce the traditional song or to replace it entirely, but here it seems that the commercial recording itself supplied the initial thrust. I cannot document this, by the way; it is just the feeling I have about the three songs, after having listened to a lot of convict songs and a lot of free world songs.

11   I'm So Glad My Time Have Come

Oh judge,   oh judge,   I liked to for - got   The
darn - dest thing   was ev - er   in   the plot:
Ly - in' and steal - in' it na   can't   be   beat,   It's the
darn - dest thing   that ev - er trav - eled the streets,   I've a
ti - died I rule,   I've a   ru - di - li - deer,   I've a
ti-died I rule,   I've a   ru - di - li - deer.

I'm so glad my time have come,
Around Sherman no more will I bum.
The last bummin' I did I remember it still,
With a long six months I stayed in the cell.
Chorus: I've a tidied I rule, I've a rudilideer,
                 I've a tidied I rule, I've a rudilideer.

Oh judge, oh judge, I liked to forgot,
The darndest thing was ever in the plot:
Lyin' and stealin' it na can't be beat,
It's the darndest thing that ever traveled the streets. (Chorus)

Oh judge, oh judge, I liked to forgot,
Darndest thing was ever in the plot:
Throw you in jail and that ain't all,
They'll give you six months for breaking the law. (Chorus)

12   Ration Blues

Well, I wonder what's the matter, what's the matter with Captain Mac,
He done got mad, he done got on to the fact,
I've got the ration blues, just as blue as I can be,
Wo me, I got those ration blues.

He done cut down all the wood, he got things lookin' clean,
He got old Ramsey lookin', the best you ever seen.
He done cut out the live oaks, all the grass has dis'peared fast,
And if you don't go to work, gonna be your yas-yas-yas.

I've got those ration blues, just as blue as I can be,
Wo me, I got those ration blues.

He done cut down on the sugar, tell me meat has disappeared fast,
I'm goin' down to Oklahoma, just to see little Carrie's . . .

(breaks off, laughs, and says, "I done got tickled.")

13   Been on the Chain Gang

Judge, he give me six months, 'cause I wouldn't go to work,
Judge, he give me six months, 'cause I wouldn't go to work,
From sunrise to sunset, I haven't got no time to shirk.

All I get is sluggin', all I get is rough of you, (2x)
Gal, I'm treated like a stepchild, I got those mean old chaingang blues.

I'm still beating on a rockpile, with a hammer in my hand,
Beating on a rockpile, with a hammer in my hand,
I forgot to tell the Captain 'bout way down yonder in no man's land.

Bug he keep a buggin', baby, that's all I know, (2x)
If I wasn't shackled down, I'd leave him standing on the turn row.

Cotton and Cane: Group Songs (14–27)

14 Please Have Mercy on a Longtime Man

A. "Walk Straight," Louis "Bacon and Porkchop" Houston and Matt Williams, Ramsey 2, 4 July 1964, 40.1, J.M.

B. Louis "Bacon and Porkchop" Houston and Matt Williams, Ramsey 2, 4 July 1964, 40.2

C. "Pull-Do," Louis "Bacon and Porkchop" Houston and Matt Williams, Ramsey 2, 4 July 1964, 40.5

Houston and Williams acted as if these were three different songs; they offered the three titles listed for the separate songs; they looked at me curiously when something I said indicated I thought they might be singing the same song again and again. In a way we were both right, but the difference is important. For most outsiders who study things like folksongs, the objects of study are specific artifacts, artifacts that can be named and measured and filed and whatever else artifact collectors do with their prizes, but for insiders in the world of the prison worksong, especially older insiders, those concepts are more or less meaningless. There are some well-known songs that have titles, but not very many. More often, there is a chorus that one knows and clusters of stanzas that can go with that chorus (many of the stanzas in this song, or group of songs, are often found in 15. "Midnight Special" and its variants), but there is nothing permanent or fixed, nothing that one might put a title to that would have any meaning the next time. These three songs have titles simply because I said after the singing, "Do you have a name for that song?" and they probably wanted to accommodate what must have been a strange request. For singers like Houston and Williams the song is always in process, while for outsiders there is always a search for a permanent state.

The B-text is painfully inclusive: it begins with the savage and arrogant response of the Captain to the black man's request (done in traditional old Southern posture, by the way, with hat in hand), then moves to the woman who comes and announces she wants her man back; she offers all she's got—"a hunderd, I got a hunderd more"—but that obviously is not enough, and so he stays where he is. He is left there with nothing but words and food—he sees the Johnny (the food wagon) and is ready for his convict beans.

William's comment on the song after the C-text is peculiar: Williams himself complained a lot about conditions, but his comment shows some disapproval of the voice in the song. A "pull-do" is an incompetent worker, someone who shirks and/or makes too many mistakes, someone who can't pull his weight; even other convicts who object to the labor disapprove of the pull-do. The aesthetic distance provided by the song allows the convict to express opinions he would not reveal in ordinary speech.

14-A   Walk Straight

Au - gust done come and gone, And left me roll - in', but I ain't got

Au - gust done come and gone, And left me ham - in', but I ain't got

long. Oh, Lord-y, oh my Lord-y Lord, Oh, Lord-y, oh my Lord-y Lord.

long. Oh, Lord-y, oh my Lord-y Lord, Oh, Lord-y, oh my Lord-y Lord.

Well the nigger like 'lasses, and the white man, too,
Well the nigger like 'lasses, and the white man, too.
Chorus: Wo Lordy, oh my Lordy, Lord,
        Wo, Lordy, oh my Lordy, Lord.

Well when I get to Dallas, I'm gonna walk and tell,
This Number One Ramsey is a burning hell. (Chorus)

Well a nigger like 'lasses, well he lick it out the can,
Well the white man like 'lasses, lick it out the nigger's hand. (Chorus)

Well I come here to hold 'em, I didn't come here to stay,
Well I come here to hold 'em, I like to have my way,
Well I come here to hold 'em, I didn't come here to stay,
Come and do my time, and get the hell away from here. (Chorus)

Well my mama and my papa done told me a lie,
Gonna get me a pardon on the Fourth a July.
Oh, July and August done come and gone,
And left me rollin', but I ain't got long. (Chorus)

Won't you look over yonder, what do you see?
Well Julie and the baby, comin' after me.
Umbrella on her shoulder, a piece a paper in her hand,
Said, "Looka here, Captain, I come a after my man." (Chorus)

If you ever go to Dallas, well you better walk straight,
Well you better not stumble and you better not fall.
Well they will arrest you, they will carry you down,
If you ain't got no money, well you Huntsville bound. (Chorus)

If I ever get able, pay this debt I owe,
I never be caught in this hole no more. (Chorus)

14-B   Please Have Mercy on a Longtime Man

Well I went to the Captain, with my hat in my hand,
Said, "A-Lordy, have mercy, on a longtime man."
Well he looked at me, and he spit on the ground,
Says, "I'll have mercy, when I drive you down."
Chorus: Wo Lordy, oh my Lordy, Lord,
            Wo, Lordy, oh my Lordy, Lord.

Well look over yonder, what in the world I see,
Pretty yella woman, a comin' after me.
Umbrella on her shoulder, a piece a paper in her hand,
Says, "Looka here, Captain, I come a after my man." (Chorus)

"Here's a hunderd, I got a hunderd more,
If this don't get him, I have to let him go." (Chorus)

I believe I spied the Johnny, oh my Lordy, Lord,
Well, I believe I spied the Johnny, oh my Lordy, Lord.

Ready for my beans, oh my Lordy, Lord,
Ready for my beans, oh my Lordy, Lord.

14-C   Pull-Do

Chorus: Wo my Lordy, wo my Lordy, Lord,
            Wo Lordy, wo Lordy, Lord.

Go marchin' to the table, you find a cup and a pan,
If you say anything about it, you have trouble out a the man.

Well my mama and pappa, well they told me a lie,
Gonna give me a pardon, on the fourth a July.

But July and August, done come and gone,
And they left me rollin', but I ain't got long. (Chorus)

You get up in the morning, when the ding-dong ring,
You go marchin' to the table, you find the same darn thing. (Chorus)

Get up in the mornin', so doggone soon,
I can't see nothin', but the stars and moon. (Chorus)

If I ever be able, and duck this blow,
Well I won't be bearin' down, this load no more. (Chorus)

Well I asked the Captain, for the time a day,
Well he looked at me, boys, with his face full a frown.
Well he looked at me, and he rode away,
Well he looked at me, and he rode away.

"That's titled to 'Pull-Do.' 'Cause he's asking for mercy. It's made to the Captain. It's a pull-do, he couldn't hold 'em. And he was trying to get the Captain to have mercy on him. That there was a person that couldn't keep up, you know, and the man was driving him and it was hot, just like it is now. And he had pulled off his hat and was trying to talk to the Captain. Ask him to have mercy on a long time man. Captain look down on him and he spit on the ground, told him he would have mercy when he drove him down" (Williams).

---

15 Midnight Special

Jesse "G.I. Jazz" Hendricks (leader), Louis "Bacon and Porkchop" Houston, Matt Williams, C. B. Kimble, Ramsey 2, 4 July 1964, 38.2, J.M.

For a discussion of Bud Russel, see the inmate comments in the introduction. Note the "If you ever go to Paris . . ." stanza; this usually appears as "If you ever go to Houston," but G.I., the group leader, was arrested in Paris, Texas (his hometown), so he made the change to fit his own career.

Mrs. McCulloh writes, "Although there are three soloists, they sing virtually in unison, so here I have transcribed what might be called in current parlance a consensus transcription rather than an actual transcription."

The group of stanzas about the woman and the convict identifying her by her dress and her approach to the captain are found throughout the Gulf South. Printed versions are found in Lomax, 1936-A, pp. 221–223 and pp. 72–75; Lomax, 1960, pp. 318–319; and Asch and Lomax, p. 71 (the version by Leadbelly on *Last Sessions*, vol. 2, Folkways FA 2942). There are a number of versions in the Archive of Folk Song, all recorded by John A. Lomax (Frank Jordan and group, Parchman, 1936 [618A1]; Gant family, Austin, 1936 [647A]; Gus Harper, Jim Henry, Herman Jackson, Parchman, 1937 [885A3]; Ledbetter [Leadbelly], State Prison Farm, Angola, 1935 [124A]; Ledbetter, Wilton, Conn., 1935 [1334]). A good Leadbelly performance is on *Leadbelly: The Library of Congress Recordings*, Electra EKL 301/2. The woman sequence noted above appears in "Jumpin' Judy," sung by a group on *Negro Prison Songs from the Mississippi State Penitentiary*, Tradition TLP 1020, recorded by Alan Lomax; those stanzas also appear in "Nashville Blues," sung by Parchman inmates and recorded by Herbert Halpert in 1939 (3090 A2 and B1, 357 A2, 357 B1).

15   Midnight Special

Let the Mid-night Spe-cial shine her light on me, Let the Mid-night Spe-cial shine her ev-er-lov-in' light on me. "Here come Bud Rus-sel." "How in the world do you know?" Well, he know him by his wag-on and the chains he wo', Big pis-tol on his should-er, big knife in his hand: He's com-in' to car-ry you back to Sug-ar-land. Let the Mid-night Spe-cial shine her light on me, Let the Mid-night

Spe - cial shine its ev - er - lov - in' light on me.   Oh, yon - der come

Ros - ie. "How'n the world do you know?"   Well, I know her by her

a - pron   and the dress   she   wore.

Let the Midnight Special shine her light on me,
Let the Midnight Special shine her ever-lovin' light on me.

"Here come Bud Russel." "How in the world do you know?"
Well he know him by his wagon and the chains he wo'.

Big pistol on his shoulder, big knife in his hand:
He's comin' to carry you back to Sugarland.

Let the Midnight Special shine her light on me,
Let the Midnight Special shine her ever-lovin' light on me.

Oh, yonder come Rosie. "How'n the world do you know?"
I know her by her apron and the dress she wore.

Umbrella on her shoulder, piece a paper in her hand,
She hollerin' and cryin', "Won't you free my man?"

Well she cause me to worry, whoopin', hollerin', and a-cryin',
Well she cause me to worry, 'bout my great long time.

Well let the Midnight Special shine her light on me,
Oh let the Midnight Special shine her ever-lovin' light on me.

If you ever go to Paris, man, you better walk right,
And you better not stumble, and you better not fight.

Po-lice he'll 'rest you, and 'll drag you down,
The judge he'll find you, you'll be penitentiary bound.

Let the Midnight Special shine the light on me,
Let the Midnight Special shine her ever-lovin' light on me.

16   My Lord Says There's Room Enough in Heaven for Us All

Jesse "G.I. Jazz" Hendricks and group, Ramsey 2, 4 July 1964, 36.5, J.M.

With very little creative effort, the group leader can keep this song going for as long as he wishes. There are several statement sequences followed by a chorus, but only the first line is changed in each stanza, which means that the lead singer need think up a new line only once every ten or twelve lines. He names a character, for example (Backslider, Little Children, and so on) or makes a statement ("I'm goin' to Heaven"), the next several lines are two or more pairs from a set group ("Come to Jesus," "He will save you," "Here's my hand, sir"), and then there is the four-line chorus. Although he does not do it in this performance, the leader can include names of other convicts working in the area (as is done in 50-A. "Drop 'em Down"). This is, of course, a free-world song that has made its way into the prison—it is not only used as a church song but also has some popularity as a children's camp song.

16   My Lord Says There's Room Enough in Heaven for Us All

My Lord says there's room e - nough, And don't stay a - way.

My Lord says there's room e - nough, And don't stay a - way.

Chorus: My Lord says there's room enough,
Room enough in the Heaven for us all.
My Lord says there's room enough,
And don't stay away.

Backslider, DON'T STAY AWAY,
Backslider, DON'T STAY AWAY.
Come to Jesus, DON'T STAY AWAY,
Come to Jesus, DON'T STAY AWAY.

He will save you . . . (*all lines repeated, with*
  burden, "DON'T STAY AWAY," as above)
Here's my hand, sir . . .
(Chorus)

Little children . . .
Come to Jesus . . .
He will save you . . .
(Chorus)

Wo, gambler . . .
Come to Jesus . . .
Here's my hand, sir . . .
I'm goin' to Heaven . . .
Here's my hand, sir . . .
Come to Jesus . . .
(Chorus)

17   Grey Goose.

Louis "Bacon and Porkchop" Houston, D. J. Miller, and group, Ramsey
2, 3 July 1964, 35.6, J.M.

The text is free world, but I have not heard of this song as active in
tradition in any place other than Texas prisons. John Lomax collected
several versions (August "Track Horse" Haggerty and group, Huntsville,
1934 [223A2]; Haggerty and another group in 1937 [A-10]; James "Iron
Head" Baker, Central Farm, 1933 [207B]; James "Iron Head" Baker and
group, Central, 1934 [205A3]). The latter Baker recording appears on
Afro-American Spirituals, Work-Songs, and Ballads, AAFS L-3; other
commercial LP performances are Leadbelly's *Last Sessions*, Folkways
FP 2941, and *Leadbelly Legacy*, vol. 1, Folkways FA 2004. Printed texts
appear in Lomax, 1936-B, pp. 109–110, and Lomax, 1936-A, pp. 242–
243.

17   Grey Goose

Miller:

Well, my papa went a-hunting, WELL, WELL, WELL,
Well, my PAPA WENT A-HUNTING, WELL, WELL, WELL.

You know he took along his shotgun . . . (*all lines are repeated, with burden, as above*)
You know he rared the hammer 'way back . . .
You know he shot at the grey goose . . .
Well down came the grey goose . . .
After six weeks a falling . . .

Houston:
Well we gave a feather picking . . .
Was a six weeks a pickin' him . . .
Well we put him on to parboil . . .
Well we put him in the oven . . .
Was a six weeks a bakin' him . . .
Well we put him on the table . . .
Well the knife couldn't cut him . . .
Well the last time I seen him . . .
He was flyin' across the ocean . . .
Well he had a string a dumplings [goslings] . . .
Well the last time I seen him . . .
Spoken: Jack, Captain!

18   Goodbye, My Lover, Goodbye

Louis "Bacon and Porkchop" Houston, Jesse "G.I. Jazz" Hendricks, and
group, Ramsey 2, 4 July 1964, 38.6, J.M.

There is one version of this in the Archive of American Folk Song
recorded by John Lomax (Fields Ward, Crockett Ward, and Mrs.
Thomas Rutherford, Galax, Virginia, 1937 [1369A2]). I first heard the
song as a child in New York State, but I haven't come across any versions of it in print. As with many other of the songs, it is expandable
("One time she blow for . . ." offers infinite possibilities) for as long
as it takes everyone to be bored with it and go on to something else.

18   Goodbye, My Lover, Goodbye

Houston:
See that train comin' round the bend,
GOODBYE, MY LOVER, GOODBYE,
You see that train comin' round the bend,
GOODBYE, MY LOVER, GOODBYE

She loaded down with the convict men . . . (*all lines*
repeat, with burden, as above)
Chorus: Well, it's bye, baby, bye,
        Bye, baby, bye, love,
        Bye, baby, bye, love,
        Goodbye, my lover, goodbye.

One time she blow for Bilo First . . .

G.I.:
He's goin' this time, ain't comin' back . . .
(Chorus)
He's got him on that one-way train . . .
You know by that he ain't comin' back . . .
(Chorus)

Houston:
One time she blowed for Bilo First . . .
(Chorus)
One time she blow for Camp Eight . . .
(Chorus)

One time she blow for Ramsey Farm . . .
(Chorus)
Bow-leg is waitin' for you . . .
(Chorus)

The final stanza is irregular:
If you can't chop cotton then get out of the way,
GOODBYE, MY LOVER, GOODBYE,
He'll worry you down.

---

19   Pick a Bale a Cotton

A. Louis "Bacon and Porkchop" Houston and group, Ramsey 2, 17 August 1965, 380.5, J.M.
B. Jesse "G.I. Jazz" Hendricks and group, Ramsey 2, 3 July 1964, 35.5

This song was well known throughout the TDC when I was there. Just about every one of the important song leaders sang it at least once (for example, Ebbie Veasley and group, Wynne, 18 August 1965, 384.12; Joseph "Chinaman" Johnson and group, Ellis, 11 July 1964, 64.51).

Mrs. McCulloh writes, "I've transcribed the first three stanzas. After this the pattern is regular . . . Usually the chorus is sung in unison."

The first line of G.I.'s version suggests that the song moved into prison from a plantation context, but I don't know of any collected versions of this song that antedate publication of prison versions. The Lomaxes recorded a number of performances by Texas convicts (James "Iron Head" Baker and group, Central, 1934, 205A1; James "Iron Head" Baker, Will Crosby, R. D. Allen, and Mose "Clear Rock" Platt, Central, 1939 [195A1]; Ledbetter [Leadbelly], Wilton, Conn., 1935 [150B1]; and so on). Leadbelly's version *Leadbelly Legacy: Take This Hammer*, Folkways FA-2004, is printed in Asch and Lomax, p. 56. Other texts are in Lomax, 1936-B, pp. 92–94, and Lomax, 1936-A, pp. 232–233.

19-A   Pick a Bale a Cotton

big e - nough and black e - nough

big e - nough and black e - nough to pick a bale a day.

Well it's never will I PICK A BALE A COTTON,
But it's never will I PICK A BALE A DAY.

Well I'm goin' to the new ground, PICK A BALE A COTTON,
Well I'm goin' to the new ground, PICK A BALE A DAY.

Chorus: How in the world can I PICK A BALE A COTTON?
         How in the world can I PICK A BALE A DAY?

Well you big enough and black enough to . . . (*all lines repeat, with
    burden, as above*)
(Chorus)
I got a little baby brother can . . .
(Chorus)
You got to jump a down and turn around to . . .
Well old Eli Hawkins . . .
(Chorus)
Well I'm goin' to the new ground . . .
Well you big enough and black enough to . . .
(Chorus)
I got a little baby sister can . . .
(Chorus)

19-B   Pick a Bale a Cotton

Well old marster told old mistress I could PICK A BALE A COTTON
Old marster told old mistress I could PICK A BALE A DAY

You big enough and black enough to . . .

Chorus: But never will I pick a bale a cotton,
         How in the world can I pick a bale a day?

You jumps around, you turns around to . . .
I went to Loosiana just to . . .
(Chorus)
Continues as 19-A

20   Stewball

A. Jesse "G.I. Jazz" Hendricks, Matt Williams, and group, Ramsey 2, 4
July 1964, 37.5, J.M.
B. Matt Williams, Ramsey 2, 4 July 1964, 39.2
C. Louis "Bacon and Porkchop" Houston and J. B. Smith, Ramsey 2, 17
August 1965, 376.4
D. Ebbie Veasley and group, Wynne, 18 August 1965, 383.2

Stewball was an Irish race horse whose fame has survived on both
sides of the Atlantic. Laws notes several versions of the song from Kentucky and quotes D. K. Wilgus on "Ten Broeck and Mollie," the American counterpart of the Irish horserace: "The July 4, 1878, march race
in which the Kentucky thoroughbred Ten Broeck defeated the mare Miss
Mollie McCarthur, went into the record books as the last four-mile heat
race in American turf history" (Laws, p. 243). But it is the Irish horse
and his race that have survived in American Negro folksong.

The song is anomalous in that there is no single chorus, but rather a
sequence of choruses that accompany different groups of verses. The
group rarely waits for the leader to begin the chorus, but shouts it immediately after the last line repeat of the previous stanza sequence, almost always in unison.

The last stanza of the C-text suggests that the song may have been
in plantation song lore even before Emancipation. The only nineteenth
century report of the song I know of is in an 1868 article by John Mason
Brown (in Jackson, 1967-B, pp. 117–119).

This song has been reported throughout the South. As "Ten Broeck
and Mollie," it appears in Laws, 1964, pp. 242–243, as entry H-27. The
Archive of American Folk Song *Check-List* names thirteen recordings of
it (including prison performances recorded by John A. Lomax from Mississippi, Virginia, North Carolina, Florida, and Texas). A version by a
group of Mississippi convicts recorded by Alan Lomax appears on *Yazoo
Delta . . . Blues and Spirituals*, Prestige 25010. Versions by Leadbelly
may be heard on Leadbelly's *Last Sessions,* Folkways FA-2941, and
Leadbelly Sings Folksongs, Folkways FA-2488; the latter performance is
printed in Asch and Lomax, p. 12. Dorothy Scarborough prints "Skew-
ball" from *The Vocal Library,* published in London in 1922, and an
American version she collected (pp. 62–63). Other versions are found
in Odum and Johnson, 1926, pp. 133–134; Work, 1940, p. 234. The Ten
Broeck version was recorded by John Byrd at Grafton, Wisconsin, in
1930 as "Old Timbrook Blues"; that appears on *Country Blues Encores,*
Origin Jazz Library OJL-8. Harry Oster recorded a group of Louisiana
convicts singing "Stewball" (on *Angola Prison Worksongs* AAFS LFS
A-5) as a woodchopping song; there is little in that version about the

race itself. Oster's recording differs from the Texas versions structurally: the group sings "Oh well" at the end of the first three lines of each four-line stanza, then repeats the fourth line after the leader sings it. The chorus is "Run, Stewball, OH WELL,/Molly gone, OH MOLLY'S GONE."

20-A   Stewball

THERE'S A BIG DAY, IN OLD DALLAS
AND I WISH THAT, MAN, I WAS THERE
I WOULD SPEND ALL, ALL MY MONEY,
ON SOME BIG LEG, OLD YELLOW GAL.

G.I.:
Won't you help me to go to Dallas,
Through the hole in the wall?
LET'S GO TO DALLAS,
THROUGH THE HOLE IN THE WALL.

Well Old Stewball, WELL OLD STEWBALL,
He was a black horse, HE WAS A BLACK HORSE,
And they painted, AND THEY PAINTED,
The pony red, THE PONY RED.
It was sworn by, IT WAS SWORN BY,
All the nation, ALL THE NATION,
That old Stewball, THAT OLD STEWBALL,
He was dead, HE WAS DEAD.

HE'S UP ON THE MOUNTAIN,
JUST A BIG-EYEIN' 'ROUND, 'ROUND, 'ROUND.
HE'S UP ON THE MOUNTAIN,
JUST A BIG-EYEIN' AROUND.

If you love me, IF YOU LOVE ME,
Like you said, LIKE YOU SAID,
We get married, WE GET MARRIED,
This Christmas day. OH CHRISTMAS DAY.

Well I wonder what's the matter,
With the hole in the wall, wall, wall.
WELL I WONDER WHAT'S THE MATTER
AT THE HOLE IN THE WALL.

Well old mister . . . (*exact repeat, as above*)
He bet a million . . .
And old master . . .
He called it all . . .
That old Stewball . . .
Beat little Molly . . .
To that little hole . . .
In yonder wall . . .

Oh look at him turnin',
At the hole in the wall, wall, wall,
OH LOOK AT HIM TURNIN'
AT THE HOLE IN THE WALL.

It's good mornin' . . .
You young ladies . . .
It's good mornin' . . .
You young men . . .

Well a my buggy . . .
Is so greasy . . .
Till a my pony . . .
They won't stand . . .

Won't you jump in my buggy,
Let's TAKE A LITTLE RIDE, RIDE, RIDE,
WON'T YOU JUMP IN MY BUGGY,
WON'T YOU TAKE A LITTLE RIDE.

Williams:
Well Mistress . . .
Told old Masters . . .
"You be savin' . . .
While I'm a gone . . .
Don't you feed them . . .
Niggers no dobies . . .
You just feed them . . .
Yellow dent corn . . ."

WELL I SURE GOT HUNGRY,
WHILE THE MASTER WAS GONE, GONE, GONE,
WELL I SURE GOT HUNGRY,
WHILE THE MASTER WAS GONE.

G.I.:
There's a big day . . .
Yonder in Dallas . . .
I wish that . . .
I was there . . .
I would spend all . . .
Nickles and quarters . . .
On some big-leg yella gal . . .

JUST RUBBIN' AND FEELIN',
ABOVE HER KNEE,
JUST A RUBBIN' AND FEELIN',
JUST ABOVE HER KNEE.

20-B   Stewball

Well old Missy, told old Marster,
"Want you be savin', while I'm gone.
Don't you give those, niggers no dobies,
You just feed them, that yellow dent corn."

Well I sure got a hungry, while the missy was gone, gone,
Well I sure got a hungry, while the missy was gone.

There is a big day, yonder in Dallas,
I wish that, I was there.
I would spend all, my nickles and quarters,
On some big-leg, yella gal.

Just rubbin' and feelin', all day long, long,
Just rubbin' and feelin', all day long.

Well old Missy, bet old Marster,
That old Stewball, beat Molly to the hole.

Won't you bet on Stewball, partner, you may win, win,
Won't you bet on Stewball, partner, you may win.

It was way back, eighteen hundred,
Eighteen hundred and forty-four,
It was proved, all the nation,
That old Stewball was a dead and gone.

He was up on the mountain, just a big-eyein' 'round, 'round,
He was up on the mountain, just a big-eyein' 'round.

It was there back, it was eighteen hundred,
When the race was, was sought to be run.
All the jockeys, they come a marchin',
Like a crimluh [criminal], to be hung.

Put your money on Stewball, boy, you may win, win,
Put your money on Stewball, partner, you may win.

Good mornin', my young lady,
How do you do, say, my young man.
Well my buggy, it's so greasy,
That my pony, will not stand.

Won't you jump in the buggy, we'll take a little ride,
Won't you jump up in the buggy, we'll take a little ride.

20-C   Stewball

Houston:
Well old Stewball, WELL OLD STEWBALL
He was a racehorse . . . (*exact repeat as above*)
And old Mollie . . .
She was too . . .
Well old Stewball . . .
He could run five miles . . .
While old Molly . . .
Tryin' to run two . . .

WON'T YOU BET ON THE RACES,
YOU MIGHT WIN, WIN, WIN,
WON'T YOU BET ON THE RACES,
BUDDY, YOU MIGHT WIN.

Well old Stewball . . .
He was a white horse . . .

And they painted . . .
Stewball red . . .
All the people . . .
Louisiana . . .
Thought old Stewball . . .
He was dead . . .

WELL HE'S UP ON THE MOUNTAIN,
JUST A BIG-EYEIN' AROUND, 'ROUND, 'ROUND,
WELL HE'S UP ON THE MOUNTAIN,
JUST A BIG-EYEIN' AROUND.

Well I don't mind . . .
Race ridin' . . .
If it wasn't for . . .
My darlin' wife . . .
On that big horse . . .
He might stumble . . .
And away goes . . .
My precious life . . .

GOT TO SLEEP IN THE GRAVEYARD
REST OF MY DAYS, DAYS, DAYS,
BE SLEEPIN' IN THE GRAVEYARD,
THE REST OF MY DAYS.

Well I went down . . .
To Kentucky . . .
Well I stopped by . . .
Old Delaware . . .
All the people . . .
In that nation . . .
Thought old Stewball . . .
He was dead . . .

WELL HE'S UP ON THE MOUNTAIN,
JUST A BIG-EYEIN' AROUND, 'ROUND, 'ROUND,
WELL HE'S UP ON THE MOUNTAIN,
JUST A BIG-EYEIN' AROUND.

Well good mornin' . . .
Young lady . . .
Well good mornin' . . .
My young man . . .

Well my buggy . . .
It's so greasy . . .
And my pony . . .
It won't stand . . .

WON'T YOU JUMP IN THE BUGGY,
OH LET'S TAKE A LITTLE RIDE, RIDE, RIDE,
OH HOP IN THE BUGGY,
OH TO TAKE A LITTLE RIDE.

Smith:
Well I went down . . .
Hey to Kentucky . . .
And I stopped by . . .
Early Delaware . . .
I got arrested . . .
Godamighty for gambling . . .
And I had no . . .
No business there . . .

JUST A SLEEPIN' IN THE JAILHOUSE,
WELL A ALL NIGHT LONG, LONG, LONG.
SLEEPIN' IN THE JAILHOUSE,
WELL ALL NIGHT LONG.

Well old Mistress . . .
Told old Master . . .
You be savin'. . .
Well-a while I'm gone . . .
Don't you feed them . . .
Doggies no biscuits . . .
You just feed them . . .
That yella dent corn . . .

WELL YOU TALKIN' ABOUT HUNGRY,
WHILE THE MISTRESS WAS GONE, GONE, GONE,
WELL YOU TALKIN' ABOUT HUNGRY,
WHILE THE MISTRESS WAS GONE.

Well old Marster . . .
He promised me . . .
Before he died . . .
Goin' set me free . . .
Well he lived so long . . .

Till his head got bald . . .
Well he got out a notion . . .
Well a dyin' at all . . .

20-D   Stewball

There is a big day, over in Dallas,
And I wish that, oh I was there.
I would spend all my nickles and quarters,
On some big-leg yella gal.

MAN, UP IN THE GRANDSTAND, JUST BIG-EYEIN' AROUND,
   'ROUND, 'ROUND,
UP IN THE GRANDSTAND, JUST BIG-EYEIN' AROUND.

Said that cuckoo, he was a pretty bird,
To that white house, wo he did fly.
And he never did holler "cuckoo,"
Till the Fourth day of July.

MAN, DIDN'T HE HOLLER, ALL DAY, LONG, LONG, LONG,
DIDN'T HE HOLLER ALL DAY LONG.

Says old Stewball, he was a white horse,
And they painted old Stewball red.
It was sworn by all the nation,
That old Stewball godamighty was dead.

HE'S UP IN THE MOUNTAIN, JUST BIG-EYEIN' AROUND, 'ROUND,
   'ROUND,
UP IN THE MOUNTAIN, JUST BIG-EYEIN' AROUND.

Well old Stewball he was a racehorse,
And old Molly, godamighty, was too,
But old Stewball he run old Molly,
Clean out of her left foot shoe.

IT WAS TROUBLE ON THE RACETRACK, ALL DAY LONG, LONG,
   LONG,
IT'S TROUBLE ON THE RACETRACK ALL DAY LONG.

21   Go Down Old Hannah

A. Jesse "G.I. Jazz" Hendricks, Louis "Bacon and Porkchop" Houston, and Matt Williams, Ramsey 2, 4 July 1964, 38.1, J.M.
B. C. B. Kimble, Ramsey 2, 4 July 1964, 37.1, J.M.
C. David Tippen and group, Wynne, 18 November 1965, 383.1
D. Johnny Jackson, Ramsey 1, 1 July 1964, 22.5

The turn rows, the roads forming the perimeter of the agricultural cuts in the rich bottom land, were where the men who collapsed or died were thrown in the days when neither happening was particularly rare, and the bodies were left there in full sight of the men working, under the hot sun until something came along to carry them away. The men still working in the field could look and see the bodies there, and know they'd better not run, they'd better not collapse, no matter how thickly laced the weed growth ("My row so grassy . . ."). They knew, too, that there was no help, so the irony of "say get up dead man, help me carry my row . . ." was obvious: no one, no one at all, could offer any help at all, and there was nothing to do but push on and think about how many more years of the same work remained, to feel the sun beating down and indulge in the absurd wish that perhaps tomorrow the sun—Hannah—would just remain wherever it was when it was not broiling the convicts working in the endless fields.

Once Johnny Jackson was talking to me about slang used in the bottoms, and he lapsed into an annotated version of the song (D-text). On another occasion, a couple of days later, Matt Williams and Johnnie B. Smith sang the song and talked about it:

> *Smith:* Boys done got real tired then. And the sun, it look like it goin' down slow.
> *Williams:* Done hung in one place.
> *Smith:* Everybody about to give out, and they hopin' for the sun to go down. Singing the sun to go down: "Go down, Hannah, don't rise no more, if you rise in the mornin' bring judgment sure." Furthermore, we so tired, we rather see judgment than see another day of hard labor like this.
> *Williams:* Hear that song when you be choppin' along, or plantin' a row or something like that. And the row done got real grassy and the hoe is hung and the boss is squabblin' or messin' with you.
> *Smith:* Long hot summer days especially. Especially long hot summer days. Like when you choppin' cotton.

"Whether singing lead or chorus," Mrs. McCulloh noted, "Hendricks likes to decorate the melody." She transcribed for the A-text two stanzas by Williams and one by Hendricks to illustrate the differences in the way the two lead the song. She noted about the B-text, "Each stanza consists of a series of four descending phrases, beginning on the 5th, 4th, or 3rd, and ending on the tonic. Like Smith's 'Poor Boy' (2-C), this is really compelling, partly because of the contrast of a free tempo and the intense quality of the voice. As for the B-natural in the last line of the transcribed stanza, I am thinking Kimble might think of it more in terms of C than of B (generally he slides up to C via a gracenote B-natural). On the other hand, he might be creating the 4th like the 3rd, that is, like a pitch area rather than one definite pitch level."

There are many recorded performances of this song. I have ten others in my collection, the AAFS *Check-List* has ten performances by Texas convicts (all recorded by John A. Lomax), including Augustus "Track Horse" Haggerty and group, Huntsville, 1934 (182 B1); and James "Iron Head" Baker and group, Central, 1933 (195 A2). The Baker recording appears on *Negro Work Songs and Calls*, (AAFS L-8). Other versions available on commercial LPs include Doc Reese, *Jazz: The South*, Folkways FJ-2801; *Negro Prison Camp Work Songs*, Folkways P-475; Doc Reese, *The Blues at Newport, I, 1964*, Vanguard VRS-9180. Leadbelly performs the song on *Last Sessions*, Folkways FA 2941; that version is printed in Asch and Lomax, p. 50. Other texts appear in Lomax, 1941, pp. 356–358; Lomax, 1936-B, pp. 118–120; Charters, 1955, pp. 16–17 (from the version sung by Lightnin' Hopkins).

21-A   Go Down Old Hannah

Williams:
Well you ought to been down on this old river, WELL, WELL, WELL,
Nineteen forty-four, NINETEEN FORTY-FOUR,
Oughta been down on this old river,
Nineteen forty-FOUR.
Well you could find a dead man, WELL, WELL, WELL,
On every turn row, ON EVERY TURN ROW,
You could find a DEAD MAN,
On every TURN ROW.

I say get up dead man, WELL, WELL, WELL,
Help me carry my row, HELP ME CARRY MY ROW,
I say get up DEAD MAN
Help me carry MY ROW.
Well my row so grassy, WELL, WELL, WELL,
I can't hardly go, CAN'T HARDLY GO.
Well my row so GRASSY,
I can't HARDLY GO.

I say go down old Hannah . . . *(burden and repetition continue as
    above)*
Don't rise no more . . .
If you rise in the mornin' . . .
Bring judgment sure . . .

G.I.:
Well I ain't tired a livin' . . .
Man, but I got so long . . .
Well they got some on the highway . . .
Little boy, they got some goin' home . . .

Well I looked at old Hannah . . .
And old Hannah looked red . . .
Well I looked at my poor partner . . .
Little boy was half mos' dead . . .

Williams:
Well my partner said, "Help me, . . .
Help me if you can". . .
I said, "Partner who fooled you . . .
Down on this long old line". . . (*repeat is* "on this river line")

"Who told you you could make it". . .
On this river line?". . .
He say, I'm not tired a workin' . . .
Pardner I got so long". . .

I said, "Write your mama . . .
Tell her the shape you in". . .
Tell her I say write the governor . . .
That your time has come". . .

"Ask the governor for a pardon . . .
And he may grant you a reprieve". . .

G.I.:
Well I see Bud Russell . . .
Little boy, with his ball and chain . . .
Little boys he gonna take you . . .
Back to Sugarland . . .

Little boys you get worried . . .
Little boy, don't try to run away . . .
Little boy you'll get to see your mama . . .
On some lonesome day . . .

And who fooled you on the river . . .
With the great long time . . .

21-B   Go Down Old Hannah

heav - y,   I can hard - ly   go.

Lord,   Lord,   Lord,   Lord,   Lord,   Lord.

Won't you go down old Hannah,
Please don't rise no more.
If you rise in the mornin',
Bring judgment on.
Lord, Lord, Lord, Lord, Lord, Lord.

I ain't tired a rollin',
But I got so long.
Lord, I ain't tired a rollin', partner,
But I got too jumpin' long to worry here.
Lord, Lord, Lord, Lord, Lord, Lord. (*Repeated at end of each stanza*)

I was lookin' at old Hannah,
And it was a gettin' dogged low,
I looked at my partner,
He was almost gone . . .

Captain, will you just spare me,
One more day,
'Cause my row is so heavy,
I can hardly go . . .

Wake up, oh dead man,
Help me carry my row.
Well the rider keep on whoopin' and hollerin',
Partner, I got to go . . .

Your shotgun and pistol,
Don't worry me.
[If] I get a letter from little Roberta,
'Cross the river I'm gone . . .

Sergeant, Sergeant,
You got to ride, you got to ride,
'Cause I be long gone . . .

21-C   Go Down Old Hannah

Go down old Hannah, WELL, WELL, WELL,
Don't rise no more, DON'T RISE NO MORE,
Go down old HANNAH
DON'T RISE NO MORE

If you rise in the mornin', WELL, WELL, WELL,
Bring judgment on, BRING JUDGMENT ON,
If you rise in the MORNIN',
BRING JUDGMENT ON.

Well I called my mama . . . (*burden and repetition continue as above*)
On the telephone . . .

I couldn't get no answer . . .
From my mom at home . . .

I'm gonna write one more letter . . .
I'm gonna telephone . . .

Well my mama answered . . .
On the telephone . . .

"How much longer . . .
'Fore you comin' home". . .

"Mama, I'm tired a rollin' . . .
But my time ain't long". . .

I'm gonna write the governor . . .
See what he can do for me . . .

If I had you governor . . .
Where you got me . . .

I'd wake up some mornin' . . .
And I would set you free . . .

21-D   Go Down Old Hannah

"You know, when it's getting ready to rain, when the convicts be working and they look up and see it's be cloudy, they say, 'I ain't no Christian, I never been baptized, but take me out a the bottom before the water rise.' Now that mean's it's gonna rain, really pour down. Storm. They sings it:"

I ain't no Christian I never been baptized,
Take me out of the bottom, Lord, Lord, Lord,
Before the water rise.

Go down old Hannah, ("Hannah means the sun")
Don't you rise no more. ("It means it's real hot")
If you rise in the mornin', Lord, Lord, Lord,
You bring judgment sure, you bring judgment sure.

Well I look at old Hannah,
She was turnin' red, ("Means it's late in the evenin'")
Well I look at my partner, ("That's the one on the row with you")
He was almost dead.

I say, "Oh, wake up, old dead man,
Help me carry my row. ("This is what his partner say when he couldn't
    hardly make it")
Well my row is so grassy,
I can't hardly go, I can't hardly go." ("And this is what he told him:")

"You ought been back on the river,
Back in nineteen ten.
They was drivin' women,
Like they was drivin' men, like they was drivin' men."

I look back at my partner,
I said, "A-partner, let's go."
Well my partner looked up at the sun,
Said, "I can't go no mo', I can't go no mo'."

22   Shorty George

A. Louis "Bacon and Porkchop" Houston and group, Ramsey 2, 17 August 1965, 381.2, N.C.
B. Matt Williams, Jesse "G.I. Jazz" Hendricks, and Louis "Bacon and Porkchop" Houston, Ramsey 2, 4 July 1964, 37.3

C. Matt Williams and Louis "Bacon and Porkchop" Houston, Ramsey 2, 4 July 1964, 39.6

D. David Tippen, Ebbie Veasley, and group, Wynne, 18 August 1965, 384.2

When I asked Johnny Jackson about Shorty George, this is what he told me:

> When I first came to the penitentiary, first day I was on the farm, I was working and all of a sudden everybody hollered "Whup!" Scared me. I said, "What's happening?" Somebody told me, "Shorty George just passed." I said, "Who is Shorty George? Where is he at?" They said they was talking about this little train just passing. I said, "Why they keep up with Shorty George?" He said, "They know when Shorty George pass it's 3:35." Same thing every day at the same time. We'd be digging ditches and suddenly everybody's hollering, "Whup!" I'd say, "What's wrong with 'em, man?" He say, "Oh, Shorty George just passed." And the bosses, they get brainwashed behind that. Shorty George and all those things. Boss look at his watch and say, "Three thirty-five. Shorty George."
>
> I don't know where that train would go. It didn't have but about three cars on the back of it, and that was why they called it Shorty George.
>
> I remember there was a girl used to come there, a Mexican girl, she used to come up on that high levee. There was big high levee built right on the side of Central farm and she'd come up there. Wind be blowin' and everybody be looking up there and they'd holler, "Sugarland Mary!" Sugarland Mary. I bet that Mexican girl never did know what they called her. They made a song: "Sugarland Mary, top of the hill/Driving me crazy." I don't remember any more of it. We'd sing that and "Shorty George" and songs like that.

Some parts of this song seem free world, but I don't know of it existing outside prison. The "Some give a nickle, some give a lousy dime . . ." stanzas seem to refer to the custom of people contributing to pay for a funeral, but none of the lead singers connected it with anything at all. Houston said, "That just means they didn't like him, that's all." The "Rosharon" in Houston's version (A-text) is the small cluster of buildings (feed store, gas station, food market, and so forth) at a road crossing a few miles from the prison on the highway to Houston.

Odum and Johnson (1925) print a song, "O My Babe Won't You Come Home?" which has the following stanza:

> Some people give you nickel, some give you dime
> I ain't goin' give you frazzlin' thing, you ain't no girl o' mine.
> O my babe, won't you come home. (p. 182)

In the same volume there is a song called "One Mo' Rounder Gone," (usually known as "Delia") with this stanza:

> Yes, some give a nickel, some give a dime
> I didn't give nary red cent, fo' she was no friend of mine.
> Well, it's one mo' rounder gone. (pp. 210–211)

The stanza also appears in a version of "Stagolee":

> Some give a nickel, some give a dime;
> I didn't give a red copper cent, cause he's no friend of mine (p. 198).

Other printed texts of the "Shorty George" song include Lomax, 1936-A, pp. 199–201; Lomax, 1936-B, pp. 142–143; Asch & Lomax, p. 69 (which is transcribed from *Leadbelly Legacy*, Folkways FA-2014). Other recorded versions are: *"Leadbelly's Last Sessions*, Folkways FP 2941, and, in the Archive of Folk Song, recorded by John A. Lomax, a version sung by James "Iron Head" Backer, Central, 1933 (210 B), and in 1934 (202 A2). A song called "Shorty George" recorded by John A. and Ruby T. Lomax at Clemens in 1939, sung by Smith Cason (2598 A1) appears on *Negro Work Songs and Calls*, AAFS L-8 and is a similar song, but different enough to be considered not the same.

22-A Shorty George

Oh well it's Shorty George, he wasn't no friend a mine,
HE WASN'T NO FRIEND A MINE,
Oh well it's Shorty George, wasn't no friend a mine.
Well he's taken all the women and left the men behind.
AND LEFT THE MEN BEHIND.

Oh, some give a nickle, some give a lousy dime . . . (*group repeats last
                                    phrase of first and third line, as above*)
Oh well, it's some give a nickle, some give a lousy dime,
I would give a quarter, but he wasn't no friend a mine . . .

That old train runnin', red green lights behind . . . (2x)
Oh red for trouble, green for a ramblin' mind . . .

Oh take me to Rosharon, [I'll] make Houston by myself . . .
If you take me to Rosharon, make Houston by myself,
Oh they tell me 'bout baby, she's got somebody else . . .

Go down old Hannah, old Hannah don't rise no more . . . (2x)
If you rise in the mornin', tell which way Shorty go . . .

Well I'm goin' to the station, I'm goin' to ask the porter there . . . (2x)
Has he seen my rider, just tell me what road she's on . . .

He said, "Describe your woman, I'll tell you what road she's on" . . .
    (2x)
"Well she's a little bitty woman, with long black curly hair". . .

Said, "If that's your woman, she's at the World Affair". . . (2x)
He says, "If that's your woman, she's at the World Affair". . .

Oh well I'm goin' to the station, I'm gonna lay my money down . . .
    (2x)
I'm gonna ask for a ticket to ride the world around . . .

Oh well I went to old Poland [Portland], come back through Tennes-
    see . . . (2x)
Oh well I didn't fine my rider, I found my used-to be . . .

A-well it's Shorty George, boys, he ain't no friend a mine . . . (2x)
Well he taken all the women, he left the men behind . . .

22-B   Shorty George

Begins with the same two stanzas as 22-A

Won't you go down old Hannah, old Hannah don't you rise no
    more . . . (2x)
If you rise in the mornin', put me at little Mary's door . . .

Oh baby, wonder where you been so long . . .
Oh I'm gonna ask you pretty baby, where you been so long.
Wo the people keep a-comin' and the train done gone . . .

Oh well a yon' stands your train with red green lights behind . . . (2x)
Well that's red for trouble, green for a ramblin' mind.

22-C   Shorty George

Similar to 22-A with the following additional stanzas, all sung in unison:

Well you see me comin', raise your window high,
Oh, if you see me comin', raise your window high.
Well, said, the more you cry, further you drive me away. Further you
    drive me away.

You got ways like the devil, wo Lordy, Lord, boy, she sleep in a hollow
    log,
She got ways like the devil, sleep in a hollow log,
She got ways like the devil, sleep in a hollow log.

Well she's a little-bitty woman, Lordy, Lordy, she weigh 'bout ninety
    pound,
She's a little bitty woman, weight 'bout ninety pounds,
She's got little'bitty legs, Lord, the noble thighs, Lord the noble thighs.

22-D   Shorty George

Well it's Shorty George, HE DIED ON THE ROAD,
Well IT'S SHORTY GEORGE, HE DIED OUT ON THE ROAD,
And how HE DIED, IT DON'T NOBODY KNOW.

Well some give a nickle, SOME GIVE A LOUSY DIME,
SOME GIVE A NICKLE, SOME GIVE A LOUSY DIME.
I would GIVE A QUARTER, HE AIN'T NO FRIEND A MINE.

If you see Roberta, PLEASE TELL HER FOR ME,
IF YOU SEE ROBERTA, PLEASE TELL HER FOR ME,
I GOT LIFE ON THE RIVER, I NEVER WILL GO FREE.

---

23   Sure Make a Man Feel Bad

J. B. Smith and group, Ramsey 2, 18 November 1965, 420.2, J.M.

This song was assembled by Smith and, like most of his songs, it has
those special qualities that move closer and closer to deliberate poetry.
There are examples of the kinds of balancing about the caesurae he
seems to favor ("Too lazy to work, too scared to run . . ." and so on).
For more on his techniques, see the comments for songs 28 through 34.

Uncle Bud in the sixth stanza is Bud Russel (see "One Lost Valley" and Glossary for convict comments on him). Smith's rhyming of "whore" with "so" in the ninth stanza is rare in these songs: it is the only time the word "whore" appears in any of the prison songs I've collected.

---

23   Sure Make a Man Feel Bad

long - time man feel bad.

long - time man feel bad.

Sure hate to see poor mother go, IT SURE MAKE A MAN FEEL BAD,
Mighta lived longer if I hadn't a grieved her so, IT SURE MAKE A MAN
FEEL BAD.
Make a longtime man feel bad, IT SURE MAKE A MAN FEEL BAD,
She mighta lived longer if I hadn't a grieved her so, IT MAKE A LONG-
TIME MAN FEEL BAD.

Can't get no letter, can't get a word from home, IT SURE MAKE A MAN
FEEL BAD,
Seem like everybody is a dead and gone, MAKE A LONGTIME MAN
FEEL BAD.
Oh it sure make a man FEEL BAD, OH IT SURE MAKE A MAN FEEL
BAD,
Seems like everybody is a dead and gone, IT MAKES A LONGTIME MAN
FEEL BAD.

(*Repeat of second line as fourth line and burdens continue as in stanza
above*)
Cotton is grassy, the sun is hot . . .
Thinkin' about all this time I got . . .

Too lazy to work, too scared to run . . .
Wish I back home where I come from . . .

Stay at home, you do as you please . . .
Come down here you got to work or leave . . .

Wouldn't mind workin' for Uncle Sam . . .
Workin' for Uncle Bud it ain't worth a damn . . .

Finally got a letter, this the way it read . . .
"Your Roberta she sick in bed". . .

Now if I had the governor like he had me . . .
Wake up in the morning I'd set him free . . .

Never had nothing to worry me so . . .
Lose my money on a no-good whore . . .

Woman I'm lovin' done left the town . . .
That ain't all, she done put me down . . .

Sometimes I have ole aches and pains . . .
Got to go on just the same . . .

Big bell toll just a while 'fore day . . .
Better get ready [to] go yonder way . . .

---

24   Old Aunt Dinah

Jesse "G. I. Jazz" Hendricks and group, Ramsey 2, 18 November 1965, 420.4, J.M.

"Carrie" and "Ida" (usually "Fort Worth Ida") figure in so many songs led by G.I. that I one day asked him about them. "They're just women in them songs," he said. "But they're in your songs and I never hear them in anybody else's songs," I said. "That's right. They're women in songs I sing." And that was where it was left.

In the text of the song, note the way in which one idea leads to the next: It would be advantageous to marry Ida, but it is Carrie the singer wants and it is Carrie he intends to have. Carrie has a baby but there is something peculiar about it—it has blue eyes! This suggests a pun on the word "rider" that shifts the context back to the prison: in the free world a rider is one's sexual partner, one's woman or man; in prison it is the guard on the horse who looks down on the convicts working in the field. Carrie, the singer's rider, has a baby with blue eyes like the prison rider. Now back in prison the song proceeds to call the Captain a devil, something none of the convicts would dare to do in speech, but something no guard would object to in song. Note the way G.I. builds up expectation. First he says, "Looka looka yonder," and the group wonders what he is going to name; then he says, "I believe I spy the devil," but he still isn't ready to name anyone. He wants one more teasing stanza, drawing it out for both the singers and whatever guards might be listening—"Who is that devil?" He answers himself in the next verse, then restates it just in case anyone missed the point. Then the singing turns to the matter of the work itself and ends with a restatement of the "Looka looka" verse, but this time leading to a brag by the singer: "I'm a timber ruler."

A musical note: the group knows the "Wo" chorus is coming when G.I. begins with the second verse melody; this is clear in the musical transcription.

24   Old Aunt Dinah

Well it's old Aunt Dinah, old Aunt Dinah, OH YEAH,
She had four daughters, she had four daughters, OH YEAH.
She wanted me to marry, she wanted me to marry, OH YEAH,
One of her daughters, one of her daughters, OH YEAH.
She give me forty dollars, she give me forty dollars, OH YEAH,
Just to marry her daughter, WO, Just to marry her daughter, WO MY
    LORD.
Here's her daughter, here's her little daughter, OH YEAH,
Girl named Ida, girl named Ida, OH YEAH.
Gonna marry little Carrie, Gonna marry little Carrie, OH YEAH.
Here's the way to call her, WO, here's the way to call her, OH MY LORD.
Wo Carrie, WO, Wo Carrie, WO MY LORD.
Hear me keep a callin', Hear me keep a callin', OH YEAH.

Carrie got a baby, Carrie got a baby, OH YEAH.
It's got blue eyes, sir, It's got blue eyes, sir, OH YEAH.
Blue eyes like the rider, WO, blue eyes like the rider, WO MY LORD.
He was always there, sir, always there, sir, OH YEAH.
Looka looka yonder, looka looka yonder, OH YEAH.
I believe I spy the devil, WO, I believe I spy the devil, WO MY LORD.
Who is that devil? Who is that devil? OH YEAH.
Captain McGaughey, Captain McGaughey, OH YEAH.
He's the devil in the bottom, WO, he's the devil in the bottom, WO MY LORD.
Help me to call 'em, help me to call 'em, OH YEAH.
This is the way to call 'em, this the way to call 'em, OH YEAH.
We gonna raise 'em up higher, WO, we gonna raise 'em up higher, WO MY LORD.
Let 'em fall like thunder, let 'em fall like thunder, OH YEAH.
Partner better watch me, partner better watch me, OH YEAH.
I'm gonna leave you doggin', WO, I'm gonna leave you doggin', WO MY LORD.
I'm troubled with a diamond, I'm troubled with a diamond, OH YEAH.
Looka looka yonder, looka looka yonder, OH YEAH
I'm a timber ruler, WO, I'm a timber ruler, WO MY LORD.
Live oak spirit, live oak spirit, OH YEAH.

---

25   Jolly

David Tippen and group, Wynne, 18 August 1965, 388.2, N.C.

A few months after this recording session I went through John A. Lomax's papers in the archives at the University of Texas in Austin and found one version of this song (*MS* 144) very similar to Tippen's. On my next visit to the prison I asked Tippen if he had ever recorded the song before. He told me that he had sung for someone with a very large recording machine in July 1933, so I assume he might be the unnamed singer in the Lomax collection. Lomax recorded the song again the following year from the singing of "Lightning and group" at Darrington, a version printed as "Johnny Won't You Ramble" in Lomax, 1941, pp. 400–402. The second time Tippen recorded the song for me (6 January 1966, 425.5) he added a descending "Yo ho ho" at the end of each stanza.

25   Jolly

Old master, don't you whip me, I'll give you half a dollar,
JOHNNY, WON'T YOU RAMBLE, JOHNNY, WON'T YOU RAMBLE,
Oh, master don't you whip me, I'll give you half a dollar,
JOHNNY WON'T YOU RAMBLE, JOHNNY WON'T YOU RAMBLE.

Old Master and old Mistress is sittin' in the parlor . . . (*repetition and burden as above*)

Well a-figurin' out a plan how to work a man harder . . .

Old Marster told Mistress, they sittin' in the parolor . . .

Old Marster told old Mistress to take the half a dollar . . .

"Well I don't want his dollar, I'd rather hear him holler". . .

Old Mistress looked at me, she told her Marster these words . . .

"Old Marster take the dollar and don't make him holler". . .

Take that dollar home.

---

26   No More Cane on the Brazos / Godamighty

David Tippen, Theo Mitchell, Ebbie Veasley and group, Wynne, 18 August 1965, 384.4, N.C.

The melody of "No More Cane on the Brazos" is complex and broad (it ranges a tenth—from B-flat to D in this transcription—an interval significantly wider than almost all other convict work songs), the song in its older versions is complex in the relation between lead singer and group. As a result it is almost never sung anymore. I met a few men who knew it, but only two or three who could sing it now. This group started and very quickly decided they didn't want to stay with the song, so they shifted into "Godamighty." The older version may be heard on *Afro-American Spirituals, Work Songs, and Ballads*, AFS L-3, a recording made from the singing of Ernest Williams and group, at Central, in 1933 by John A. and Alan Lomax. The printed text is in Lomax, 1936-A, pp. 58–59.

26   No More Cane on the Brazos / Godamighty

Tippen:
Well, 'tain't no more cane on the Brazis, WELL, WELL, WELL,
Well, 'tain't no more cane on the Brazis, WELL, WELL, WELL

Well it's yonder comes the sergeant, WELL, WELL, WELL,
YOUNDER COMES THE SERGEANT, WELL, WELL, WELL.

Well he's ridin' in a hurry . . . (*burden and repetition as in previous stanza*)

Well he's ridin' like he's angry . . .
Well I wonder what's the matter . . .
Well I b'lieve it's comin' up a norther . . .

Mitchell: (to second melody)
Oh yon' come the Captain, GODAMIGHTY, GOD KNOW IT,
OH YON' COME THE CAPTAIN, GODAMIGHTY GOD KNOWS.

HE RIDIN' IN A HURRY . . . (*all sing in unison, with burden and repetition as in previous stanza*)

SAY YOU BETTER GO TO ROLLIN' . . .

HE'S RIDIN' LIKE HE'S ANGRY . . .

GO TO JUMPIN' AND DODGIN' . . .

WELL YOU BETTER GET YOUR LOAD BOY . . .

Veasley:
If you don't want trouble, GODAMIGHTY GOD KNOWS IT,
IF YOU DON'T WANT TROUBLE, GODAMIGHTY GOD KNOWS.

'Cause the captain's a little angry . . .
Don't want no trouble . . .

---

27 Captain Don't Feel Sorry for a Longtime Man

Marshall Phillips, Ebbie Veasley, and Theo Mitchell, Wynne, 18 August 1965, 383.6, N.C.

The dynamics of this song make it most difficult to transcribe textually, so I ask the reader to refer carefully to Norman Cazden's music transcription. A sequence of rather complex parallel and antiphonic musical activities go on that simply do not make much sense when printed as words alone; one must either hear the song or try to follow the various musical lines. Because of the interesting variations, Mr. Cazden decided to transcribe the song in its entirety.

Basically, the song consists of three parts: (I) the opening section of four stanzas; (II) the five-line stanza in which Veasley shifts the meter and melodic form somewhat ("Tell mama, a-tell mama") which leads into another regular section with the full group; and (III) the part in which Veasley and Phillips sing while Mitchell drops to his knees and chants the Lord's Prayer, with a final pair of stanzas in the form of "Mama, I got a life time" in part II.

27   Captain Don't Feel Sorry for a Longtime Man

Well I'm gonna write my MAMA
And tell her to PRAY FOR ME.
Mama, I got lifetime on this old RIVER, river,
LITTLE GIRL AND NEVER WILL GO FREE.

Well I'm gonna write my MAMA,
And tell her [if] she wanna SEE ME FREE (*one sings:* "free, alive")
Mama, just send me a box a CARTRIDGE,
Mama, 'n' a FORTY-FIVE.

Captain, don't you never feel SORRY, sorry,
Captain, for a LONGTIME MAN.
He say, "Little boy, I don't never feel SORRY, OH SORRY,
Little boy, till I DRIVE YOU DOWN."

Well I called my MAMA,
And she COULD NOT COME.
Well I called my PARTNER
Little boy, and he BROKE AND RUN

Veasley: (*Others are calling and chanting during this stanza, which is used to shift the meter; Veasley's words only are printed here. For the words sung or called by the others, see the music transcription.*)

Tell mama, a-tell mama,
A-tell mama, tell-a mama not to worry.
Mama, don't you worry, Godamighty don't worry.
Goin' tell mama, goin' tell my mama,
Goin' tell my mama, goin' tell my mama,
Godamighty don't you worry.

DON'T YOU WORRY 'BOUT MY TIME-muh (*group joins in, as indicated*)

DON't YOU WORRY 'BOUT MY TIME-muh
DON'T YOU WORRY 'BOUT MY TIME-MUH,
DON'T YOU WORRY 'BOUT MY TIME.

Mama, I got a LIFE TIME,
MAMA, I GOT a LIFE TIME,
Mama, I got LIFE TIME,
Don't you WORRY 'BOUT MY TIME.

Godamighty, look-a YONDER,
GODAMIGHTY, LOOK-A YONDER,
GODAMIGHTY, LOOK-A YONDER.
Well a-YONDER COME THE SERGEANT,
WELL A-YONDER COME THE SERGEANT.
WELL, HE'S RIDING IN A HURRY,
WELL HE'S RIDING IN A HURRY,
WELL, HE'S RIDING IN A HURRY,
GODAMIGHTY, LOOK-A-YONDER,
Godamighty, look-a YONDER.
I gotta break and RUN, SUH,
I gotta BREAK AND RUN, SUH,
I GOTTA BREAK AND RUN, SUH.

I'M GONNA CALL RATTLER,
WELL, I B'LIEVE I'LL CALL RATTLER,
Well, I B'LIEVE I'LL CALL RATTLER,
THAT A MAN DONE GONE, SUH.

WELL, I B'LIEVE I'LL PRAY NOW
WELL, I B'LIEVE I'LL PRAY NOW,

WELL, I B'LIEVE I'LL PRAY NOW,
GODAMIGHTY, GOD KNOWS.

(*While Veasley and Phillips continue the song, Mitchell drops to his knees and begins to chant the Lord's Prayer. Transcribed below are the lines Veasley and Phillips sing; for the parallel chant by Mitchell, see the music transcription.*)

I gotta pray in a hurry, (3x)
Godamighty, God knows.

Well, he ridin' in a hurry, (3x)
Godamighty, God knows.

I got to make it to my mama,
I'm gonna make it to my mama,
I got to make it to my mama,
Godamighty, God knows-suh. (6x)

(*As they sing the last "Godamighty, God knows-suh," Mitchell chants, "Well, I done prayed now." The other two continue as below; for Mitchell's responses and interactions while they are singing, see the transcription.*)

Pray a little longer,
Oh, pray a little longer,
Won't you pray a little LONGER,
GODAMIGHTY, GOD KNOWS-suh.

Godamighty, don't worry,
Godamighty, don't worry,
Godamighty, God knows it.

The Songs of J. B. Smith (28–34)

Although part of the solo nonmetered worksong group, these songs by Johnnie B. Smith—132 separate stanzas—form so coherent a document and so magnificent a piece of composition that they deserve a section by themselves. (Smith sings lead in a number of other songs in this collection, but note particularly 2-C. "Poor Boy Number Two" and 23. "Sure Make a Man Feel Bad," both of which bear the stamp of his particular genius.) The songs were taped on a number of occasions, and Smith sometimes gave them titles, but he meant them as part of *one* song; he sometimes talked of them that way, and they will be considered that way here. The melody used throughout is basically the same; what varies is the speed and degree of ornamentation—more a function of his mood on any particular day than anything else. Transcriptions from three different sections are included to give some idea of the variety Smith achieves within the form of that basic melody. Three of these songs—28-A, 29-B and 31— appear on Smith's record, *Ever Since I Have Been a Man Full Grown*, Takoma B-1009.

When I met Smith he was in the eleventh year of a forty-five-year sentence for murder. He had been in prison three times previously on charges of burglary and robbery by assault. He said about his murder charge:

> I got out of here on those ten-year sentences, that robbery by assault. I lost my people while I was in here and I just felt like I was kind of in the world alone. I wanted to find me a pretty girl to settle down with and marry. I was thirty-five years old then. And I just wanted to marry and settle down. I left my home down at Hearn, Texas, other side of Bryant, and went to west Texas, out in the Panhandle country, to Amarillo. And I married a beautiful girl. She was about three-quarters Indian, I guess. A lot of mixed-breed girls out there, 'specially around Mexico and Oklahoma and Amarillo. I found me that pretty girl, the girl of my dreams I thought, and I had good intentions. But now, I fell in love with her, was what I did, and I got insane jealousy mixed up with love. So many

of us do that. Lot of fellas in here today on those same terms. I was really insane crazy about the girl and I had just got out of the penitentiary and I was working, just trying to make an honest living and to keep from coming back. But I couldn't give her all she wanted and she'd sneak out a little. That went to causing trouble. I was intending to get in good shape, but I hadn't been out there long enough, not to make it on the square, you know. She wanted a fine automobile, she like a good time, a party girl, she liked to drink, she liked to dress nice. So did I, and so I was living a bit above my income. And she would sneak out to enjoy these little old pleasures and that caused us some family trouble. On a spur of the moment I came in one day, we had a fight and I cut her to death. And regret it! Because I loved her still and still do and can't get her back.

So Smith returned to Ramsey with a forty-five-year sentence, which, because of his age, looked pretty much like life. (He was paroled in 1967, lived in Amarillo for awhile and did some preaching; I heard recently that he'd returned to the prison for a parole violation.) While working in the prison on that long sentence, he began putting verses to his melody (I've never heard anyone else use it). He said about such composition:

> Now these songs, we can, you know, you stay here so long, a man can compose them if he want to. They just come to you. Your surroundings, the place, you're so familiar with them, you can always make a song out of your surroundings. I read about some great poetry, like King David in the Bible, he used to make his psalms from the stars and he wrote so many psalms. A little talent and surroundings and I think it's kind of easy to do it.

Smith's talent is considerably more than "a little." Working within a traditional framework and using some traditional elements, he has woven an elaborate construct of images that brilliantly details the parameters of his world.

Musically and textually, Smith's style is extremely ornamental. He frequently adds words, repeats phrases, and shifts the locations of stresses while maintaining the metric base. The most striking aspect of his verbal style is the device, used in most stanzas, of making a quatrain of a couplet by reversing the lines. Sometimes the turn just fills out a four line verse with what is essentially a mere couplet, or acts as a simple restatement:

What you do, buddy, get so jumpin' long?
"Man, I kill Roberta, my woman, in the high sheriff's arms.
Well I kill Roberta, oh man, in the high sheriff's arms."
What you do, oh partner, get so jumpin' long? (14)

but on other occasions the turn is more functional. Consider,

Said she'd be back tomorrow, partner, but she carried her clothes,
She don't be here tomorrow, she will the next day sure,
Mmmm, she don't be here tomorrow, oh partner, she will the next day
   sure,
Said she be home tomorrow, but she carried her clothes. (87)

The first line (A) reveals the situation with the woman and suggests mendacity; the second line (B) presents what appear to be the singer's conclusions about the meaning of A. He repeats the line (B') and then, when he sings A', we know—rather than suspect—that he is consoling himself merely, that no matter what he wants to think and what she said, the fact remains that she did take her clothes and she will not be back and he knows that only too well. The movement is: promise and evidence that the promise is untrue (A), statement of hope and restatement of hope (B and B'), then revelation of the futility of hope (A')— which suggests that the deeper thematic content of the stanza is not really different than the stanzas about his long sentence, for in those stanzas, also, hope is lacking or minimal or artificial.

The mode is statement and comment, as in blues, but instead of the statement being given three times and the comment once (AAAB), we have the comment repeated immediately (ABB'A'), as if to reconsider first the comment by visiting it twice, then to reconsider the original remark by viewing it in inverted order. This does more than affirm merely. We are able to see A and A' in light of the insight gained through B and B', a re-view lost in the regular blues form. The hyperbata sometimes creates dramatic monologue out of stanzas that in the AAAB form would be scenic only.

The device also increases the intensity of stanzas that are more direct:

Sometime I wonder, oh, where all the good men gone,
Mmmm, some in the building, poor boy, some gone home
Mmmm, some in the building, some gone home,
Sometime I wonder where the high-rollin' men gone. (23)

There is a poignancy to this stanza, a touching sense of sadness or wistfulness, a sense of epigonism even within prison, but it isn't really apparent to the listener until A'. The first couplet is a simple query and answer; it is the second couplet, with its inversion, that shifts focus to the sense of loss itself.

Almost all stanzas in Smith's songs rhyme; two of the nonrhyming stanzas (there are approximately ten) were taken directly from other songs. There is considerable variation in the rhyme sounds (he uses about forty-five different word pairs), and, more important, there is hardly any repetition even with the sounds used frequently. The "i" sound, for example, is rhymed in eight stanzas; each pair includes "me," which is rhymed with five different words: Stagolee (34), free (1, 16, 40, 58), eternity (5), see (33), pee (95); each of the four "me/free" stanzas is different in content. Another common rhyme is "ei," which appears eight times, none of the pairs repeated: buy/try (11), mine/line (17), die/eye (48), why/by (92), die/buy (97), by/fly (102), try/eye (106), try/crossfired (124).

It is difficult, maybe useless, to talk about slant or partial rhyme in this song context. Slant rhyme is quite common in Negro folksong, and I suspect that many singers do not distinguish between full and slant, or, if they do, feel that both are equally acceptable. Smith's mixture of "air" and "ear" illustrates this best. (This is a rhyme equivalent of the refusal to distinguish between the major and minor seventh.)

Except for "rightaway/getaway" (39), all the rhymes are masculine. "Try/crossfired" (124) is the only apocopated rhyme. *Rime riche* occurs twice (9, 85), but one of those stanzas is of two lines only, A and A', and probably shouldn't be considered a rhyme. In one pair of stanzas that do not rhyme there is an interesting prosodic element: Stanza 20 is "year/twelve" and stanza 21 is "here/hell"; the two are not necessarily consecutive dramatically, but they are sung that way, and as a pair they happen to rhyme abba, abba.

Smith's rhyming displays considerable variation in terminal sounds and an obviously deliberate avoidance of complete repetitions. Considering that the author had no high school education and that his song is 264 lines long, one cannot help but be astounded by the natural talent here revealed.

Most of Smith's verses are his own, but he frequently uses lines or parts of lines from the prison repertory. Twelve stanzas are in versions of other Texas prison songs in my collection (2, 3, 14, 16, 22, 28, 29, 50, 51, 52, 53, 68); in nine stanzas he has taken the first line only (9, 11, 27, 29, 41, 62, 71, 72, 84); in seven stanzas he uses the second line only (1, 10, 23, 36, 45, 61, 123). When Smith does use one of these lines more than once he usually changes the context and part of the word structure. The second line of each of the stanzas that follow is essentially the same (with some formulaic changes), but the first line — and hence the sense of the verse — is quite different in each case:

Sometime I wonder, oh, where all the good men gone,
Mmmm, some in the building, poor boy, some gone home (23)

Captain, captain, captain, you can count your men,
Well it's some goin' to the building, and it's some gone in (68)

You can tell 'em I'm a leavin', a leavin', you can tell 'em when,
Oh some goin' to the bushes, partner, and there's some goin' in (123)

Several of the stanzas appear in free world songs. The stanza,

Man, they accuse me a murder, oh murder, and I ain't raised my hand,
They accuse me a forgery, I can't write my name (72)

appears in Texas Alexander's "Levee Camp Moan," recorded in 1928 and republished on *The Country Blues*, RBF-9, Eddie Boyd's "Third Degree," recorded in 1950, Chess 4374; Skip James sings a similar verse in his "22–20" (my own collection; a version of this song is on *Devil Got My Woman*, Vanguard VSD-79273; the verse appears in partial form in "If You See My Mother," song 9 in this collection (recorded on *Negro Folklore From Texas State Prisons*, Electra EKS-7296). Most of the free world stanzas in Smith's songs are from levee camp songs (the first six stanzas of "Ever Since I Been a Man Full Grown," 49–54, and 44, 71, 83, 115–116, and possibly a few others).

Smith, of course, also uses many phrases and partial lines from the traditional prison songs. I think one might make a case for the sort of formulaic composition, *mutatis mutandis*, Albert Lord describes in the *Singer of Tales*.

28-A   No More Good Time in the World for Me
(17 November 1965, 414.1)

This song begins with a *double entendre:* "good time" means both a pleasurable experience (the ordinary usage) and the time a man is given off his sentence for good behavior; the "I" of the song expects to have neither. Note that the song is full of temporal images: "Lifetime skinner," "I been down on this old river, man, so jumpin' long," "I got from now on, baby, to eternity," and so forth. Even in a lyric form, Smith manages a rare coherence of imagery, one of the qualities which make him so notable an oral composer.

He uses three expressions in this song not found in any of the other convict worksongs: *running time, danger line,* and *sundown man.* The first two terms are well known in prison argot; the third seems idiosyncratic with Smith. "Running time" is an indeterminate sentence, such as two-to-ten or ten-to-twenty years. Modern penology favors such sentences over "flat time" (twenty years or ten years or fifty years) because a man who shows what authorities consider great progress may be paroled early. The majority of inmates dislike the running sentence because, they say, they do as much time as they do under flat time and are burdened with many years of uncertainty and unfulfilled hope. The argument is loaded, for the inmates for whom the hope *is* fulfilled go home and aren't around to complain. The "danger line," Smith says, "is the dividing line between the state land and the free land, the penitentiary and the free world. We always call that the danger line no matter whichaway you're goin'. 'Cause when you leave the state property you's in the free world, and so there's always somebody at the danger line to keep you, try to keep you from going, of course. The dog sergeant, high rider, dog boy, somebody. But now, usually, if you beat them to the danger line you got a pretty good chance—there's nobody on the other side to shoot at you right away." Smith says, "sundown man," relates to "the way they used to work here years ago. They'd work right up to just about as long as they could, long as it was day. We'd often say we glad God made day and night, 'cause if it stayed day all the time they'd work a man to death the way we used to work here."

28-A   No More Good Time in the World for Me

No more good time, buddy, oh man, in the wide, wide world for me,   (1)
'Cause I'm a lifetime skinner, never will go free.
Well a lifetime skinner, buddy, I never will go free,
No more good time, buddy, in the wide, wide world for me

Lifetime skinner, skinner, hold up your head,   (2)
Well you may get a pardon if you don't drop dead.
Well you may get a pardon, oh man, if you don't drop dead,
Oh well lifetime skinner, partner, you hold up your head.

I been on this old Brazos, partner, so jumpin' long,   (3)
That I don't know what side a the river, oh boy, my home is on,
Don't know what side a the river, oh man, oh boy, my home is on,
'Cause I been down on this old river, man, so jumpin' long.

Well I lose all my good time, 'bout to lose my mind,   (4)
I can see my back door slammin', partner, I hear my baby cryin'.
Yeah, I'm a hear my back door slammin', man, I hear my baby cryin',
I done lose all my good time, partner, I'm 'bout to lose my mind.

You can go 'head on, an' marry, woman, good girl don't wait on me,   (5)
I got from now on, baby, to eternity.

Well I got from now on, woman, poor girl, to eternity,
You can go 'head on and marry, don't you wait for me.

If I ever get lucky, man, pay the debt I owe,   (6)
Whoa, boy, I won't be guilty of the charge no more.
Hmmm and I won't be guilty of this charge no more,
If I ever get lucky, pay the debt I owe.

If I ever go free, buddy, just goin' walk and tell,   (7)
'Bout this lowland Brazos, it's a burnin' hell.
Well this lowland Brazos, partner, sure a burnin' hell,
Ever go free, man, just goin' walk and tell.

"Little boy, why you keep on a runnin', just keep runnin' on your   (8)
   mind?"
Captain, I never had nothin' but that old runnin' time.
Well I ain't never had nothin', captain, this old runnin' time,
That's why I keep on runnin', just keep runnin' on, on my mind.

Little girl make your bed up higher, higher woman, let your hair   (9)
   grow long,
Oh I be by to see you if I don't stay long.
Well I'll be by to see you woman, if I can't stay long,
Make your bed up higher, woman, let your hair grow long.

Well if I ever make it, rider, ever make it to the danger line,   (10)
I'm goin' be long gone, partner, goin' be hard to find.
Well I'm goin' be long gone, rider, sure be hard to find,
If I ever make it 'cross that danger line.

If you lookin' for heaven, lookin' for heaven, you better go 'head by, (11)
But if you lookin' for trouble, you can stop and try.
Well if you lookin' for trouble, oh man, you can stop and try,
But if you lookin' for heaven, you better go 'head by.

Got your piece a pistol, rider, you know you playin' half bad,   (12)
Gonna be mine in the morin', if you just make me mad.
Well it'll be mine in the mornin', rider, you just make me mad,
Got your piece a pistol, goin' 'round playin' half bad.

Had my thirty-two-twenty, rider, just one round a lead,   (13)
I wouldn't leave enough livin', oh man, to bury the dead.
Oh wouldn't be enough livin', rider, oh man, to bury the dead,
Had my thirty-two-twenty, and a round a lead.

What you do, buddy, get so jumpin' long?   (14)
"Man, I kill Roberta, my woman, in the high sheriff's arms.
Well I kill Roberta, oh man, in the high sheriff's arms."
What you do, oh partner, get so jumpin' long?

Well if I never no more to see you woman, oh black gal, do the (15)
    best you can,
I got a home on the river for a sundown man.
Well I got a home on the river, on the river, for a sundown man,
If I never see you no more woman, do the best you can,

If you see my woman, buddy, buddy, please tell her for me,   (16)
I'm a long time skinner, never will go free.
Well I'm a long gone skinner, man, and I never will go free,
If you see my woman, oh man, tell her for me.

28-B   No More Good Time in the World for Me
(17 August 1965, 375.1, N.C.)

This version consists of stanzas 1, 7, 9, 10, 11, 12, and 13 of 28-A,
plus two additional stanzas. Note that the text printed with the music
for the first stanza of 28-B differs slightly from the text of the first
stanza of 28-A. Such minor variation is common in lyric folksong.

28-B   No More Good Time in the World for Me

free,   Hmm,   No more   good time,   bud-dy,   in the

wide,   wide   world   for   me.

If I just had me a buddy, a buddy with a mind like mine,   (17)
Oh 'fore sunrise in the mornin', I'd be way down the line.

I done been on this old river, Lord, so jumpin' long,   (18)
Don't know what side of the river my home is on.
Well I don't know what side a the river my home is on,
Been down on this old river so jumpin' long.

29-A   Too Much Time for the Crime I Done
(23 August 1965; 406.1, N.C.)

Few convicts feel their sentence is appropriate to their crime, hence the first stanza of this song, which says, in effect, "If I had known how long a sentence they would actually give me I would not have permitted myself to be captured and brought to trial." The metaphor in stanza 21 is brilliant: if the Devil has gotten religion and given up the business of keeping prisoners, then the only functioning hell left is this prison he's in. "Hot Springs" (stanza 25) seems to have a peculiar fascination for Smith; he has never visited the resort, but he regards it as a kind of promised land and mentions it several times in his songs. The irony in stanza 28 (the B-text of "Too Much Time for the Crime I Done") appears frequently in the inmate cotton and cane songs. "Kilroy Junior" and "Stagolee" (stanza 34) are obviously inmate nicknames. The "two-barrel derringer" (stanza 36) is a reference to the shotgun the guards used to carry (the riders carry .38 caliber pistols now, the high rider a .30 caliber rifle); when I asked Smith about this metaphor, he said, "That's what we call 'down talkin' it,' makin' it small." The "line" in stanza 37 is the danger line, discussed in the headnote to song 28-A.

29-A   Too Much Time for the Crime I Done

I got too much time, buddy, oh Lord, for the crime I done.   (19)
Whoa, I got too long, for the crime I done
If I just had a knowed it, could a broke and run.
Well, if I just had a knowed it, I'd a broke and run,
Hmmm, got too long, partner, oh, for the crime, crime I done.

Well I don't mind a doin', buddy, no two, three year,   (20)
Hmmm, hate like hell, partner, hmmm, do these ten or twelve.
Well I hate like hell buddy, to do ten or twelve,
Hmmm, wouldn't mind doin', partner, maybe two, three years.

Well the time a gettin' better, better, everywhere but here,   (21)
Devil got religion, no more, no more hell . . . (*line B repeats, followed
                                        by line A*)

Little boy, you ought a been here, been in here, back in nineteen   (22)
    oh four,
Mmmm, you could find a dead man, partner, on every turn row . . .

Sometime I wonder, ohh, where all the good men gone,   (23)
Mmmm, some in the building, poor boy, some gone home
Mmmm some in the building, some gone home,
Sometime I wonder where the high-rollin' men gone.

If I don't get drowned, don't get washed away,   (24)
Mmmm, goin' to see my woman [if I] have to swim the Mobile Bay . . .

Spoken: Yeah, if I don't get washed away or don't get drowned. Man
behind me got a double-barrelled shotgun loaded with double-ought
buckshot. If I don't get washed away or don't get drowned I'm goin' to
see my woman. When I get there, girl, I'm gonna take a long chance to
get to you, get back to ya. I want you to be good to me. I'm riskin' my
life tryin' to make it back home.

If I call you woman, [and] you refuse to come,   (25)
Mmmm, Hot Springs water, girl, won't help you none.
Well the Hot Springs water won't help you none,
If I call you, black gal, and you refuse to come.

29-B   Too Much Time for the Crime I Done
(17 November 1965, 414.1)

I done too much time, buddy, whoa man, for the crime I've done,   (26)
Well if I had a knowed it, oh, I'd a broke and run,
Well, I just had a knowed it, oh boy, I'd broke and run,
I got way too long, buddy, for the crime I done.

"What you do, buddy, get your great long time?"   (27)
Whoa, man, they accuse me a robbin', poor boy, with a fire iron . . .

Well, wasn't I lucky, please 'sider me lucky, now when I got my   (28)
    time,
I got it cut from one hundred, oh boy, down to ninety-nine . . .

Oooo, well I soon have one hundred, whoa boys, as ninety-nine   (29)
Whoa, man, ain't no difference, partner, for they both lifetime . . .

Well I been here rollin', buddy, so jumpin' long   (30)
But I be here rollin' when the boys all gone,
Well I be right here rollin', hamin', when the boys all gone,
Well I been on this old river, partner, so jumpin' long.

I done lose all my power, captain, out a my right arm,   (31)
'Cause I'm way overloaded for the crime I done.

Well ain't no more loud hollerin', hey man, you may's well   (32)
     mumble low
You'll find hell on the river, partner, everywhere you go . . .

Would you take money, hmmm, from a boy like me?   (33)
"I take money, partner, from the blind [who] can't see . . .

Well they hung my partner, oh man, shook the chain at me,   (34)
Doublecrossed Kilroy Junior, framed poor Stagolee . . .

If I had my German Luger, oh my Luger, just one round a ball,   (35)
Man, I'd leave here walkin', I wouldn't run at all . . .

Rider, your two-barrel derringer, yeah, your derringer, it don't (36)
     worry my mind,
Oh, the way I'm a lookin', that's the way I'm goin' . . .

Well I never got worried, never got worried, 'till I cross the line,   (37)
Got to thinkin' about dog sergeant and the twelve bloodhound . . .

Well, she told me not to worry, not to worry, but I got to worry (38)
     some,
'Cause I'm way overloaded for the crime I done.

---

30   I Heard the Reports of a Pistol
(23 August 1965, 406.2, N.C.)

It might be instructive to note the stanzaic progression in this song, for it illustrates nicely the kind of thematic coherence possible even in loosely structured lyric.

The opening stanza has about it a cinematic quality: one envisions the men working the field, knowing that one of their group has escaped a while before and that the dogs and some of the guards have taken off after him; the afternoon is punctuated by a brief burst of pistol fire, then there is silence; the other men continue working, knowing the man was killed at close range (it was a pistol, not a rifle they heard) and that it is all over for him now. The singer then thinks of his own life sentence and considers running off, but everyone has such thoughts from time to time and they don't mean much; his thoughts turn immediately to something positive, something expressing power—instead of the passive convict in the second stanza he becomes a Badman, as the record at Sugarland (another one of the prison units) will prove, someone who fills graveyards. But that brag doesn't work for long either, for the real power in the prison is held by the guards and by the guards only, so the next two stanzas (43 and 44) have to do with their options of control— first how the guards can make the men work in awful conditions, second how they can withold pay or money mailed from home (stanza 44 is from the free world levee camp tradition). In stanza 45 there is another expression of his longing for escape, but it is not at all as assertive as the escape lines in stanza 40. Stanza 46 doesn't really fit, but it leads him to a wistful rememberance of a woman in Abilene. Then he remembers where he is and how long he will be here, and the song ends with two thoughts: a lament that he may rot there forever (until "the last man die") and a passive wish that he not be troubled by Marble Eye, the guard, the man with the gun.

30   I Heard the Reports of a Pistol

Well, I heard the reports of a pistol, whoa man, down the right-   (39)
   a-way,
Hm hm, must a been my partner, hm hm hm, tryin' a make a getaway.
Whoa, they killed my partner, ho, tryin' a get away,
Hmmm, just heard reports of a pistol, a down the right-a-way.

If I leave here runnin', don't you follow me,   (40)
Mmmm, I'm a longtime skinner, mmmm, want to be free.
Well I'm a longtime skinner, oh, sure want to be free,
I hate to be charged with murder in the first degree,
Mmmm, hate to be charged with murder, oh, in the first degree,
Now if I leave here runnin', don't you follow me.

If you don't believe, partner, that I killed a man,   (41)
Send and get my record, buddy, from Sugarland.
Well you can see my record, buddy, in Sugarland,
If you don't believe, partner, I have killed a man.

Old Boot Hill over yonder, strictly belong to me,   (42)
Partner, a cold-blood murder is my pedigree . . . (*line B repeats,*
                                       followed by line A)

I got a red-eyed captain, squabblin' boss,   (43)
Oh, work in the mud and the water, but he won't knock off . . .

Well, I asked the captain, did my money come.   (44)
"What the hell you care, don't owe you none.
What the hell you care, mmmm, don't owe you none,
Better get to rollin', get my levee done."

I done lose all my good time, buddy, 'bout to lose my mind,   (45)
Mmmm, the way I'm a lookin', that's the way I'm a goin' . . .

Mmmm, everybody is talkin', mmmm, 'bout Mary Blair,   (46)
Mmmm, the poor girl is crippled, mmmm, and the clothes she wears.
Oh nothin' to the black gal, just the clothes she wear,
Everybody talkin', talkin' 'bout Mary, Mary Blair.

If I go west Texas, drop in Abilene,   (47)
I got the cutest little woman, huh, you ever seen . . .

Well I don't want to be here when the last man die,   (48)
I don't want no trouble out a Marble Eye,
I don't want no trouble, oh, out a Marble Eye
I don't want to be here, partner, when the last man die.

---

31   Ever Since I Been a Man Full Grown
(17 November 1965, 414.6–415.1)

Ever since I been a man, oh boy, a man full grown,   (49)
I been skippin' and a dodgin' for old farmer Jones.
Well I been skippin' and dodgin', hey man, for old farmer Jones,
Ever since I been a man, I mean a man full grown.

Well my lead mule's crippled, partner, whoa, my wheel mule's   (50)
    blind,
Was the best in the country, but done been drove down . . .

Well I done a been all around, partner, in the whole corral,   (51)
Couldn't find a mule, buddy, with his shoulder well . . .

All you long line skinners, you better learn to skin,   (52)
Man comin' here in the mornin', want a hundred men . . .

Well talkin' 'bout your hamstrings poppin' them old leather lines, (53)
Ought heard the back bands stretchin', partner, and the
    collars cryin' . . .

I done worked old Rhody, hey man, I worked old Moll,   (54)
But I ain't gon' stop rollin' till I work them all.

Little boy, little boy, if you can't hold 'em, you can't hold 'em, (55)
    don't let 'em fool you here,
'Cause old Jesse James Seefus, partner, a walkin' 'lectric
    chair . . .

Well, but me and my partner, oh rider, and my partner's friend,   (56)
We could pick more cotton in the country than your gin can
    gin . . .

When I get up the country, hey, goin' tell all the boys,   (57)
"Don't you come no further south, buddy, than Illinois . . ."

I want some missionary woman, oh woman, please pray for me,   (58)
Don't pray that I go to heaven, just pray that I go free . . .

Sometimes I wonder, oh, can I get my long time done,   (59)
Oh, boy, I prayed for better, man, but worser come . . .

If I had the good luck, buddy, oh like I had bad,   (60)
I'd win a barrel a dollars and keg a halves . . .

Life been a long lone gamble, I just can't seem to win,   (61)
If you don't believe I'm a sinkin', look what a hole I'm in . . .

Long lane, buddy, it's a long lane, buddy, that ain't got no end,   (62)
You may call me lucky, but I'm goin' up again . . .

"What you want me to tell your mama, tell your mama, oh boy,   (63)
    when I go home?"
Tell her you left me rollin', buddy, but I ain't got long.

I got a high yella woman, woman, man, in the world somewhere,   (64)
She got three gold teeth, long black curly hair . . .

Well if you don't tell her, tell her, man, she will never know,   (65)
I got a home in Pocatella, oh man, Idyho . . .

Well I'm goin' to Oklahoma, marry a Indian squaw,   (66)
When I get her daughter, I be her son-in-law . . .

If I beat you to the Brazos, sergeant, oh man, you can blow your   (67)
    horn,
Well I done got worried, I'll be gone 'fore long . . .

Captain, captain, captain, you can count your men,   (68)
Well it's some goin' to the building, and it's some gone in,
Well it's some gone to the bushes, some gone in,
Well it's cool kind captain, you better count your men.

Everybody talkin', talkin' man, 'bout old Danger Blue,   (69)
If I had my big horse pistol, I'd be dangerous, too . . .

Had my big horse pistol, buddy, just one round a ball,   (70)
I would leave here walkin', I wouldn't run at all.

"Mornin', mornin', captain." He said, "Good mornin', Shine."   (71)
"I don't want no trouble, captain, I want that gal a mine."

Man, they accuse me a murder, oh murder, and I ain't raised my   (72)
     hand,
They accuse me a forgery, I can't write my name . . .

Now I'm further up the river, oh man, than I ever been,   (73)
Me and my partner, nothin' but a walkin' gin . . .

Well I been here rollin', partner, ever since nineteen and ten,   (74)
But if you keen on gamblin', partner, I know you bound to
     win . . .

It's gonna rain, rain, rain, partner, oh boy, then turn cold,   (75)
But I don't mind the weather if the wind don't blow . . .

Saddest word in history, buddy, that I ever read,   (76)
"You got to do one hundred for the life you led . . ."

Well you may be a bully, but you no bad man,   (77)
Uncle Bud will get you, put you on the ball and chain . . .

Man, wasn't I lucky, wasn't I lucky, when I didn't get killed?   (78)
Got in a Saturday night ruckus, partner, with old Trigger Bill,
Whoa, Saturday night ruckus, mean old Trigger Bill,
Wasn't I lucky that I didn't get killed?

Rather been in Loosiana, partner, down with the whipporwill,   (79)
Than to be here in Texas treated like I feel . . .

Due to be in Butte, Montana, oh man, oh boy, this very day,   (80)
If I ever get lucky, goin' be on my way.

But it ain't but one thing, partner, oh boy, I done wrong,   (81)
I stayed in Texas just a day too long . . .

32   Woman Trouble
(17 November 1965, 415.2)

Note the interesting sequence of relatives in stanzas 89–93: he is first asked by his mother if he is tired, then the father asks why he stays if he is tired, then his woman suggests he leave, and he answers (92, 93) with resignation. Most of the stanzas of the song have to do with being left by a woman or being kept in jail; there is little linking them together. The erotic and slightly obscene notes of stanzas 94 and 95 (which have to do with a vagina and gonorrhea, respectively) are rare in the prison worksongs—women are mentioned frequently, but there are seldom direct references to sexuality or the consequences of sexual activity; in stanzas 96 and 97 the protagonist of the song tells us his disease is incurable, and he will never again be purchasing sexual companionship. The life sentence of impotency reminds him of his life sentence as convict, and he returns in the rest of the song to several inmate themes.

32   Woman Trouble

Spoken: Here's a little short one here, titled "Woman Trouble." He's worried about some old woman in the free world. Guy down here, if he's thinkin' about anything at all, he's thinkin' about his freedom and his woman.

She left me this mornin', never said a word,   (82)
Whoa man, nothin' I done partner, just on somethin' she heard.
Well wasn't nothin' done, buddy, just somethin' she heard.
Woman left me this mornin', never said one word.

"What you do partner, with your summer change?"   (83)
Man, I spent it all on the women for a great big name . . .
                    (*line B repeats, followed by line A*)

Waterboy, waterboy, waterboy, won't you bring your water 'round, (84)
I got a great big notion to lay the hammer down . . .

I don't see no fire, oh man, but I'm burnin' down   (85)
Hmmm, don't see no fire, partner, but I'm burnin' down.

Well you hear a shotgun a blastin', oh man, know somebody's lost (86)
Jumped in Big Muddy, whoa, and tried to cross . . .

Said she'd be back tomorrow, partner, but she carried her clothes,   (87)
She don't be here tomorrow, she will the next day sure . . .

You don't feel like a hollerin', oh rider, you wave your hands,   (88)
It's the man at the crossin', he gon' let me by . . .

Well my mama, heard her call me, poor boy, answered, "Ma'm?"   (89)
"Ain't you tired a rolling for Mister Cunningham?
Well ain't you tired a haming, poor sonny, for Mr. Cunningham?"
Poor boy, my mama she call me, and I answered, "Ma'm?"

Well my papa he called me, "Sonny," so I answered, "Sir?"   (90)
"If you tired a rollin' what you stay there fur?
Mmmm, if you tired a haming, sonny, what you stay there fur?"
Poor boy, my papa called me and I answered, "Sir?"

Well my woman finally called me, she called me, oh I   (91)
    answered, "Hey."
"If you tired a rolling, why don't you run away?" . . .

Can't run away, woman, tell you the reason why,   (92)
They got a man at the crossing, he won't let me by . . .

Well I ain't tired a rollin', hmmm, I just got so long   (93)
Just to keep down trouble, guess I'll go 'head on . . .

She got a hole in her belly, boy, and it won't get well,   (94)
And the more you rub it, well the more it swell . . .

Everytime, buddy, everytime, partner, man, I go to pee,   (95)
Mmmm, chills and fever come down on me.

I went to see my doctor, boy, he said "I can't tell,   (96)
You may get better but you can't get well . . ."

Long as I live, partner, long as I live, poor boy, never die,   (97)
No more lovin' will I have to buy . . .

I know you're gonna murder me, rider, rider, why don't you   (98)
    set a day?
I don't have religion, I need time to pray . . .

Ain't nothin' but Tom Devil make a man do wrong,   (99)
Well I'm gonna do better, man, from this day on.

I believe that lead row bully, rider, got a mojo hand,   (100)
He's a seven day roller, captain, and a sundown man . . .

I got a free transportation, oh man, in the world somewhere,   (101)
Been a longtime a comin', but you welcome here . . .

If you stay in Huntsville, partner, oh boy, you may get by,   (102)
You come down on the Ramsey, you got to rise and fly . . .

"When you get your big old money, hey man, whichaway you   (103)
    goin'?"
I'm goin' a way up the country, oh boy, around Des Moines . . .

---

33   The Major Special
(12 June 1966, 463.3)

This song expresses considerable respect for Major Eska McGaughy, the officer in charge of Ramey Two Camp. This is not as surprising as it probably seems to an outsider: Smith has known McGaughy for about thirty years, off and on, easily as long as anyone else he knows presently; they get along and understand one another. Smith says of the song, "This is mostly true. It sorta correlates with some of the past and the present. And it's sort of nice to think about him in his old age. We been knowin' each other a pretty good while." Warden C. L. McAdams, who was on Ellis when I did most of my work in the TDC (he is now Warden of the Wynne Unit in Huntsville), is the strictest and most highly respected warden in the system; many of the men on his unit were proud of that strictness, proud that they got along with "Captain Mac." That the keepers and convicts are both prisoners of the same system is an ancient insight. For a discussion of a similar kind of symbiosis among police and drug addicts, see my "Exiles from the American Dream," *Atlantic Monthly*, 219 (January 1967), 44–51.

A paragraph McGaughy wrote for the TDC *20-Year Progress Report* in 1967 might have been composed by an old-time inmate: "I began working for the Prison System in 1926 for $50.00 a month. Uniforms were not furnished and the guards wore khakis or overalls. Food for both employees and inmates was pretty skimpy. The typical meal consisted of potatoes, salt bacon, cornbread, and molasses. If you got an egg for breakfast, you had to bring it from home. If you wanted preserves or jelly for breakfast, you had to bring that also. We worked from daylight until dark, with only time off at noon to eat our 'John Henry,' which usually consisted of black-eyed peas, fat meat, and cornbread" (p. 87).

Note that McGaughy is mentioned as a devil in 24. "Old Aunt Dinah."

The "Moreland Brothers" (stanza 114) aren't any real farmers. Smith says, "We call the 'Moreland Brothers' any man with a whole lot of land around this penitentiary. He don't have to be blood-related. Just if he's a big farmer, owns a lot of land. They yoke him in with all the farmers. They got more land than anybody else."

---

33   The Major Special

Oh you come down on this Ramsey, partner, 'specially Ramsey   (104)
    Two,
Hmmm, fix it in your mind, buddy, you got your time to do.
Well fix it on your mind, partner, got your time to do,
Come down on Ramsey, 'specially Ramsey Two.

Don't try to punch it, partner, you can't get away,   (105)
Under the supervision of Major McGaughy [Muh-gay-hay]
Well under the supervision [of] Major McGaughy,
Don't try to punch it, partner, you can't get away.

No, you can't beat the rider, ain't no use to try,   (106)
He's a well-experienced river ranger with a eagle's eye.
Well-experienced river ranger, oh boy, got a eagle's eye,
Hmmm, don't try to beat the rider, ain't no use to try.

Horse he used to ride was pretty, oh, I long remember Prince,   (107)
Tread water like old Rattler, jump a shallow fence . . .
                    (*line B repeats, followed by line A*)

Way back in the '30's, whoa, in the '30's, partner, I hooked up   (108)
    with [him] then,
Whoa, he made me a roller, partner, I learned under him . . .

Well he raised plenty a watermelon, cotton a bumper crop,   (109)
Sugar cane don't you mention, boy, that's all he's got . . .

Major he know the river, oh he know the river, from the upside   (110)
    down,
Sandy land, old original, black land and the new ground.

He's a man a law and order, ain't no doubt about it,   (111)
Please don't break the monopoly, you'll regret you ever started.

If you come down to this old Ramsey, why you plannin' and a   (112)
    figurin',
Plan on leavin' legal, workin' for your livin'.

Well the summer gone and a comin', keep a comin', I may be   (113)
    here to stay,
I got a home under supervision [of] Major McGaughy.

Now you talkin' about all your troubles, ho you troubles man,   (114)
    but, boy, I had mine,
Ho, workin' Moreland Brothers, got the best go here.
Well the Moreland Brothers, partner, got the best go here,
Talkin' 'bout your troubles, well I had my share.

---

34   No Payday Here
(12 June 1966, 463.2)

The two opening stanzas are probably from a levee camp song, but Smith has used them as the basis for a song quite his own. The inmates in the TDC are not paid, but the difference between a levee camp boss who won't come through with a payroll on time and a prison system that doesn't bother with one is slight enough to make the song transfer easily.

Note that stanza 116 is a variant of stanza 44 above. Stanzas 128–131 are similar to Leadbelly's various songs to governors pleading for release, such as "Had you, Governor Neff, like you got me, /I'd wake up in the mornin' an' I'd set you free" (Lomax, 1936-B, p. 228), and a similar song to Louisiana Governor O. K. Allen (Lomax, 1936-B, p. 235).

---

34   No Payday Here

I used to weigh two hundred, two hundred, now I'm skin and   (115)
    bone,
Ever make a payday, captain, Hot Spring I'm goin'.
Ever make a payday, captain, Hot Spring I'm goin'.
Oh I used to weigh two hundred, now I'm just skin and bone.

Well I asked the captain, asked the captain, "Did the payroll   (116)
    come?"
"What the hell you care, partner, I don't owe you none."

If I never make a payroll, captain, if they never call my name,   (117)
Can't see the healing water, never make Hot Spring . . .
                    (*line B repeats, followed by line A*)

[They] tell me in Louisiana, big Louisy, oh boy, the murder[er]'s   (118)
    home,
Hmmm, may be a cemetery, partner, that's where I belong.

Got a one more letter, one more letter, I got to go myself,   (119)
I done lose my woman, everything I have left.

Well I heard a Winchester chargin', Winchester chargin', just a   (120)
    while 'fore day,
Hmmm, [if] you can't beat a bullet, partner, you can't get
    away . . .

Well don't let me catch you, rider, rider, see you foolin' round,   (121)
Lord I'd rather be shot to pieces, [than] stay here hobbled
    down . . .

Well the shotguns keep on blastin', just a blastin', somebody   (122)
    may be lost,
Sometime they shoot just to stop you partner, sometime where
    the [sus]spender cross,
Sometime they shoot just to stop you from runnin', man,
    sometime where your 'spenders cross,
When you hear the shotguns a blastin', somebody may be lost.

You can tell 'em I'm a leavin', a leavin', you can tell 'em when,   (123)
Oh some goin' to the bushes, partner, and there's some goin'
    in . . .

Well you never know who be lucky, whoa boy, if you never try,   (124)
You may run on from under the gun, partner, you may be
    crossfired,
Well if you run from under the gun, partner, you may beat the
    crossfire,
Never tell who be lucky if you never try.

Well when you wake up here every mornin', every mornin',   (125)
    then it's all day long
Whoa boy, you can't hear nothing, buddy, but just "Roll 'head
    on" . . .

Captain, he said, "Hurry, hurry, man," well the rider said, "Run."   (126)
Had my way, partner, wouldn't do neither one . . .

Ain't made a payday, captain, captain, since I been gone,   (127)
Rain or shine, buddy, got to go right on . . .

Sure like to see the Governor, Governor Connally, I don't   (128)
    have my fare,
Hmmm, sure like to see you Governor, we don't have no
    payday here . . .

Governor John Connally, please Governor, if you see me as a   (129)
    man,
Please consider me in your working, working, your release
    working plan.

Hmmm if you hold 'em here, buddy, if you hold 'em here, part-   (130)
    ner, you hold 'em anywhere,
But we just don't have no payday here.

I'll make you this promise, oh this promise, to three or four relia-   (131)
    able men,
Whoa, if you sign my release this time, Governor, won't have
    to do it again.
Well if you sign my release Governor, Governor Connally, won't
    have to do it again,
Oh I promise the good Lord above, Governor, three or four
    responsible men.

Hmmm we never have had, oh, no payday here,   (132)
Talkin' 'bout your trouble, boy, I had my share.

Axe Songs: Crosscutting (35–44)

---

35   Jody

A. Benny Richardson and group, *crosscutting*, Ellis, 24 March 1966,
451.2, N.C.

B. Benny Richardson and group, *crosscutting*, Ellis, 22 March 1966,
447.1

C. Benny Richardson and group, *crosscutting*, Ellis, 22 March 1966,
447.2

D. "Jody's Got My Wife and Gone," W. Sandell and group, Ellis, 21
August 1965, 386.10

Life in an army during wartime and life in prison anytime have a
number of aspects in common, so it is not surprising that items of
folklore are shared by both camps. One mutual concern is who is doing
what with, and to, the woman one left at home. In Negro folklore, this
concern is voiced in the songs and toasts about Jody the Grinder—"Jody"
is a contraction of "Joe the," and "Grinder" is a metaphor used for a
certain kind of coital movement.

Jody's activities and life style are perhaps best described in the toast
bearing his name:

Say, old Joe the Grinder was coppin' a snooze,
when the world got hip to some solid news.
Say, now, there was a no-good whore with a man overseas,
sayin', "Now get up, Jody, wake up please!"
Say, "I know you'd rather burn in hell,
but it's all over the headlines: Japan just fell."
Then old Jody turned over and his eyes all red,
he say, "I beg your pardon, baby, now what is that you said?"
She said, "I know you're high, motherfucker, and restin' fine,
and I know you heard me the first damned time."

He said, "Baby, I know that can't be right,
because I know those damned Japs just begin to fight.
And, anyway, I know those Japs they have to be invaded before they
     scrap."
She said, "No, no, Jody, back in Pearl Harbor the Japs had their day
but General Douglas MacArthur made a comeback play."
Say, "There may have once been a time when those Japs wouldn't quit,
but that atomic bomb has stopped all that shit."
Jody said, "I don't dig this play,"
said, "I'm goin' up on the cuts and see what the other cats say."
She said, "Jody, darlin', don't be mad,
but whilst you up on the cuts try to dig you up another pad."
Say, "I'm sorry, darling, but that's all she wrote,"
say, "my old man may be here on that next damn boat."
Jody said, "Don't front me with that shit because it's not anywhere,
and this is Joe the Grinder, and damn that square."
Say, "Now I'm not interested in your point of view,
now turn on the radio and get me the news."
Now the news he got, Jack, was a solid sender,
old Tojo was just signin' unconditioned surrender.
He said, "Turn it off, baby," say, "I don't want to hear no more
and see who's knockin' at that motherfuckin' door."
He said, "Wait a minute, baby, before you answer that knock,
will you get me that bottle and pour me a shot?"
He [G.I.Joe] said, "That's all right, Jody, I'm already in,"
said, "now let's all sit down and have a drink of gin."
Said, "Now I can tell by the look in both a your eyes
that I took this joint completely by surprise."
He said, "Hush, whore, I know what you gonna say before you even
     begin—
that you and Jody are just damned good friends.
But I'm gonna put you and Juanita wise,"
said "there's a lots a firepower in this forty-five."
He said, "And before some dreadful mistake is made,
Jody, will you kindly pocket that old rusty blade."
Say, "I heard you say you didn't give a damn,
but will you hip him, baby, to who I am."
She said, "Yes, daddy, if you want him to know.
Mr. Jody Grinder, meet Mr. G. I. Joe."
Said, "Now you people pull me up a seat
and I'll make my little story short and sweet."
He said, "Jody, ever since Pearl Harbor, back in '41,"
say, "you've played the cuts and had your fun."
Say, "You even shucked my old lady, and that ain't all,

You even carried her to the Allotment Balls.
You carried her to the park and you carried her to the zoo,
then you finally decided you'd just move in, too."
Say, "Now you know you and Juanita didn't play it fair,
but now you face to face with this same damn square."
He said, "Oh, yes, I picked up on your wardrobe as I came down the line,
and from what I hear about it, it's awful fine.
Now that's all right, babe, I'll get around to you;
I picked up on your wardrobe and it's foxy, too."
Say, "Now I have a little chick over across the way
and those togs may come in handy for her some day."
Say, "Now if you people will be cooperatin' and give me a helpin' hand,
we can soon have all this jive in my movin' van."
Boy, he took the rug off the floor, he took the mattress off the bunk,
he took the divan, cookstove, and the wardrobe trunk.
He took her shoes and stockings, her highest priced dress,
he took a combination Victrola and a cedar chest.
He said, "Load up, Jody, and load up fast,"
say, "I'm about ten seconds off your motherfuckin' ass."
Say, "Now when you load this van you don't have to be ashamed,
'cause lots of other Jodys are doing the same damned thing."
Say, "I know you people are interested in what I'm goin' to do,"
say, "I'm gonna open up a hopjoint on Cedar Avenue.
And you can pick up on me most any old day,
when me and my new old lady step out to play."
Now he made a military bow as he backed through the door
and he said goodbye to Jody and his dogassed whore.
He said, "Oh, yes, Jody, I want to you meet my Japanese queen—
and will you please hand me over that Longine?"

                    (Sam, Wynne Unit, 18 August 1965)

The toast is well dated by its content and slang: "solid news" and "solid sender" were out of style by the early 1950's; Japanese war brides didn't start receiving much attention until sometime after the American occupation of Japan was well under way, probably around 1947. The atom bomb and fall of Japan are so central to the story that they insure an early cutoff date. One would be safe in assuming composition sometime between 1947 and 1950. But Jody was around earlier. He is named in the brief blues "Joe the Grinder," recorded by John A. Lomax from the singing of Irvin Lowry in Gould, Arkansas, in 1939 (the song appears on *Afro-American, Blues and Songs*, AAFS L-14).

Roger Abrahams collected a version of "Jody the Grinder" in Philadelphia in the early 1960's (Abrahams, 1964, 170–171). If his version of the toast is at all representative of its current condition, it seems the toast is wearing down with age—younger performers have dropped the allusions and slang they don't understand, and concomitantly, some of the narrative elements. The man who performed the longer version printed above was sixty-four and, fortunately, one of those uncreative folk performers incapable of altering or destroying anachronisms in a text.

Newman White reports a four-line stanza (from an anonymous student, who, he says, probably found it in Durham, North Carolina) that is probably about an earlier avatar of the same character:

> Jones, he's got my gal and gone,
> When I get him I'm goin' to cut him, bite him,
> I'm goin' to cut him through an' through—
> Jones, he's got my gal an' gone.
>
> (White, 336)

During the war years, Jody figured in the marching song "Sound Off," a version of which is printed in Alan Lomax, 1960, p. 595. Lomax says there that, "In many variants this was sung by all Negro outfits in World War II." Abrahams says "This song is often called 'Jody's Song' and other similar ones 'Jody Calls'" (p. 170). Woody Guthrie has a sample in *Born to Win*, (p. 22). And John Greenway suggests George G. Carey's "A Collection of Airborne Cadence Chants," *Journal of American Folklore*, 77 (January–March 1965), 52–61, for adaptations of Jody rhymes.

The song has fared better than the toast. It was sung during the Korean War; I've been told that it is still sometimes sung in military camps. And it has gone to prison.

The first regular stanza of the D-text below, "Jody's Got My Wife and Gone," is similar to the one quoted by Guthrie. Most of the verses have to do with conditions of prison labor: the singer describes his various tasks, the weather, the field captain, parole, his loneliness, the Jody theme. That recording session was indoors, late at night in 1965.

When I returned to the prison in March 1966, I asked whether anyone else around knew it. This time we were out in the woods where the men were clearing timber. Benny Richardson, who told me he had put the song together, offered to sing lead while a group of sixteen inmates chopped down trees. Richardson at first called the song "Jody's Got Your Girl and Gone" (an interesting shift from the first singer's title), but later referred to it simply as "Jody."

The versions led by Richardson with the men at work were much better in text and tune than the one recorded earlier indoors. He had probably thought about the song a bit in the seven months between sessions. All his verses rhyme, as compared with only nine in the first version. Richardson's song (the A-text) has more structure: he sings two verses

about the work; one about his physical situation; the next three have to
do with the guards—their severity, power, soft life: the captain sits in
the shade and receives a salary, the inmates work all week (he does ex-
aggerate here—they work a five-day week now) for two sacks of rolling
tobacco and a movie; he thinks about going home and then is reminded
of Jody, who got not only his girl, but his sister as well; he closes with
a decision to avoid prison in the future.

The song is important for several reasons. Some of the stanzas have a
haiku-like brevity and force; the rhymes are not contrived or strained;
the melody is lovely. Unlike the sketchy World War II songs or chants
and their Korean counterparts, this "Jody" forms itself into several de-
scriptive and thematic blocks, each covered or developed before the
singer moves on. The song represents a survival of two traditions: one
is thematic and deals with Jody and the threat he has continued to represent in the folk culture, the threat of the man who steals your woman
when you are not there; the other has to do with the genre—the song is
one of the few that are of obviously recent adaptation and incorporation
into the prison worksong structure, and the composer is a young man,
still in his thirties, which suggests that the worksong tradition may yet
survive a little while even though many of the work situations that pro-
duced it are being replaced by modern machinery, and the prison conditions that maintained it have been replaced by modern penology. (I have
quoted freely in this note from my article, "What Happened to Jody,"
Journal of American Folklore, 80 [October–December 1967], 389–396.)

35-A   Jody

Stanzas 6, 11, 17, 22, 25

I've been workin' all day long
YEAH, YEAH, YEAH, YEAH,
Pickin' this stuff called cotton and corn,
YEAH, YEAH, YEAH, YEAH.

We raise cotton, cane and a corn . . . *(group sings burden at end of each line, as above)*

'Taters and tomatoes and that ain't all . . .

[My] back is weak and I done got tired . . .
Got to tighten up just to save my hide . . .

Boss on a horse and he's watchin' us all . . .
Better tighten up, [if you] don't, you'll catch the hall.

Wonder if the Major will go my bail . . .
[Or] give me twelve hours standin' on the rail . . .

Yeah, yeah, YEAH, YEAH,
Yeah, yeah, YEAH, YEAH.

I see the Captain sittin' in the shade . . . *(group resumes as in first stanza)*

He don't do nothin' but a he gets paid . . .

We work seven long days in a row . . .
Two sacks a Bull and a picture show . . .

In the wintertime we don't get no lay . . .
Cuttin' cane and makin' syrups every day . . .

When it get wet in the cane field . . .
All the squads work around the old syrup mill . . .

Yeah, yeah, YEAH, YEAH,
Yeah, yeah, YEAH, YEAH.

Two more months and it won't be long . . .
I'm gonna catch the chain 'cause I'm goin' home . . .

Goin' back home to my old gal Sue . . .
My buddy's wife and his sister, too . . .

Ain't no need of you writin' home . . .
Jody's got your girl and gone . . .

Ain't no need of you feelin' blue . . .
Jody's got your sister, too . . .

First thing I'll do when I get home . . .
Call my woman on the telephone . . .

Yeah, yeah, YEAH, YEAH,
Yeah, yeah, YEAH, YEAH.

Gonna settle down for the rest of my life . . .
Get myself a job and get myself a wife . . .

Six long years I've been in the pen . . .
I don't want to come to this place again . . .

Captain and the boss is a drivin' us on . . .
Makin' us wish we'd a stayed at home . . .

[If] we had listened what our mama say . . .
We wouldn't be cuttin' wood a-here today . . .

Yeah, yeah, YEAH, YEAH,
Yeah, yeah, YEAH, YEAH. (*repeat both lines*)

Captain and the boss is drivin' us on . . .
Makin' us wish we'd a stayed at home . . .

We had listened what our mama say . . .
We wouldn't be droppin' big timber here today . . .

Yeah, yeah, YEAH, YEAH,
Yeah, yeah, YEAH, YEAH.

Spoken: Jack, jack! Hold it up here boys.

35-B   Jody

Similar to 35-A, but with the following variant or additional stanzas:

Know old Major won't go my bail . . .
Standin' twelve hours on the mean old rail . . .

Captain settin' over yonder under the shade . . .
He don't do nothin' but a he gets paid . . .

You know I work seven days in a row . . .
Two sacks a Durham and a one picture show . . .

When I go home I'm goin' to stay . . .
Ain't gonna do no wrong for quite a few days . . .

Gonna settle down and get me a job . . .
A pretty little girl and a great big yard . . .

One a these mornings, it won't be long . . .
I'm gonna catch the chain, 'cause I'm going home . . .

When I get there the first thing I will do . . .
Look up my old good girl Sue . . .

35-C   Jody

Similar to 35-A and 35-B, but with the following variant or additional stanzas:

Goin' back home to my old girl Sue . . .
Sport 'em up a wife for me and you . . .

Don't worry, buddy, I ain't comin' back . . .
Don't want no fine clothes and no Cadillac . . .

First thing I'll do when a I'll get home . . .
Call Marie on the telephone . . .

Get myself a wife and get myself a job . . .
Anything but pickin' cotton and a-parkin' cars . . .

Don't you worry, fella, 'bout a-me . . .
Won't steal no more, now you watch and see . . .

Never been a place like this before . . .
All they do is pick cotton and a use a hoe . . .

35-D   Jody's Got My Wife and Gone

Yeah, yeah, YEAH, YEAH,
Yeah, yeah, YEAH, YEAH.

Jody's got my wife and gone,
YEAH, YEAH, YEAH, YEAH,
Jody's been here and now he's gone,
YEAH, YEAH, YEAH, YEAH.

Got me pickin' cotton and corn . . . (*group continues burden as above*)
A come on, fellas, let the hammer ring . . .

And tell the waterboy to brink some water . . .
I got to wash my hands one time . . .

Cleaned my heart and left my feet . . .

But Jody done got ya in my house . . .
A come on, fellas, let the hammer ring . . .

The hotter the day . . .
The cooler the afternoon . . .

Let the hammer ring . . .
Drive on boys . . .
Spoken: Drop 'em.

I think I see the captain comin' around . . .
He's fixin' to let us go down . . .
Spoken: Drop 'em.

Come on, Captain, won't you raise your hat . . .
Talk for me and go to bat . . .

Talk to the parole board and let me go . . .
I got to drop this o-mighty hoe . . .

I got a diamond in my hand . . .
Now you know I'm a lonesome man . . .

Yeah, yeah, YEAH, YEAH,
Yeah, yeah, YEAH, YEAH.

Jody's got my wife and gone . . .
I got to get some more cotton and corn . . .

Listen here, fellas, now listen to the song . . .
Jody done got my wife and gone . . .
Spoken: Oh drive 'em.

Come on, Captain, a raise your hat . . .
My heart is worried and I just got the bat . . .

I got to go, I can't stand no more . . .
So here's your sack and here's your hoe . . .

Yeah, yeah, YEAH, YEAH (4x)

---

36 I Need Another Witness

A. Joseph "Chinaman" Johnson and group, *crosscutting*, Ellis, 21 August 1965, 396.5, N.C.
B. Johnny Jackson, Houston Page, and group, *flatweeding*, Ramsey 1, 22 August 1966, 403.3, J.M.

This well-known spiritual exists in two forms in the prison. The older form—as straight spiritual—is the crosscutting version lead by Chinaman. The prison adaptation—using calls for various guards, inmates, and even visitors, and omitting the narrative spoken verses—is the flatweeding version led by Jackson and Page. It is uncommon for one song to be used for two different kinds of work activity, but there is so much difference in performance styles between the axe and hoe versions that perhaps they might be considered almost different songs, sharing a similar melody and a chorus. (The tune for the hoe version is similar to 42-B. "Timber Gettin' Limber," sung by Johnny Jackson and David Tippett.)

The humorous last spoken stanza is more complex than it may appear. It is not an irrelevant addition to the sequence of biblical narrations preceding it, but rather a stanza that brings it all back home. An old man goes to church, is possessed by some kind of spirit, is symbolically damaged (he falls down lame), bringing discomfort to the churchgoers; he continues his shout (see Parrish, 1942, for more on the "shout" and what it means in the folk community), strikes a "certain sister" (that is, "*You* know who—might be you"), and then quietly returns to his seat, having transferred the affliction in different form to the proper sinner, his messenger function fulfilled. All the previous stanzas are about situations in which God was involved in people's activities; this stanza suggests that the use of messengers and agents might continue.

The sequence of persons in the flatweeding version deserves some note. It begins with Jack O Diamonds, Captain Duncan, and the Major —one dead, the other two in different parts of the field. It shifts to a "brother," then says "you" can join in also. Jack O Diamonds is mentioned again, then "Boss Calvin"—a guard riding nearby. The Beartrack stanza produced some chuckles by some of the singers; Calvin and I laughed, and when they saw us laughing, they decided to throw me into the song, too, whereupon they all laughed. As many of the simpler axe songs, this could be continued until the lead singer became bored with it.

Printed versions of the A-text are found in Odum and Johnson, 1925, 132–133; Johnson and Johnson, 1962, 130–133. The *Lomax MS* (A9/143) has a song, "Preaching in the Wildnerness," collected by W. H. Thomas in south Texas, that has in it some of Chinaman's spoken stanzas. On *Negro Prison Camp Worksongs*, Folkways P 475, recorded in 1951, the talking part of "You Got to Hurry" is similar to Chinaman's talk here.

36-A   I Need Another Witness

Sung:
Oh well I need another witness, FOR MY LORD,
A well I need another witness, FOR MY LORD.
I need a witness like old Jonah was, FOR MY LORD,
I need a witness like old Jonah was, FOR MY LORD.

Chanted:
Oh well the angel come from the cloud, YEAH!
Spoke to Ezekiel and voice sound loud, YEAH!
Angel individual spoke to Ezekiel, YEAH!
In his hand-a was a golden shekel, YEAH!
Got my shekel and people all stared, YEAH!
Moses ground up golden calf, YEAH!
Calf in the water turned bitter as gall, YEAH!
Children of Israel couldn't drink it at all.

Sung:
Oh, Moses was a witness, FOR MY LORD,
Oh, Moses was a witness, FOR MY LORD.
Well I need another witness, FOR MY LORD,
Well I need another witness, FOR MY LORD.

Chanted:
Oh Moses on-a the mountain 'lone, YEAH!
Where he broke God's table stones, YEAH!
When old Moses was comin' down, YEAH!
Children in the valley did give alarm, YEAH!
Then old Moses got worried in mind, YEAH!
Went to God oh his second time, YEAH!
God told Moses leadin' part, YEAH!
'Graved that law in Moses' heart, YEAH!
Stamped that law in Moses' mind, YEAH!
Told him not to leave that law behind.

Sung:
Oh, Moses was a witness, FOR MY LORD,
Oh, Moses was a witness, FOR MY LORD.
A-well I need another witness, FOR MY LORD,
A-well I need another witness, FOR MY LORD.

Chanted:
A-well-a God told Jonah, "Go Niniveh land," YEAH!
Jonah saw a ship a goin' over there, YEAH!
Paid his way and got on board, YEAH!

A God sonamighty went from the shore, YEAH!
Captain and the mate, they got troubled in mind, YEAH!
Search that ship a-from bottom to top, YEAH!
In that ship they found a knock, YEAH!
Found old Jonah layin' fast asleep, YEAH!
"A wake up man." A-says, "A-who art thou?" YEAH!
"Child a God please tell me so," YEAH!
"If it rain, a-please let me know," YEAH!
Heaved old Jonah overboard, YEAH!
'Long come a whale and swallowed him whole, YEAH!
Made his way to Nineveh land, YEAH!
Spewed out on a banks of sand, YEAH!
'Long come a little bird, dropped the seed, YEAH!
From that seed it sprung a root, YEAH!
From that root it sprung a vine, YEAH!
'Long come a greedy one, cut it down, YEAH!
Well it's bored another hole and broke Jonah's crown, YEAH!

Sung:
Brother Jonah was a witness, FOR MY LORD,
Brother Jonah was a witness, FOR MY LORD.
Well I need another witness, FOR MY LORD,
Well I need another witness, FOR MY LORD.

Chanted:
A-well old man Adam never been out, YEAH!
Go to the church and he jump up and shout, YEAH!
Fall down and gets up lame, YEAH!
All the church a members became ashamed, YEAH!
Shouted till he give a certain sister a blow, WHOOO!
Set right down, didn't shout no mo', YEAH!

Sung:
Brother Adam was a witness, FOR MY LORD,
Brother Adam was a witness, FOR MY LORD.
I want you come and be a witness, FOR MY LORD,
I want you come and be a witness, FOR MY LORD.

36-B   I Need Another Witness

Jackson:

A-well I need another witness, FOR MY LORD,
A-well I need another witness, FOR MY LORD.

A-well my mother was a witness . . . (*group repeats burden after each
line*)
A-well my mother was a witness . . .

Come on and be a witness . . . (2x)
A-Jack a Diamonds was a witness . . . (2x)

He was a sinnerman witness, FOR MY LORD (2x)
Come on and be a witness, HEY, FOR MY LORD,
Come on and be a witness, HEY, HEY, FOR MY LORD.

Page:

Oh well, Cap'n Duncan was a witness, FOR MY LORD,
Oh well, Cap'n Duncan was a witness, OH, FOR MY LORD.
Well I need another witness, OH, FOR MY LORD (2x)
A-well the Major was a witness, FOR MY LORD,
A-well the Major was a witness, WITNESS FOR MY LORD.

Jackson:
One a these mornin's . . .
I said, goin' to be a witness . . .

Well my brother was a witness . . .
Well Lordy have mercy . . .

I say, now you can be a witness . . . (2x)
I said, Jack Diamonds was a witness . . . (2x)
Boss Calvin was a witness . . . (2x)
Anybody can be a witness . . . (2x)
I say no raise up higher man . . . (2x)
Come on and be a witness . . . (2x)
I mean a truly born witness . . . (2x)

A-Beartrack he was a witness . . .
Down in the bottom man . . .

I say, now you can be a witness . . .
I say, man, you can be a witness . . .

A-well come and be a witness . . .
I said, a come and be a witness . . .

A Mister Bruce he is a witness . . .
Bruce Jackson is a witness . . .

Bruce Jackson is a witness . . . (2x)
He is a truly born witness . . . (2x)
I says the warden is a witness . . . (2x)
Well he's a true born witness . . . (2x)

---

37   Grizzly Bear

A. Benny Richardson and group, *crosscutting*, Ellis, 22 March 1966, 447.4

B. Benny Richardson and group, *crosscutting*, Ellis, 24 March 1966, 452.3

C. Johnny Jackson, Houston Page, and group, *spading*, Ramsey 1, 22 August 1965, 402.4, N.C.

D. Joseph "Chinaman" Johnson and group, *crosscutting*, Ellis, 22 March 1966, 447.7, N.C.

Many inmates believe this song is about Carl Luther McAdams, presently warden at the Wynne Unit, long warden of Ellis (unit for hardcore redicivists and troublemakers), and before that warden of Ramsey (which served the function Ellis now does before that prison was constructed in the early 1960's). McAdams is known as the toughest and fairest warden in the system; there are many folktales about how in the old days he broke up riots by walking into the riot areas alone and taking off rioters one by one until there were none left because most ran away before he had finished whatever he was doing. Most of those stories are true. McAdams nickname is "The Track" or "Beartracks," and the song is probably connected with him because his nickname is so similar to the subject of the song.

Whatever inmates *now* think about the song's inspiration, oldtimers say it wasn't McAdams at all, but someone who worked in the prison system long before he joined it in the late 1930's, a man named Joe Oliver. One inmate said, "Jack O Diamonds had a man up under him, his name was Joe Oliver and they named him 'Jack the Bear.' And that's where the song come from. You could see him comin' from the bottom and they'd say, 'There come Bear.' Then other guys, if they foolin' around in any kind of ways, then they know that the captain is coming and they'll tighten up a little bit. And so guys just got together, got to practicing, and someone said, 'You just follow me.' Got out there in the woods and we just got to hollering and eventually they made a song out of it. And that's where it started from."

"It didn't start with Captain Mac then?" I asked him.

"McAdams? Oh, he wasn't even in the system when that song come down, don't let nobody tell you he was. He got the name of Big Bear. See, Warden McAdams, I don't know how long he been in the system, but he ain't been in *that* long. Don't let nobody tell you that song was built up behind McAdams because it wasn't. Originally that song was built behind Joe Oliver. Joe Oliver was the one they called Jack the Bear, he was the assistant warden under Jack O Diamonds. Oliver left the first of '41."

It may be true that the song existed before McAdams came into the prison system or got his nickname, but it is peculiar that there are no versions recorded before 1951. The Lomaxes did an extremely good job of covering the TDC field when they visited the prisons in the 1930's, and it seems peculiar that they should have missed completely a song as popular as this one is. It is, of course, possible that the song was in circulation then, perhaps on only one or two prison farms they did not visit. In any event, the song is widely known now, and many inmates connect it with Warden McAdams, "The Bear." I recorded twelve versions performed by five different song leaders. "Grizzly Bear," "Hammer Ring," and "Crooked-Foot John" are the three most frequently heard crosscutting songs.

In 1965 Benny Richardson (who sings lead on the A- and B-texts) told me he never sang lead. When I saw him again in March 1966, he sang lead for two songs, both of them magnificent texts: 35. "Jody" and "Grizzly Bear."

Richardson's first text is really a ballad, rare in convict worksongs. He begins by singing "I wanna tell you a story," and he concludes, "That's a my story." He is not only *singing* a ballad, but is conscious enough of what he is doing to point it out in the text of the song. There is something approaching the epic mood in this text. His bear travels widely (all over the southwest—Texas, Oklahoma, Louisiana—and even north to Tennessee) killing stock and people, eluding trackers every-where. When first trapped, he kills two men; he is captured in Tennessee and escapes again; he is caught somewhere else and put in a zoo, then escapes again. Finally there comes "a little man . . . that been a-huntin' bears long time now," and the bear is killed. Like Faulkner's bear, his track is unmistakably his; like Faulkner's bear, he cannot be killed by just *anyone*—it requires a special person.

Richardson's B-text is also a ballad. It isn't as compelling as the first text, but it is closer to the usual versions. In this performance we are told about the bear, we hear that the singer's father went off after him (fathers are rarely mentioned in the worksongs, by the way; the words used are evocative of the hunting sections of 17. "Grey Goose"), then a stanza that a "workin' squad they killed him there . . ." which brings it back to the prison context.

The texts by Jackson and Page (C) and Johnson (D) are more *about* prison than Richardson's. Jackson's begins with mention of Jack O Diamonds, who is mentioned more often than anyone else in perform-ances of this song. They link it to McAdams: "Oh don't you let that Bear catch you, man . . ." is understood to mean Beartracks, not any mythic animal. Chinaman first establishes the personality of the bear by tieing it to Jack O Diamonds, then transfers it to two other guards, Stormy Weather and Boss Rainey.

The text transcriptions refer to "Grizzly Bear," but Texas convict singers never pronounce that word with two syllables—it is always *grizz-a-ly*, and should be read that way. Norman Cazden used that vari-ant spelling for the lines with the musical transcriptions because of the metrics.

An unidentified singer who I am sure is Chinaman sings lead to "Grizzly Bear" on *Negro Prison Camp Worksongs*, Folkways P-475, re-corded in 1951 (printed in Courlander, 1963-B, p. 106). Grover Dickson and group, on Retrieve, who recorded on the same excursion that pro-duced the previous record, sing it on *Treasury of Field Recording, I*, Candid 8026. The notes to that album state that "In myths and fairy tales the bear is the traditional totem of the evil mother. 'Grizzly Bear' seems to contain parallels to all these images, and yet on another level, is poking fun and innuendo at the homosexual relationships of the convicts themselves. Given this interpretation, it's merely another term for the hairy, old homosexual, (called 'Wolf' by white convicts, 'Bear' by Negroes), of the dormitory." That is not true: not only does this song lack any homosexual connotation for the prisoners, but the word "bear" is never used by them in that context. There is a commercialized version sung by Harry Belafonte and chorus which appears on *Swing Dat Hammer,* RCA LPS-2194.

37-A   Grizzly Bear

I wanna tell you a story 'bout a GRIZZLY BEAR,
I wanna tell you a story 'bout a GRIZZLY BEAR.

He was a great big grizzly, GRIZZLY BEAR,
He was a great big grizzly, GRIZZLY BEAR.

You know he laid a track like a GRIZZLY BEAR,
He had great big paws like a GRIZZLY BEAR.

I said a grizzly, grizzly, GRIZZLY BEAR,
Oh Lord have mercy, GRIZZLY BEAR.

You know they tracked him through a Texas now, GRIZZLY BEAR,
He went down to Oklahoma now, GRIZZLY BEAR.

You know the people tried to catch him now, GRIZZLY BEAR,
Because he was a-killing stock now, GRIZZLY BEAR.

I said a grizzly, grizzly, GRIZZLY BEAR,
Well a Lord have mercy, GRIZZLY BEAR.

You know 'way down in Louisiana now, GRIZZLY BEAR,
He was a-runnin' in the swamp now, GRIZZLY BEAR.

He was killin' every thing, GRIZZLY BEAR,
He got a woman on a plain, GRIZZLY BEAR.

You know the people got a-scared a the GRIZZLY BEAR,
They wouldn't come a out to see him, GRIZZLY BEAR.

He stood ten feet tall like a GRIZZLY BEAR,
He had a big bone paw like a GRIZZLY BEAR.

I said a grizzly, grizzly, GRIZZLY BEAR,
Oh Lord have mercy, GRIZZLY BEAR.

You know we caught the big grizzly, GRIZZLY BEAR,
You know he killed two men and he, GRIZZLY BEAR.

They hemmed him up in Tennessee again, GRIZZLY BEAR,
He didn't do nothin' but to get loose again, GRIZZLY BEAR.

He was a mean old grizzly, GRIZZLY BEAR,
He was a mean, mean grizzly, GRIZZLY BEAR.

Oh grizzly, grizzly, GRIZZLY BEAR,
Oh Lord have mercy, GRIZZLY BEAR.

Well they finally caught him now, GRIZZLY BEAR,
They tried to put him in the zoo and now, GRIZZLY BEAR.

You know he knocked down a man and he, GRIZZLY BEAR,
He tried to enter twelve times and he, GRIZZLY BEAR.

He stood up on his two feet and he, GRIZZLY BEAR,
He growled all day long and he, GRIZZLY BEAR.

But they had a little man and now, GRIZZLY BEAR,
That been a-huntin' bears long time now, GRIZZLY BEAR.

Well a grizzly, grizzly, GRIZZLY BEAR,
Oh well a-Lord have mercy, GRIZZLY BEAR.

Well they finally caught old grizzly, GRIZZLY BEAR,
Well they finally caught old grizzly, GRIZZLY BEAR.

And they decided they would kill him, GRIZZLY BEAR,
Because they couldn't do nothin' with him, GRIZZLY BEAR.

Well you know they caught old grizzly, GRIZZLY BEAR,
That's a my story, GRIZZLY BEAR.

37-B   Grizzly Bear

I'm gonna tell you a story about a GRIZZLY BEAR,
I'm gonna tell you a story about a GRIZZLY BEAR.

He was a great black a-grizzly, GRIZZLY BEAR (2x)
Chrous: Well-a grizzly, grizzly, GRIZZLY BEAR,
Lord have mercy, GRIZZLY BEAR.

He went a-trackin' through the bottom like a GRIZZLY BEAR (2x)
He had a long white tushes like a GRIZZLY BEAR (2x)
(Chorus)
You know my mama was afraid of the GRIZZLY BEAR (2x)

You know my papa went a-huntin' for GRIZZLY BEAR,
He went a-huntin' in the mornin' for GRIZZLY BEAR. (Chorus)

Well he went a track through the fields like a GRIZZLY BEAR,
He was a-makin' big tracks-a like a GRIZZLY BEAR.

He had a long black hair like a GRIZZLY BEAR,
And every mornin' he will be there, GRIZZLY BEAR. (Chorus)

You know my papa went a huntin' for GRIZZLY BEAR,
He died a-huntin' on the Brazis for GRIZZLY BEAR.

It was early one mornin', GRIZZLY BEAR,
I heard a shootin' and a callin' and GRIZZLY BEAR. (Chorus)

He find the bear on old Brazos, GRIZZLY BEAR,
He found him down on old Brazos, GRIZZLY BEAR.

You know I ain't scared a no bear, GRIZZLY BEAR,
Because the workin' squad they killed him there, GRIZZLY BEAR.

Well-a grizzly, grizzly, GRIZZLY BEAR,
Well Lord have mercy, GRIZZLY BEAR.

37-C   Grizzly Bear

Jackson:
Jack O Diamonds ain't nothin' but a GRIZZLY BEAR,
Oh, Jack O Diamonds ain't nothin' but a GRIZZLY BEAR.

Well he's a grizzly, grizzly . . . (*repeat and burden continue as above*)

He make big tracks down in the bottom like a . . . (2x)
Well he's a grizzly, grizzly . . . (2x)

Page:
Well he's a great big, great big . . . (2x)
He gonna hold you if he catch you now . . . (2x)

A-well he hold you if he catch you now, GRIZZLY BEAR,
He gonna hold you if he catch you, GRIZZLY BEAR.

Well he's a great big, Lord now, GRIZZLY BEAR,
Well he's a great big, fuzzy-leg, GRIZZLY BEAR.

A-well the Captain is a ridin' like a . . . (2x)

Jackson:
Now if he hit you he will kill you that, GRIZZLY BEAR,
I say if he hit you he will kill you that, GRIZZLY BEAR.

Well that grizzly, grizzly . . . (2x)
Oh don't you let that Bear catch you, man . . . (2x)
He will stomp you in the ground, man . . . (2x)
Well that grizzly, grizzly . . . (2x)
Well I'm afraid, I'm afraid of that . . . (2x)
Well that grizzly, grizzly . . . (2x)

Well he will catch you and he'll kill you that GRIZZLY BEAR,
I say he'll catch you and he'll kill you that GRIZZLY BEAR.

He don't know his own strength that . . . (2x)
Well that grizzly, grizzly . . . (2x)

37-D   Grizzly Bear

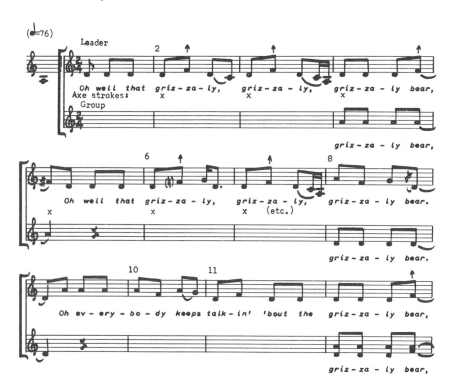

Oh well that grizzly, grizzly, GRIZZLY BEAR,
Oh well that grizzly, grizzly, GRIZZLY BEAR.

Oh everybody keeps talkin' 'bout the . . .   (*repeat and burden continue*
                                                        as above)

Oh everybody keeps wonderin' who the . . .
Oh if I tell you don't you tell it to the . . .
Oh Jack O Diamonds ain't nothin' but a . . .
He come walkin' and talkin' like a . . .
I heard Mama tell Papa 'bout the . . .
Well Lordy that grizzly . . .
Oh well I b'lieve I go to lookin' for the . . .
I looked all in Loosiana for the . . .
Well Lordy that grizzly . . .
He makes a track in the bottom like a . . .
Oh everybody keeps a talkin' 'bout the . . .
Oh Jack O Diamond ain't nothin' but a . . .
He got two white tushes like a . . .
He make a echo in the bottom like a . . .
Wo Lordy that grizzly . . .
Oh everybody keep wonderin' who the . . .
Well Stormy Weather ain't nothin' but . . .
He makes a track all in the bottom like a . . .
He comes a reelin' and rockin' like a . . .
Well Boss Rainey ain't nothin' but a . . .
He come walkin' and talkin' like a . . .
He make a track all in the bottom like a . . .

38   Hammer Ring

A. Joseph "Chinaman" Johnson and group, *crosscutting*, Ellis, 21 August 1965, 395.1, N.C.
B. "Don't You Hear My Hammer Ring," Matt Williams (lead) and Louis "Bacon and Porkchop" Houston, 4 July 1964, Ramsey 2, 43.7
C. Henry Scott and group, *crosscutting*, Ellis, 21 August 1965, 389.6, N.C.
D. "Black Betty," Jesse "G. I. Jazz" Hendricks, Matt Williams, and group, Ramsey 2, 4 July 1964, 36.1
E. J. C. Spring and group, *crosscutting*, Ellis, 22 March 1966, 447.3
F. Joseph "Chinaman" Johnson and group, Ellis, 11 July 1964, 63.3
G. David Tippen and group, Wynne, 6 January 1966, 424.4

This might be regarded as two songs: one the Noah (sung *Norah*) sequence, best presented in Chinaman's A-text, the other the group of prison verses. The story of Noah's trying to warn people too foolish to listen to him, then having the same people pound his door in vain when it is too late, has an obvious interest, but the link between the two lyrics sets is more practical: Noah goes to the woods to cut down timber for his Ark, and the timber-cutting convicts sympathize with him in his labors; the B-text, led by Matt Williams, drifts from mention of Jack O Diamonds to someone working early in the morning in the bottoms to God and Noah.

There is a curious progression in the E-text, led by J. C. Spring. He names or "calls" several people and prison camps — the captain, the baby, Central, the rider, and so on — then says "I going to ring it for a diamond man." That line means "ring it for a good axe man." But he quickly shifts to what the word "Diamond" evokes — Jack O Diamonds — and sings several stanzas about him. Jack O Diamonds is also mentioned in the A- and B-texts. Chinaman's A-text sequence about Black Betty's crazy baby sired by Jack O Diamonds illustrates the peculiar Southern perceptual quirk: what a black man sings doesn't count, so he can sing things in peace which if spoken would infuriate whites. Chinaman puns on Black Betty — it is of course the truck that carries people around the farms, but he makes it mean a woman, also.

This song, in which all verses are made up of one line sung twice with the group joining in only on the brief chorus, is probably the best-known axe song in the TDC. I have recorded nineteen versions by thirteen different leaders. The Archive of American Folk Song catalog lists nine performances, all but one from Texas. A version can be heard on *Negro Prison Camp Worksongs,* Folkways P-475 (that version is transcribed in Courlander 1963-B, 99–101). A sequence of stanzas like the Noah sections of "Hammer Ring" but with a chorus of "ump-humph" is in the *Lomax MS* (A9/142) from Juanita I. Sawyer, La Grange, Texas. There is a "Black Betty" in Lomax, 1936-A, pp. 60–61; no singer's name is given, but it seems similar to Leadbelly's versions. (The song is about a *whip* named Black Betty, but no singer I met in any Texas prison had ever heard the whip called "Black Betty"—the term there means the transfer wagon that moves the men from town to jail or from unit to unit. The whip was the "red heifer" or, more commonly, the "bat.") In the same volume is a group of verses called "The Hammer Song" (pp. 61–62), sung to the tune of "Black Betty," which is a variant of the "Hammer Ring" texts here.

38-A   Hammer Ring

ham - mer   ring,   Well,   soon   one   morn - in',   let your ham - mer   ring.

ham - mer   ring,   ham - mer   ring.

Var.
2   2   2   2

Oh Black a Betty, Black a Betty, let your HAMMER RING,
Oh Black a Betty, Black a Betty, let your HAMMER RING.

Oh Black a Betty's in the bottom, let your . . . (*repeat and burden continue as above*)

Oh Black a Betty's got a baby . . .
A-well he crazy like his daddy . . .
Tell me who was his daddy . . .
Oh if I tell you don't you tell it, let your . . .
A Jack O Diamonds was his daddy, let your . . .
A-well it's God told Norah, let your . . .
"I want you to build me a ark-a," let your . . .
"Oh, how high do you want it," let your . . .
"I want it one hundred cubies," let your . . .
"Oh and go and warn the people," let your . . .
"Want you tell everybody," let your . . .
"I want you to tell 'em 'bout the water," let your . . .
Well old Norah went to walkin', let your . . .
He want a walkin' and talkin', let your . . .
He went to talkin' bout the water, let your . . .
You oughta heard them sinners laughin', let your . . .
They made fun a poor Norah, let your . . .
Well soon one mornin', let your . . .
A-well the lightnin' went to flashin', let your . . .
Well the thunder start to rollin', let your . . .
A-well the water start to risin', let your . . .
You oughta heard them sinners cryin', let your . . .
They cried, "Lord, have mercy!" let your . . .
Well early in the mornin', let your . . .
I could hear 'em call Norah, let your . . .
They said, "Lord, have mercy," let your . . .
"A Norah letta me in-a," let your . . .

"It do you no good," let your . . .
"A-well the angels got the keys," let your . . .
"And they gone back to glory," let your . . .

38-B   Don't You Hear My Hammer Ring

Goin' tell everybody, DON'T YOU HEAR MY HAMMER RING,
Goin' tell everybody, DON'T YOU HEAR MY HAMMER RING.

Say my hammer's striking fire . . . (*repeat and burden continue as above*)
I'm gonna ring it for the Major . . .
I'm gonna call him like I used to . . .
Say early in the morning . . .
It's bullin' Jack O Diamonds . . .
Say early in the morning . . .
I say down in the bottom . . .
And say, "Partner what's the matter?". . .
God told Norah . . .
"I'm gonna 'stroy this world". . .
"Ain't gonna be no more fire". . .
"A-won't you go the the forest". . .
"I want you build me a cubit". . .
"I want it forty-two cubits". . .
"I want you go to the forest". . .
"I want a beast of every kind". . .
Oh a Norah, Norah . . .
A-well he picked up his hammer . . .
He went a-marchin' to the forest . . .
And start to hewin' out the timber . . .
Oh Norah, Norah . . .
"I want you build me a cubit". . .
He's got a beast of every kind . . .
Wo Lordy have mercy . . .
Oh won't you help me out of trouble . . .
Well I'm troubled in this bottom . . .
Oh Norah, Norah . . .
Well he went to the forest . . .
Well he hewed out the timber . . .
Well he fell on his knees . . .
He begin to pray . . .
"Wo Lord have mercy". . .

"Wo help me out a trouble". . .
"Been in trouble so long". . .
"Won't you please have mercy". . .
"If you help me this time". . .
"Well I won't be worried". . .
Don't you knockin' in the timber . . .
Well you knock in the timber . . .
JACK!

38-C   Hammer Ring

I'm gonna ring my hammer, OH LET YOUR HAMMER RING,
I'm gonna ring my hammer, OH LET YOUR HAMMER RING.

I'm gonna ring it in the bottom . . . (*repetition and burden continue
as above*)

I'm gonna ring my hammer . . .
I got a nine-pound hammer . . .
I'm gonna take it to the river . . .

Oh just to cool my hammer . . .
I b'lieve my partner's got worried . . .
A-well, he worried 'bout his hammer . . .
I'm gonna call him li'l louder . . .
Oh well I wonder can he hear it . . .
I'm gonna call li'l louder . . .
Oh well I thought I'd call my baby . . .
Oh well my baby's in Houston . . .
Oh Evalina, Evalina . . .
Oh Evalina was my baby . . .
Oh I wonder can she hear it . . .
I'm gonna call a li'l louder . . .
Oh Evalina, Evalina . . .
Oh Evalina was my baby . . .
Oh well my baby's in Houston . . .
I got a letter from my baby . . .
Oh I wonder can she hear it . . .
I'm gonna call her in the bottom . . .
Oh well the bottom on Ellis . . .
I'm gonna cool my hammer . . .

38-D   Black Betty

G.I.:
Oh Black Betty, Black-a-Betty, LET YOUR HAMMER RING,
Oh Black Betty, Black-a-Betty, LET YOUR HAMMER RING.

We got to cut until we find her . . . (*repetition and burden continue as
above*)
Oh well it's partner quit your doggin' . . .
Wo man and let's go to loggin' . . .
I'm gonna tell you 'bout the rider . . .
Oh well the rider done a tol' me . . .
Oh well there's trouble in the bottom . . .
Oh well I told you I's the devilman . . .
Oh well the timber keeps a bendin' . . .
Oh well a Fort Worth a Ida . . .
Oh well she used to be my rider . . .
Oh well I'm goin' back to Austin . . .
I'm gonna talk to the governor . . .
Oh well it's maybe he will help me . . .
Oh! I b'lieve I'll go crazy . . .
I'm goin' crazy with my hammer . . .

Wo partner quit your doggin' . . .
Oh well a help me to log 'em . . .
Oh ain't nothing but a spirit . . .
A-well it's a liveoak spirit . . .
Oh well it's be no more jackin', LET YOUR HAMMER RING
Until the timber starts to crackin', LET YOUR HAMMER RING.

Williams:
Oh hamber keep a ringin', let your HAMMER RING,
I say my hamber keep a ringin', let your HAMMER RING.

I say Lordy have mercy, let your HAMMER RING (*all lines repeated*)
I say the Major's gone to Dallas, HAMMER RING
I say he's gone to get me a partner, HAMMER RING
He gonna find me in the bottom, HAMMER RING
I got a four-pound hamber, HAMMER RING
I says bring me a drink a water, let your HAMMER RING
I says I don't want to drink it, let your HAMMER RING
I want to pour it on my hamber, HAMMER RING
I say my hamber's on fire, HAMMER RING
I say my hamber's strikin' fire, HAMMER RING
I say Lord have mercy, HAMMER RING
I say I b'lieve I spied the rider, HAMMER RING

Spoken: Ohhhh! Timber, timber, timber's fallin'—

38-E   Hammer Ring

I says I'm down in the bottom, Lordy, HEAR MY HAMMER RING,
I says I'm down in the bottom, Lordy, HEAR MY HAMMER RING.

I got a nine-pound hammer, Lordy, HEAR MY HAMMER RING,
I got a nine-pound hammer, Lordy, HEAR MY HAMMER RING.

I'm gonna ring it for the Captain, Lord . . . (*repetition and burden
continue as above*)

I'm gonna ring it for the Captain, Lord . . .
I'm gonna ring it for this story, Lord . . .
I'm gonna ring it for the baby now . . .
A-well I rung it on the Central, Lord . . .
I says I rung 'em on the Dangton [Darrington], Lord . . .
I says I rung 'em on the Ramsey now . . .

I says away 'cross the Brazos, Lord . . .
I was a-ringin' for the Major, man . . .
I says oh tell-a my dear brother Lord, HEAR MY HAMMER RING
(sung once)

A-won't you raise your window my good gal, HEAR MY HAMMER RING
(sung once)

I'm going to ring my hammer, Lord . . .
I'm going to ring it for the rider, Lord . . .
I got all lifetime to ring it now . . .
I going to ring it for a diamond man . . .
I says ole Diamond like the ringing now, HEAR MY HAMMER RING
(sung once)

I says oh ring it for the Diamond now, HEAR MY HAMMER RING
(sung once)

I says ole Diamond's in the bottom, Lord . . .
I says he ain't nothin' but a man, HEAR MY HAMMER RING
(sung once)

A Jack O Diamond was a ruler, Lord . . .
I says the ruler of the Brazos now . . .
I'm going to ring it in the morning, man . . .
I'm going to ring it in the evening, Lord . . .
I'm going to ring-a for the Colonel, Lord . . .
I'm going to ring it late in the evening, Lord . . .

38-F   Hammer Ring

Why don't you ring old hammer, let your HAMMER RING,
Why don't you ring old hammer, let your HAMMER RING,

I keep a talkin' to my hammer, let your HAMMER RING
(all lines sung twice)
"Won't you please ring, hammer," let your HAMMER RING
Oh well my hammer's striking fire, let your HAMMER RING
"What's the matter, what's the matter?" let your HAMMER RING
I b'lieve I take it to the grinder, let your HAMMER RING
A-well the grinder won't grind it, let your HAMMER RING.
Oh what's the matter with my hammer, let your HAMMER RING
I b'lieve I take it to the Brazos, let your HAMMER RING
Oh well I dipped in the water, let your HAMMER RING
Well the water won't cool it, let your HAMMER RING
I b'lieve I take it to the Major, let your HAMMER RING
Well the Major gone to Houston, let your HAMMER RING

Gonna get me a hammer, HAMMER RING
Coming back by Darrington, HAMMER RING
A-gonna get my partner, HAMMER RING
Well we goin' to the bottom, HAMMER RING
I set the woods on fire, HAMMER RING
Well I b'lieve I spy a spirit, HAMMER RING
Tell me what is the spirit, HAMMER RING
A-well it's nothing but a liveoak, HAMMER RING
Won't you ring old hammer now, HAMMER RING
I'm gonna ring it for Alberta, HAMMER RING
I'm gonna ring it all day long, HAMMER RING

38-G   Hammer Ring

Won't you ring old hammer, HAMMER RING
Ring old hammer, HAMMER RING

Well my hammer keep a-ringin' . . .   (*all lines sung twice with burden
                                              as above*)
Won't you ring old hammer . . .
Well my hammer strikin' fire . . .
I got one more hour . . .
Won't you ring old hammer . . .
Well it lookin' mighty cloudy . . .
Well I believe it's gonna rain, sir . . .
Bring along my slicker . . .
Well I don't want to get wet . . .
Don't want to get sick yet . . .
Well the Captain gonna drive me . . .
Well you ring old hammer . . .
Well my hammer keep a ringing . . .
It's gonna ring all day long . . .
Well it's strikin' fire . . .
Give me one more hour . . .
Well I spied a little shower . . .
Well in just about an hour . . .
I'm gonna call old Maybelle . . .
Maybelle, don't you hear me? . . .
Gal, if you can't hear me . . .
Whyn't you write me a letter . . .
I'm wanna hear from you gal . . .
I'm comin' home soon gal . . .
A by the stars and moon sir . . .

39   Crooked-Foot John

A. Johnny Jackson and group, *spading,* Ramsey 1, 22 August 1966, 402.2, J.M.

B. "Lost John," Joseph "Chinaman" Johnson and group, *crosscutting,* Ellis, 21 August 1965, 395.2, N.C.

C. "Lost John," Joseph "Chinaman" Johnson and group, *crosscutting,* Ellis, 22 March 1966, 448.1

D. "This Old Tree," J. B. Smith and Louis "Bacon and Porkchop" Houston, Ramsey 2, 17 August 1965, 375.6

E. "Long Gone," Matt Williams, Jesse "G. I. Jazz" Hendricks, and group, Ramsey 2, 4 July 1964, 36.2

F. "Lost John," J. B. Smith, Ramsey 2, 23 August 1965, 407.2, J.M.

G. "Long Gone," Jesse "G. I. Jazz" Hendricks and group, Ramsey 2, 8 November 1965, 420.6, J.M.

This well-known prison song, which documents the exploits of the clever convict who escapes his trackers by using the ruse of a double-heeled pair of shoes, seems to have many sources. The character of Long John may be popular because he bears the name of the famous trickster in Negro narrative tradition. There are stories about trickster John which date from slavery times; in the years after the war he became a worker on the plantations, who always engaged in a battle of wits and display of trickery with the boss. Indeed, there may be a real connection between the two. (For more on John the Trickster, see Dorson, 1967, pp. 124–171.)

Notice the splendid verse sequence beginning with "This old tree" in Chinaman's B-text. The first time I heard Chinaman sing those lines I was so impressed by the image of the aged tree hewed down by the little man with his diamond that I was sure the lines must have had an independent existence. A few days later Johnny Smith said, yes, it did exist as a separate song, and he sang the D-text, which begins with the "This old tree" group then immediately goes back into the regular verses. If the verses ever did have a separate existence, it has been lost and they now are locked within the "Crooked-Foot John" song.

Mrs. McCulloh notes that the A-text has "three melodic units: *a,* working from a third or fourth below the tonic up to the tonic; *b,* from the third down to the tonic; and *c,* from the sixth down to the tonic. Generally, the chorus, 'Well he long gone' has *c c a b,* while the intervening passages alternate *a* and *b.*"

The F- and G-texts by Smith and Hendricks are free-world versions, both of which antedate the prison song. The clown of Smith's "Lost John" (F) is transmuted to a hero in prison. (That text, by the way, includes the only "gwine" I've ever heard sung by any Negro anywhere —and as he says, he learned it in school.) A free-world version of the F-text found in Ohio appears in Buckley, 1953. Hendricks' free-world version is similar to a song published by the Pace and Handy Music Company in New York in 1920, reprinted in Scarborough, p 268; that song is about one Long John Dean, "a bold bank robber from Bowling Green."

There are several published texts of this song. Odum and Johnson (1925, p. 277) report a dance song, "Lost John," which goes,

> Lost John, Lost John, Lost John (2x)
>
> Lost John, Lost John, Lost John,
> Help me to look for Lost John.
>
> Lost John done gone away,
> Help me to look for Lost John (and so on)

They also print a song, "Jesus Done Bless my Soul" (p. 65), one verse of which is,

> One day, one day, while walkin' along
> Jesus done bless my soul;
> I heard a voice an' saw no one,
> Jesus done bless my soul.

There is a long text in the *Lomax Ms.* (A/9–144); though the notes give no source for that text, internal allusions indicate that it is from Texas prisons. An unidentified solo singer performs the song on *Negro Prison Camp Worksongs,* Folkways P-475; a version recorded by John A. Lomax in 1934 from the singing of "Washington (Lightnin') and group, Darrington," may be heard on *Afro-American Spirituals, Work Songs and Ballads* AAFS L-3; the Lomaxes published a composite text (1936-A, pp. 76–79).

39-A   Crooked-Foot John

One day, one day, ONE DAY, ONE DAY,
I was walkin' along, I WAS WALKIN' ALONG,
Well I heard a little voice, WELL I HEARD A LITTLE VOICE,
Didn't see no one, DIDN'T SEE NO ONE.
Well it must a been John . . . (*group repeats leader's lines, as above*)
Ole Crooked-Foot John . . .
With a heel in the front . . .
And a heel behind . . .
Well you never could tell . . .
Whichaway John run . . .

Chorus:
Well he long gone . . .
Well he long gone . . .
Like a turkey through the corn . . .
With his long drawers on . . .

Well you read on down . . .
To the Chapter Five . . .
If a sinner man die . . .
Where will he go . . .
If he don't go to HEAVEN . . .
To hell you know . . .
(Chorus)

Did a you boys a hear . . .
What the rider says . . .
"If a you boys a work . . .
Gonna treat you mighty well . . .
If a you don't work . . .
Gonna give you plenty hell . . .
(Chorus)

One day, one day . . .
I was walkin' along . . .
Well I heard a little voice . . .
And I seen someone . . .
And that was old John . . .
Old Crooked-Foot John . . .
Had a heel in the back . . .
And a heel in the front . . .
And you never could tell . . .
Whichaway John run . . .
(Chorus)

Well you read on down . . .
To Chapter number Four . . .
If a sinner man die . . .
Where will he go . . .
Well he didn't go to Heaven . . .
Went to Hell you know . . .
(Chorus)

39-B   Lost John

Old John, Old John, OLD JOHN, OLD JOHN,
Old Crooked-Foot John, OLD CROOKED FOOT JOHN,
Old Crooked-Foot John, OLD CROOKED FOOT JOHN,
Had a funny pair a shoes . . . (*group repeats leader's lines, as above*)
Had a funny pair a shoes . . .
I ever did see . . .
That I ever did see . . .
Had a heel in the front . . .
And a heel behind . . .
Well you never could tell . . .
Well you never could tell . . .
Whichaway John go . . .
Whichaway John gone . . .

Well, he's long gone, YES, HE'S LONG GONE
Well, he's long gone, WELL HE'S LONG GONE
Like a turkey through the corn . . . (2x)
With his long clothes on . . . (2x)

One day, one day . . .
I was walkin' along . . .
Well I heard a little voice . . .
Couldn't see no one . . .
Well it must a been John . . . (2x)
Well-a old Lost John . . . (2x)

Well I'm long gone . . .(2x)
Like a turkey through the corn . . .
With my long clothes on . . .

Well a this old tree . . .
Be a-standin' right here . . .
For a many, many year . . . (2x)
Well along come a man . . .
With a diamond in his hand . . .
Well he hewed it down . . .
And he hewed it down . . .
Hewed it down to the ground . . . (2x)

Well it's long gone . . . (2x)
Like a turkey through the corn . . . (2x)
With his long clothes on . . . (2x)

Give me two, three minutes . . .
Let me catch a my wind . . .
Give me four, five minutes . . .
I be gone again . . .

Well I'm long gone . . . (2x)
Like a turkey through the corn . . .
With his long clothes on . . .

Well you read on down . . .
To the Chapter four . . .
If a sinner man die . . .
Where will he go . . .
If he don't go to Heaven . . .
Go to Hell you know . . .

Well I'm long gone . . . (2x)
Like a turkey through the corn . . . (2x)
With my long clothes on . . . (2x)

Spoken: "Move some of them heavy chips out of the way!"

39-C   Lost John

Similar to 39-B, but with one additional stanza:

Well you read on down . . .
To the Chapter Five . . .
If a sinner man die . . .
In the front of his wife . . .
And she shake a that thing . . .
Bring him back to life . . .

39-D   This Old Tree

Well a this old tree, WELL A THIS OLD TREE,
Been a standin' here, BEEN A STANDIN' HERE,
For many, many year, FOR MANY, MANY YEAR,
For many, many year, FOR MANY, MANY YEAR.
Till along come . . . (*Houston repeats Smith's lines, as above*)
Three-and-One . . .
And he hewed it down . . .
Down to the ground . . .
Won't you fall tree . . .
Won't you fall tree . . .

Well along come . . .
Old Three-and-One . . .
And hewed it down . . .
Down to the ground . . . (3x)

If I had a listened . . .
What my mama said . . .
Could a been at home . . .
In my mama's bed . . .
But I wouldn't listen . . .
Kept running around . . .
The first thing I knowed . . .

I was jailhouse bound . . .
Now I sit in the cell . . .
With my mouth poked out . . .
Now I'm in the pen . . .
And I can't get out . . .

Well I'm long gone . . .
Yes long gone . . .
Like a turkey through the corn . . .
With my long clothes on . . .
With my long clothes on . . .
Give me two, three minutes . . .
Let me catch my wind . . .
Give me four, five minutes . . .
Be gone again . . .
Well long gone . . .
You know I'm long gone . . .
Like a turkey through the corn . . .
With his long clothes on . . .
Be gone 'fore long . . .

_____

39-E   Long Gone

Williams:
Did a you boys hear, DID A YOU BOYS HEAR,
Did a you boys hear, DID A YOU BOYS HEAR,
What the rider said? . . . (*group repeats leader's lines, as above*)
"If a you boys work . . . (2x)
Gonna treat you mighty swell . . .
If you don't go to work . . .
Gonna give you plenty hell". . .

I'm a long gone . . . (2x)
Like a turkey through the corn . . .
With my long drawers on . . .

On a frosty mornin' . . .
Well a John said, "Oh". . .
Then he made a pair a shoes . . .
Had a heel in the front . . .
Like the heels behind . . .
Well you never could tell . . .
Whichaway John's goin' . . .

He was long gone . . . (2x)

If you read on down . . .
At the Chapter Fourteen . . .
If a sinner man die . . .
And he live again . . .
Have to be baptized . . .
And his soul may be . . .
Be saved again . . .

Or be long gone . . . (2x)
Like a turkey through the corn . . .

G.I.:
Gonna call him this summer . . .
Gonna call no more . . .
Next time I call him . . .
Be in Baltimore . . .
Wo, Lord, Lord . . .
Wo, John, John . . .

Well they crucified Jesus . . .
And they nailed him to the cross . . .
Sister Mary cried . . .
"My child is lost". . .
But the third day . . .
King Jesus rose . . .
Just to save our souls . . .

Wo, Lord, Lord . . .
I'm long gone . . .

39-F   Lost John

(♩ = 130)

'Long come a Dix - ie Fly - er just be - hind time,

Missed the cow - catch-er and he caught the blind, And he's

Long gone, well, he's long gone.

"This one I heard when I was a little boy. We had it in a school closing play. I remember it a long time ago. I was probably twelve or thirteen years old, something like that. In a school play. When I got down here, I heard 'em singing 'Lost John' in a little different way. But the first time I heard it, it was this way."

Lost John settin' on a railroad track,
Waitin' for the freight train to come back.
Train come back, it didn't make no stop,
Lost John thought he had to ride the top.
He's long gone, he's long gone.

'Long come a Dixie Flyer just behind time,
Missed the cowcatcher and he caught the blind.
And he's long gone, well he's long gone.

Lost John came by a country woman's house,
Everything there was as quiet as a mouse.
Lost John asked the woman about buyin' some beer,
Says, "You better get it in a hurry 'cause I can't stay here.
The hounds on my trail, I can't stay here.
And I'm long gone, well I'm long gone."

Lost John came to Bowling Green,
And was the funniest thing that you ever have seen.
Shoes had heels in front and heels behind,
Couldn't tell whichaway Lost John is gwine.
But he was long, well he was long gone.

39-G   Long Gone

Little Boy Blue come blow your horn,
Sheep's in the meadow and the cow's in the corn.
Where's the little boy tend to the sheep?
He's under the haystack fast asleep.

Chorus:
He's long gone, WASN'T HE LUCKY?
Long gone, FROM KENTUCKY.
Long gone, WHAT I MEAN,
LONG LOST JOHN FROM BOSTON BEAN.

Long Gone settin' on a railroad tie,
Waitin' on a freight train to come by.
Long come a freight train puffin' and flyin',
Oughta seen Long Gone grabbin' the blinds.
(Chorus)

Where is the boy tend to the sheep?
He's under the haystack fast asleep.
He's this little boy, "Wake your sheep.
You know what: you got to sleep."
(Chorus)

I had a little dog, his name was Jack,
Rode his tail just to save his back.
His tail broke and I feel back,
Everybody laughin' at poor little Jack.
(Chorus)

"I been hearin' that song a lone time. That's one a them old minstrel songs . . . I did blackface work. I traveled with Bill Haines, John T. Weston. 'Way back long years ago. I was nothin' but a kid."

---

40   I'm in the Bottom

A. Johnny Jackson and group, *spading,* Ramsey 1, 22 August 1965, 402.1, N.C.
B. Johnny Jackson and group, *spading,* Ramsey 1, 22 August 1965, 401.6

This song was improvised while Jackson and three others were doing some work with spades one afternoon; I never heard it before or after that session. A year later when Jackson was asked if he remembered it, he said, "No, but I could make another one up." The meter is the same as that of the crosscutting songs—the workers slap the backs of the spades on the ground on the return stroke to pick up the extra beat. They do the same thing when singing 37.C "Grizzly Bear" and 39.A "Crooked-Foot John."

40-A   I'm in the Bottom

In the bottom, OH LORDY NOW, WO,
I'm IN THE BOTTOM, WO LORD.

I'm shovelin' dirt, LORDY NOW, WO,
I'M SHOVELIN' DIRT, WO LORD.

I'm gettin' tired, LORDY NOW, WO,
I'M GETTIN' TIRED, WO LORD.

It's in the mornin' . . . (*burdens and repetition continue as above*)
I'm shovelin' cinder . . .
It's in the evenin' . . .
It's for the Captain . . .
I started achin' . . .
All in my shoulder . . .
The boss don't believe it . . .
That here in my side, man . . .
I'm hurtin' all over . . .
Take me to the building . . .
I need some water . . .
I need a doctor . . .
My heart is aching . . .
Boss say I'm faking . . .
What I'm gonna do, man . . .
Gonna write my mother . . .
Tell her see the governor . . .
Ask him do something . . .
I can't move now . . .

40-B   I'm in the Bottom

Similar to 40-A, but with these additional verses:

I'm making a ditch . . .
Even at dinner . . .
Even at breakfast . . .
Raise 'em up higher . . .
Drop 'em down together . . .
Can't tell the difference . . .
Make a day easy . . .
The boss don't know it . . .
The Captain sees it . . .
My back is achin' . . .
My side is hurtin' . . .
The Boss don't believe it . . .
I'm achin' all over . . .

41   Plumb the Line

A. Joseph "Chinaman" Johnson and group, *crosscutting*, Ellis, 21 August 1965, 397.3, N.C.
B. Joseph "Chinaman" Johnson and group, *crosscutting*, Ellis, 24 March 1966, 452.5
C. "Down the Line," David Tippett and group, *crosscutting*, Ellis, 21 August 1965, 389.3, N.C.

The lyrics suggest this may derive from a railroad tie-tamping song or chant, but I don't know of any collected texts from such a source. Like many worksongs, it consists mainly of a series of brags about good workers. The chorus "Jestice done plumb the line!" appears in a religious song in an article by Octave Thanet, "Folk-Lore in Arkansas," *Journal of American Folklore*, 5 (January–March 1892), 124–125. See also the song "Plumb the Line," Parrish, pp. 67–70, and Courlander, 1963-A, p. 55. It is similar to 58. "Down the Line" in this collection, a flatweeding song.

41-A   Plumb the Line

plumb the line. A - won't you ham-mer on, part - ner, let's

plumb the line.

plumb the line, A - won't you ham-mer on, part - ner, let's

plumb the line,

plumb the line, A - won't you ham-mer on, part - ner, let's

plumb the line,

plumb the line, It takes a num-ber one tam-per to plumb the line.

plumb the line, It takes a num-ber one tam-per to plumb the line.

Well-a I'm so glad I can PLUMB THE LINE,
Oh well-a I'm so glad I can PLUMB THE LINE.
Oh well-a I'm so glad I can PLUMB THE LINE,
It takes a NUMBER ONE DRIVER TO PLUMB THE LINE.

A-won't you hammer on, partner, let's PLUMB THE LINE, (3x)
IT TAKES A NUMBER ONE TAMPER TO PLUMB THE LINE.

I got a little baby brother can PLUMB THE LINE, (3x)
It takes a NUMBER ONE TAMPER TO PLUMB THE LINE.

A-well I come here partner, just to PLUMB THE LINE, (3x)
It takes a NUMBER ONE TAMPER TO PLUMB THE LINE.

Well I know Louella, she can PLUMB THE LINE (3x)
It takes a NUMBER ONE TAMPER TO PLUMB THE LINE.

A-well I know John Henry can PLUMB THE LINE, (3x)
It takes a NUMBER ONE DRIVER TO PLUMB THE LINE.

A-well I'm so glad I can PLUMB THE LINE, (3x)
It takes a NUMBER ONE TAMPER TO PLUMB THE LINE.

A-well my little baby brother can PLUMB THE LINE, (3x)
It takes a NUMBER ONE TAMPER TO PLUMB THE LINE.

41-B   Plumb the Line

A-won't you come on buddy, we can PLUMB THE LINE, (2x)
A-won't you come and go with me, PLUMB THE LINE,
It takes a number one tamper, PLUMB THE LINE.

I got a girl named Rosie, PLUMB THE LINE (2x)
A big-leg Rosie, PLUMB THE LINE,
It takes a number one tamper, PLUMB THE LINE.

I got to do it all over, you can PLUMB THE LINE, (2x)
Got my buddy on the Ellis and I can PLUMB THE LINE,
It takes a number one tamper, PLUMB THE LINE.

I got a nine-pound hammer, PLUMB THE LINE,
It's a nine-pound hammer, PLUMB THE LINE, (2x)
It takes a number one tamper, PLUMB THE LINE.

I got a need all over, PLUMB THE LINE, (2x)
Well my daddy was a bully, PLUMB THE LINE,
It takes a number one tamper, PLUMB THE LINE.

I got a silver ring and you can PLUMB THE LINE, (2x)
Big timber in the bottom, you can PLUMB THE LINE,
It takes a number one tamper, PLUMB THE LINE.

Oh won't you come along buddy, we can PLUMB THE LINE, (2x)
Come along with your partner, we can PLUMB THE LINE,
It takes a number one tamper, PLUMB THE LINE.

Well that pull-do can't hold me, we can PLUMB THE LINE, (3x)
It takes a number one tamper, PLUMB THE LINE.

Well-a watch my hammer, we can PLUMB THE LINE, (2x)
Watch my hammer ringin', partner, PLUMB THE LINE,
It takes a number one tamper, PLUMB THE LINE.

Won't you chop down timber, you can PLUMB THE LINE, (2x)
Let your timber get limber, you can PLUMB THE LINE,
It takes a number one tamper, PLUMB THE LINE.

Won't you help me holler, we can PLUMB THE LINE, (2x)
Help me holler in the bottom, we can PLUMB THE LINE,
It takes a number one tamper, PLUMB THE LINE.

41-C   Down the Line

Oh, won't you hear me when I call you, DOWN THE LINE,
Oh, won't you hear me when I call you, DOWN THE LINE,
Oh, won't you hear me when I call you, DOWN THE LINE,
IT TAKES A NUMBER ONE TAMPER DOWN THE LINE.

Oh, won't you help me to holler . . . (*repetitions and burdens continue
as above*)
Oh partner can't you hear me call you . . .
A-well I'm callin' on you Sidewinder . . .
Oh won't you help me when I call you . . .
It takes a tamper like old Henry . . .

---

42   Fallin' Down

A. Joseph "Chinaman" Johnson and group, *crosscutting*, Ellis, 21 August 1965, 397.4, N.C.
B. "Timber Gettin' Limber," Johnny Jackson and David Tippett, Ramsey 1, 2 July 1964, 26.6, J.M.

43   Fall Tree

J. B. Smith, Ramsey 2, 17 August 1965, 376.2, N.C.

A few minutes before a big tree falls, it begins to "get limber," that is, it starts rocking slowly back and forth in a narrow arc that increases a few degrees with each rock and as more and more chips are cut out closer to the center. As the tree rocks there are splintering noises— "crackin'" in the song—made as uncut fibers are ripped apart. If the men happen to be singing when that process starts, they sometimes change to one of these songs to warn the other workers in the area that the tree will be falling soon. Jackson said, "When the tree get ready, when they cut that tree almost down and it's almost ready to fall, some a them will be draggin' brush and so they [the axemen] be singing to the ones that's draggin' brush to tell them to get out of the way: 'Timber gettin' limber.'"

Chinaman's opening line, "A-well my hammer keep a-hangin'," refers to the tendency of the axe to stick in the rocking tree, caught by the compression caused by the weight of the entire tree on a decreasing center.

42-A   Fallin' Down

A-well my hammer keep a-hangin', 'cause it's FALLIN' DOWN,
A-well my hammer keep a-hangin', 'cause it's FALLIN' DOWN.

A-well my timber gettin' limber, 'cause it's FALLIN' DOWN,
A-well my timber gettin' limber, 'cause it's FALLIN' DOWN.

A-well my diamond strikin' fire, 'cause it's . . . (*all lines sung twice,*
with burden, as above)
A-well the tree is gettin' limber 'cause it's . . .
You better watch him, better watch him, 'cause it's . . .
Oh if it hit you don't you holler, 'cause it's . . .
I done warned you, if . . . 'n' done told you 'bout it's . . .
You better watch him, better watch him, 'cause it's . . .
A-well my timber gettin' limber, 'cause it's . . .
Oh well my diamond strikin' fire, 'cause it's . . .
If it hit you don't you holler, 'cause it's . . .
I done warned you 'n' done told you 'bout it's . . .
You better watch it everybody, 'cause it's . . .
So soon in the mornin' and it's . . .

42-B   Timber Gettin' Limber

Oh well my timber gettin' limber and it's FALLIN' DOWN,
Oh well my timber gettin' limber and it's FALLIN' DOWN.

I done a-warned you, done told YOU THAT IT'S FALLIN' DOWN,
I done a-warned you, done told you that it's FALLIN' DOWN.

Well if it hits you, don't you holler, man, IT'S FALLIN' DOWN,
WELL IF IT HITS YOU, don't YOU HOLLER, Lord, IT'S FALLIN'
    DOWN.

Oh well my timber start to crackin' and IT'S FALLIN' DOWN,
I say my timber start to crackin' and FALLIN' DOWN.

There will be no more jackin' 'TILL IT'S FALLIN' DOWN,
'Till my timBER START TO CRACKIN' AND IT'S FALLIN' DOWN.

I done a-warned you, done told you that it's FALLIN' DOWN,
Oh that this timber gonna hold you man, FALLIN' DOWN.

Oh well my timber gettin' limber man, IT'S FALLIN' DOWN,
I say MY TIMBER GETTIN' LIMBER AND IT'S FALLIN' DOWN.

43 Fall Tree

($\downarrow$=126)

You bet-ter watch it, bet-ter watch it, bet-ter watch-a my tim-ber,

Watch, you bet-ter watch, you bet-ter watch   my   tim - ber,

Warn you, done told you, if it hit you, don't you hol - ler, If it

hit you, don't you hol - ler, Done - a warn you, done   told   you.

Tim-ber get-tin' lim - ber, Tim-ber get-tin' lim - ber, Watch-a my tim-ber

Fall,   tree,   Watch-a my tim-ber, won't you fall,   tree,

Watch-a my   tim - ber,   tim-ber get-tin' lim-ber, Done - a

warn you, done   told you. [Spoken]: Better get back out the way over
there, boss, the tree's gettin' weak here, it's fixin' to fall here, y'all
better watch my timber. [Sung]: Done warned you, done told you, if it

hit you, don't you hol - ler,   Watch-a my   tim - ber, 'cause my

tim-ber get-tin' lim-ber, Won't you fall,   tree,   fall,   tree,

Fall,   tree, won't you fall,   tree. [Spoken]: All right, gang, let's
get it down. Watch out, it's fixin' to fall now. Timber out there!

You better watch it, better watch it,
Better watch-a my timber,
Watch, you better watch,
You better watch my timber.
Warn you, done told you,
If it hit you, don't you holler,
If it hit you, don't you holler,
Done-a warn you, done told you.
Timber gettin' limber,
Timber gettin' limber,
Watch-a my timber.
Fall, tree,
Watch-a my timber,
Won't you fall, tree.
Watch-a my timber,
Timber gettin' limber,
Done a warn you, done told you.

Spoken: "Better get back out the way over there, Boss, the tree's gettin' weak here, it's fixin' to fall here, y'all better watch my timber."

Done warned you, done told you,
If it hit you, don't you holler.
Watch-a my timber,
'Cause my timber gettin' limber.
Won't you fall, tree,
Fall tree, fall tree,
Won't you fall, tree.

Spoken: "All right, gang, let's get it down. Watch out. It's fixin' to fall now. Timber out there!"

---

44   So Soon This Evenin'

A. David Tippett and group, *crosscutting*, Ellis, 21 August 1965, 389.3, N.C.
B. "Done Had My Dinner," David Tippett and group, *crosscutting*, Ellis, 22 March 1966, 448.3

These two short lyrics are not songs in themselves, but are used to get the axes together before the start of a regular worksong. In both instances Tippett stopped chanting as soon as the workers on the surrounding trees were alternating regularly, in time with his group; then a minute or two passed in which the only sounds were the axes hitting the trees, then another singer began leading 38. "Hammer Ring."

44-A   So Soon This Evenin'

*Axe strokes at irregular and erratic intervals.

> So soon this evenin', hey now, mmmm,
> So soon this evenin', oh Lord.
> Back in the bottom, hey now, MMMM,
> Back in the bottom, oh Lord.
> Just hewin' down timber, hey now MMMM,
> Just hewin' down timber, OH LORD.

44-B   Done Had My Dinner

> Done had my dinner, hear now, mmmmm,
> Done had my dinner, oh Lord.
> Don't feel no better, Lordy now, mmmm,
> Don't feel no better, oh Lord.

Axe Songs: Logging (45–56)

45 Julie

W. D. Alexander and group, *logging*, Ellis, 21 August 1965, 394.4, N.C.

There is a poignancy to this song that gets lost on the printed page. It is simple and direct, it is about loss and absence, about the woman and child somewhere else, the woman who cannot or will not hear the lonesome calls from the convict whose real sentence is the loss of his youth, the silence of his family. It is Alexander's song, though some of the lyrics are from the general repertory (just as 9. "If You See My Mother," is Mack Maze's song even though most of the lyrics are from general circulation). I recorded "Julie" on four separate occasions; Alexander sang lead each time.

45 Julie

Jul - ie   Oh   my   Lord - y.   Raise 'em up to -

geth - er,   Raise 'em up to - geth   - er,

Raise 'em up to - geth - er,   Oh   my   Lord - y.

Julie, hear me when I call you,
Julie won't hear me,
JULIE WON'T HEAR ME.

B'lieve I'll go to Dallas,
B'lieve I'll go to Dallas,
Got to see my Julie,
OH MY LORDY.

Raise 'em up together, (3x)
OH MY LORDY.

Julie, hear me when I call you,
Julie and the baby,
JULIE AND THE BABY.

Better get the sergeant, (3x)
OH MY LORDY.

My feet is gettin' itchy, (3x)
OH MY LORDY.

Got to see my Julie, (3x)
OH MY LORDY.

Child's gettin' hungry, (3x)
OH MY LORDY.

Rattler can't hold me, (3x)
OH MY LORDY.

Raise 'em little higher, (3x)
OH MY LORDY.

Spoken: "One more time!"

Julie, hear me when I call you,
Julie won't hear me,
JULIE WON'T HEAR ME.

Julie,
Julie won't hear me.

Spoken: "Water, water."

---

46   John Henry

A. Johnny Jackson and group, *logging,* Ramsey 1, 22 August 1965, 400.3, N.C.

B. Johnny Jackson, Ramsey 1, 16 August 1965, 369.3

C. David Tippett, Ramsey 1, 3 July 1964, 32.4

Jackson uses the song for logging, but Tippett said, after performing the C-text, "You sing this when you pickin' cotton, pullin' corn, where you don't need a heavy beat. You know, you just sing it mostly as a mind reliever."

"John Henry" is probably the most frequently recorded traditional song in America. The *Checklist . . . in the Archive of American Folk Songs* gives fifty-two recordings. A few representative versions available on commercial LP records are: Guitar Welch, Hogman Maxey, and R. P. Williams on *Prison Worksongs,* Folk-Lyric LFS A-5; Arthur Bell on *Afro-American Spirituals, Work Songs and Ballads,* AAFS L-3; Big Bill Broonzy, *Last Session: Part Three,* Verve V-3003; *John Jacob Niles,* Folkways FA-2373; *Henry Thomas Sings the Texas Blues,* Origin Jazz Library OJL-3; Leadbelly, *Last Sessions,* Folkways FP-2941.

There are two books concerned specifically with this song: Louis W. Chappell, *John Henry: A Folk-Lore Study* (Jena, 1933); and Guy B. Johnson, *John Henry: Tracking Down a Negro Legend* (Chapel Hill, 1929). Among the many published versions are Lomax, 1941, pp. 258–261; Lomax, 1936-A, pp. 3–10; Courlander, 1963-A, pp. 64–72; Courlander, 1963-B, pp. 110–115 and 280–281; White, 189–191; Odum & Johnson, 1926, pp. 221–240. Two recent articles of especial interest are Leach, 1966, and Dorson, 1965. Further references can be found in many of the above, or in Laws, entry I–1, p. 246.

46-A   John Henry

John Henry was a little baby,
You could hold him in the palm a your hand,
Well the first word I heard the little baby say,
He said, "I wanna be a steel drivin' man, Lord, Lord,
I wanna be a steel drivin' man."

John Henry told-a his mother,
"You better cook my breakfast soon,
I got ninety-nine a bald steel to lay,

I'm gonna lay it by the light a the moon,
I'M GONNA LAY IT BY THE LIGHT A THE MOON."

John Henry told-a sister Mary,
"Little Mary let's go to bed."
She said, "A wait and let me lay the little baby down,
I'm gonna shake it all over your head, Lord, Lord,
GONNA SHAKE IT ALL OVER YOUR HEAD.

John Henry was up on the mountain,
Way up on the mountain high.
Well the mountain so tall and little Johnny so small,
Until he lay down his hammer and he cried, Lord, Lord,
WELL HE LAID DOWN HIS HAMMER AND DIED.

John Henry told-a the Captain,
He said, "A man ain't but a man,
And before I'll stand to let you drive me down,
I will die with the hammer in my hand, Lord, Lord,
I WILL DIE WITH THE HAMMER IN MY HAND.

46-B   John Henry

Similar to 46-A, with the following final stanza:

Everybody in a-Houston, Texas,
Thought little John Henry was dead.
Well he was layin' at home with a big hard-on,
With his shirt-tail over his head, Lord, Lord,
With his shirt-tail over his head.

46-C   John Henry

John Henry was a baby,
You could hold him in the palm of your hand.
Well the first word I heard John Henry say,
"I wanna be a steel spike drivin' man,
I wanna be a steel spike drivin' man."

John Henry was a little boy,
He was sittin' on his daddy's knee.

"Well that rocks and gravel on that Rock Island Line,
Is gonna be the death a me, good Lord,
Is gonna be the death a me."

John Henry told-a the Captain,
"Captain, I need a job.
Well it makes no difference what the job might be,
For the work never gets too hard,
And the work never gets too hard."

Well the Captain asked-a John Henry,
"Little boy, what can you do?"
"Well I can lay some track and I can ball the jack,
And I can drive more spikes than two,
And I can drive more spikes than two."

Well the Captain told-a John Henry,
"I can use a man like you.
I got ninety-nine miles a Walker steel to lay,
I want to lay it by the light of the moon,
I want to lay it by the light of the moon."

John Henry told-a his mama,
"Mama, cook my breakfast soon.
I got ninety-nine miles a Walker steel to lay,
I'm gonna lay it by the light a the moon,
I'm gonna lay it by the light a the moon."

Well the Captain told-a John Henry,
"This old track is cavin' in."
"Well you just step back, Captain, and have no fear,
It's just my hammer suckin' wind,
It's just my hammer suckin' wind."

Well John Henry told-a the Captain,
"Captain, you step back out a the way.
If my hammer miss this ten-inch spike,
Tomorrow be your burying day,
Tomorrow be your burying day."

John Henry told his shaker,
"Shaker, why don't you sing?
I'm dropping thirty pounds from my hips on down,
Listen to this cold steel ring,
Listen to this cold steel ring."

John Henry had a little woman,
Her name was Polly Ann.
The day John Henry laid down and died,
Polly Ann drove steel like a man,
Polly Ann drove steel like a man.

Oh John Henry went up on the mountain,
'Way up on the mountain top.
Mountain so tall and little Johnny so small,
He laid down his hammer and he died, good Lord,
He lay down his hammer and he died.

Well John Henry's little old woman,
The dress she wore was red.
Well she hit the track and she didn't look back,
She said, "I'm goin' where my man fell dead,"
She said, "I'm goin' where my man fell dead."

---

47   Take This Hammer

A. "This Old Hammer Killed John Henry," Joseph "Chinaman" Johnson
and group, *logging*, Ellis, 21 August 1965, 393.4, N.C.
B. Johnny Jackson and David Tippett, Ramsey 1, 2 July 1964, 26.3

This song has been reported throughout the South. See White, 1928,
p. 259; Lomax, 1941, pp. 380–381 (stanzas from Virginia, Georgia,
Alabama, North Carolina, Florida); Parrish, p. 223; Leach, 1966; and
the two "John Henry" studies—Chappell, 1933; and Johnson, 1929.

Among the many recorded versions are Guitar Welch, Hogman
Maxey, and Andy Mosley on *Prison Worksongs*, Folk-Lyric LFS A-5;
Clifton Wright and group, State Penitentiary, Richmond, Virginia, re-
corded by John A. Lomax, 1936 (726B1); Eugene Rhodes, *Talkin' About
My Time*, Folk Legacy FSA-12; Leadbelly, *Take This Hammer*, Folkways
FA-2004; Mississippi John Hurt, "Spike Driver Blues," Okeh 8692
(republished in *American Folk Music, III*, Folkways FA-2953. A tran-
scription of Hurt's version is in Courlander, 1963-B, pp. 285–286.

47-A   This Old Hammer Killed John Henry

This old hammer killed John Henry,
This old hammer KILLED JOHN HENRY,
THIS OLD HAMMER KILLED JOHN HENRY,
But it WON'T KILL ME, OH BOYS, WON'T KILL ME.

Take this HAMMER, TAKE IT TO THE SERGEANT, (3x)
Tell him I'm GONE, OH BOYS, TELL HIM I'M GONE.

If he asks you WHAT GOT THE MATTER, (3x)
Had too long, OH BOYS, HAD TOO LONG.

If he asks you, was I laughin', (3x)
Tell him I was CRYIN', OH LORD, TELL HIM I WAS CRYIN'.

If he ask you, was I runnin', (3x)
Tell him I WAS FLYIN', OH LORD, TELL HIM I WAS FLYIN'.

If he ask you any more questions, (3x)
You don't KNOW, OH BOY, YOU DON'T KNOW.

47-B   Take This Hammer

Sung unison:
This is the hammer kill John Henry, (3x)
But it won't kill me, oh Lord, it won't kill me.

I'm goin' to burn this ole hammer at the handle, (3x)
Throw the hammer away, oh Lord, throw the hammer away.

Pick up my hammer, take it to the sergeant, (3x)
Tell him I'm gone, oh Lord, tell him I'm gone.

If he ask you, was I runnin',
If he ask you, partner, was I runnin', (2x)
You can tell him I was flyin', oh Lord, tell him I was flyin'.

If he ask you, partner, any more questions, (3x)
You don't know, oh Lord, you don't know.

This old hammer, mos' too heavy,
This old hammer, partner, mos' too heavy, (2x)
For a lightweight man, wo Lord, a lightweight man.

Every time I raise up my hammer,
Every time, partner, raise up my hammer, (2x)
I burn down, oh Lord, I burn down.

If he ask you, partner, was I laughin', (3x)
You can tell him I was cryin', oh Lord, tell him I was cryin'.

Every time I get a letter from my baby, (3x)
It's, "Daddy, come home, wo Lord, daddy come home."

Every time I get a letter from the gov'nor, (3x)
It's, "Bully, roll on, oh Lord, bully, roll on."

I'm gonna roll on just a few days longer, (3x)
Then I'm goin' home, wo Lord, then I'm goin' home.

---

48   Haming on a Live Oak Log

A. Johnny Jackson and group, *logging,* Ramsey 1, 22 August 1965, 400.1, J.M.
B. "I Was Down in the Bottom," David Tippett and Johnny Jackson, Ramsey 1, 2 July 1964, 28.7
C. Joseph "Chinaman" Johnson and group, *logging,* Ellis, 21 August 1965, 394.1

I know of two recorded versions of this song, both lead by Chinaman but with different titles: "Shake it, Mister Gator" recorded by Chester Bower, John Lomax, Jr., and Pete Seeger in Texas in 1951 (*Treasury of Field Recording, I,* Candid 8026); and "Move Along 'Gator" on *Negro Folklore From Texas State Prisons* (Elektra EKS-7296), recorded on Ellis by me in 1964.

Tary Owens recorded a performance by a group on Wynne lead by Ebbie Veasley (23 July 1965) that suggests there might have been some railroad tradition in the song's background. It contains these verses:

God made a 'gator, God made a whale,
Well God made a 'gator, with notches all on his tail

Well go 'head, gator, to your muddy hole, hole, hole,
Go head 'gator, 'gator to your muddy hole.

Yes captain's got a section, first, second and third, third, third,
Got a nigger in the mountain, whistle like a mockin' bird

Well go 'head 'gator, doggone your soul, soul, soul
Go 'head 'gator, make it to your muddy hole

If you ever get a section, let me be your straw [boss], **straw, straw,**
If you ever get a daughter, let me be your son-in-law

Well go 'head 'gator . . . (etc.)

I found that Veasley usually performed older versions of the prison songs and tended to retain free-world stanzas dropped by younger convicts. The song was reported earlier, in part, in a number of sources, some going as far back as the nineteenth-century minstrel stage. (See White, pp. 194–195, 229.) Some stanzas are in both white and black tradition. Lomax, 1936-A, p. 19, prints a "Tie-Tamping Chant" with a similar stanza: "Godamighty made a monkey, Godamighty made a whale,/Godamighty made a 'gator wid hickies all over his tail." See also, Lomax, 1941, pp. 398–399, "Godamighty Drag," from the singing of Alan Lomax, who learned it from Augustus Haggerty and group in Huntsville in 1934; and Talley, p. 6, 1922, for a verse called "Crossing the River." Several unpublished texts from Texas are in the Lomax papers. Among them are "Cotton Field Song":

> Ain't no need of you—pping on the steal
> Hotter the sun shine the better I feel
> I been in the notion long enough to know
> I got a home in the territo
> Went to the river and couldn't get across
> Paid four dollars for an old gray horse
> Put him in the river and he wouldn't swim
> Hit it across the head with a mulberry lim'.
> (*Lomax, Ms.* A9/144)
> Went down to the river an' couldn't get across
> Pay ten dollars fo an ole gray hoss
> He wheel about an' turn about an' do jes so,
> An every time he turns about he jump Jim Crow.
> (*Lomax, Ms.* A9/142)

This last text was sent to Lomax by a John Jones of Houston who said it was from the singing of a Negro as he worked. It is almost exactly the text sung by nineteenth-century minstrel Thomas "Daddy" Rice, quoted by White, p. 194.

The song is well known in Texas prison tradition now. Sometimes, as in the B-text by Jackson and Tippett, it appears as a coherent ballad; more often it is a collection of verses about the "captain and sergeant" who "come riding along," often coupled with the "Midnight Special" (15) stanzas that make up most of Chinaman's C-text.

The group's participation varies, depending upon how well they know the stanza. They always sing the repeat of the second half of the second line; they usually sing a repeat of the last word in the first line (sometimes repeating only the vowel sound, as in stanzas 5 and 6 of the A-text). If the verses are known to the group (this happens most often when they have been with the lead singer a long time and know *his* stanzas), they will join in before the first caesura in the first line; an interesting concomitant of this is that such groups tend *not* to sing the repeat at the end of the second line, as in the C-text printed here.

48-A   Haming on a Live Oak Log

I was down on the river, on a live oak log, LOG, LOG
Well the way I was haming, partner, LIKE A LOWDOWN DOG, LIKE A
  LOWDOWN DOG

Well the sergeant and the captain came a riding a-LONG, LONG, LONG,
Well you better go to haming, partner, IF YOU WANT TO GO HOME,
  IF YOU WANT TO GO HOME.

Well I hooked on a 'gaTOR, and I THOUGHT HE WAS A LOG, LOG,
  LOG,
Well the way I was haming, partner, like a LOWDOWN DOG . . .

Well the 'gator wasn't movin', and the gator wouldn't SWIM, SWIM,
  SWIM,
Well I cut me a pole and BEAT THE HELL OUT A HIM . . .

Well I swat him in the side, and I bust him in the SIDE, IDE,
Ought a seen that a-gator hustlin' to THE OTHER SIDE . . .

Didn't come here to worry, didn't come here TO STAY, AY, AY,
Well I'll do my time, boys partner, get the HELL AWAY FROM
  HERE . . .

I was down on the river, on a live oak LOG, LOG, LOG,
Well the way I was haming, partner, like a LOW DOWN DOG . . .

Well you wake up in the morning, hear the big bell ring, RING, RING,
Well you march in the DININ'ROOM, PARTNER, SEE THE SAME
  DAMN THING . . .

If you say anything about it, better hush your head,
'Cause the bosses get together, yeah, you know they cut your head . . .

Well the sergeant and the captain CAME A RIDING ALONG, LONG
  LONG,
WELL YOU BETTER GO TO HAMING, PARTNER IF YOU WANT TO
GO HOME . . .

I was down on the river, on a live oak LOG, LOG, LOG,
Well the way I was HAMING, PARTNER LIKE A LOWDOWN
  DOG . . .

48-B   I Was Down in the Bottom

Sung unison:
I was down in the bottom, under a live oak log, log, log,
And the way I was haming, partner, like a low-down dog, like a low-
  down dog.

Well the captain and the sergeant, come a ridin' along, long, long,
Says, "You better go to haming, bully, if you want to go home". . .

Well I went to the captain, with my hat in my hand,
"Captain please have mercy, captain, I'm a longtime man". . .

Well the captain looked on me, and he spit on the ground,
Says, "I won't stop this drivin', bully, till I drive you down". . .

Well I looked at the captain, from his head to his toe,
"You don't stop this drivin', captain, to the Brazos I'll go". . .

Well I went to the Brazos, and I couldn't get across, cross, cross,
Well I stepped on a 'gator, partner, and I thought it was a log . . .

Well the 'gator wasn't movin', and the 'gator wouldn't swim,
Well I picked up a club and, partner, knocked the hell out a him . . .

Hollerin', "Move along 'gator, doggone your soul,"
Hollerin', "Move along 'gator, 'gator to your muddy hole". . .

48-C   Haming on a Live Oak Log

I was down in the BOTTOM, up on a LOG,
I was whoopin' and a-HOLLERIN', HAMIN' LIKE A DOG.

Well the captain and the SERGEANT, COME A RIDIN' ALONG, LONG,
"Hey you better go to hamin', want to MAKE IT BACK HOME."

Partner don't you talk ABOUT IT, if you DO I'LL CRY-Y,
Partner, DON'T TALK ABOUT IT, IF YOU DO I'LL CRY.

Got a letter from ROSIE, she SICK IN THE BED, BED,
All a my CHILDREN IS A CRYIN' FOR BREAD.

Partner don't you talk ABOUT IT, IF YOU DO I'LL CRY-Y
Well don't talk ABOUT IT, IF YOU DO I'LL CRY.

Well a yon' come Rosie. "How in the world do you know?"
Well I know her by her APRON AND THE BONNET SHE WORE.

Umbrella on HER SHOULDER, piece a PAPER IN HER HAND, AND,
"HEY LOOKA HERE, CAPTAIN, I COME AFTER MY MAN."

"Well-a here's a hundred DOLLAR, HERE'S A HUNDRED MORE, ORE,
WELL IF THAT DON'T GET HIM, LET THE MISTREATER GO."

Cryin' oh LORDY, LORDY, LORD, LORD,
CRYIN' OH MY LORD, LORDY, LORDY, LORD.

Well you wake up IN THE MORNIN', SO JUMPIN' SOON, OON,
WELL YOU CAN'T SEE NOTHIN', BUT THE STARS AND THE MOON.

Go to marchin' to the TABLE, get your pan and YOUR SPOON,
If you say anything about IT, YOU IN TROUBLE WITH THE MAN.

Cryin' oh LORDY, LORDY, LORDY, LORD, LORD,
CRYIN' OH MY LORD, LORDY, LORDY, LORD.

Well a my old LAWYER TOLD A DIRTY LIE, -IE,
WELL HE SAID HE'S GONNA PARDON ME, BY THE FOURTH A
    JULY.

June July AND AUGUST DONE COME AND GONE, GONE,
WELL THEY LEFT ME ROLLIN', BUT I AIN'T GOT LONG.

Cryin' oh LORDY, LORDY, LORDY, LORD, LORD,
CRYIN' OH MY LORD, LORDY, LORDY, LORD.

---

49   Drinkin' That Wine

Joseph "Chinaman" Johnson and group, *logging,* Ellis, 21 August 1965,
394.4, N.C.

Lydia Parrish prints a song, "Drinkin' of the Wine" (pp. 249–251),
that has the same chorus and as this song, as well as one similar stanza

(of her four stanzas). She says she heard it as a convict song. Odum and Johnson, 1925, p. 136, publish a text that goes:

> If my mother ask you for me, tell her I gone to Gallerlee,
> I ought to a been there four thousand years ago,
>   To drink of the wine.
>
> Drinkin' of the wine, drinkin' of the wine,
> Drinkin' of the wine, drinkin' of the wine.
> Christ was there four thousand years ago,
> Drinkin' of the wine.
>
> You may mourn, sinner, mourn, the Lord help you to mourn;
> Christ was there four thousand years ago,
>   Drinkin' of the wine.

Chinaman's version is, obviously, far more secularized than the above. "Galilee" survives in the song primarily because it rhymes with "send for me" and happens to be three syllables. The prison text here is very much of this world—most of the singing time is spent in the two choruses, which are almost entirely about wine, not theology. Like many other songs in this collection, it could be expanded indefinitely: the lead singer has to introduce only one noun every three sung stanzas.

I recorded two other performances of this song in the TDC, one solo by J. B. Smith (407.5), and another led by Chinaman when the group was flatweeding (22 March 1966, 445.1). Both texts were similar to this one.

---

49   Drinkin' That Wine

($\mathbf{d}$=56)

Axe strokes:
Drink-in' that wine, wine, wine, Drink-in' that
good old cher - ry wine, Ought to been there ten thou - sand
years drink-in' that wine. (Whooh, hah!). If my moth - er send for
me, Tell her I'm gone to Gal - i - lee, Ought to been there ten thou - sand

years drink-in' that wine. (Whooh, hah!). Drink-in' that wine, wine,

wine, Drink-in' that W, I, N, E, wine, Ought to been

there ten thou-sand years drink-in' that wine. (Whooh, hah!).

Drinkin' that wine, wine, wine,
Drinkin' THAT GOOD OLD CHERRY WINE,
Ought to been there ten thousand years,
DRINKIN' THAT WINE.

If my mother send for me,
Tell her I'M GONE TO GALILEE,
OUGHT TO BEEN THERE TEN THOUSAND YEARS,
DRINKIN' THAT WINE.

Chorus 1:
Drinkin' that WINE, WINE, WINE,
DRINKIN' THAT GOOD OLD CHERRY WINE,
OUGHT TO BEEN THERE TEN THOUSAND YEARS,
DRINKIN' THAT WINE.

Chorus 2:
Drinkin' that WINE, WINE, WINE,
Drinkin' that W, I, N, E, wine,
OUGHT TO BEEN THERE TEN THOUSAND YEARS,
DRINKIN' THAT WINE.

If my sister send for me,
Tell her I'm GONE TO GALILEE,
OUGHT TO BEEN THERE FOR TEN THOUSAND YEARS,
DRINKIN' THAT WINE.
(Chorus 1 and chorus 2)

If my father send for me . . . (*pattern continues as in
    "mother" and "sister" stanzas above*)
(Chorus 1)
If my sister send for me . . .
(Chorus 2)
If my uncle send for me . . .
(Chorus 1, chorus 2, chorus 1)
If Elvessey send for me . . .
(Chorus 1)

50   Drop 'Em Down

A. David Tippett and group, *logging,* Ellis, 22 March 1966, 446.4, J.M.
B. David Tippett and group, *logging,* Ellis, 24 March 1966, 452.2
C. Joseph "Chinaman" Johnson and group, *logging,* Ellis, 21 August
1965, 393.4, J.M.
D. Matt Williams and group, Ramsey 2, 17 August 1965, 379.2

In his two texts, Tippett runs through the names of the people around
him, the standard descriptions of the work ("strikin' fire," "With my
diamond," and so on). The song is strikingly simple: a short line, not
thematically connected to anything before or after most of the time, is
sung twice and followed by a simple chorus. Chinaman's text (C) has
similar melody and pacing, but manages to incorporate a line twice as
long syllabically. Chinaman has been singing lead for many years more
than Tippett, of course, and perhaps for that reason is better able to
handle isochronic expansion. Chinaman's lines are similar to the lines
he sings for 38-F. "Hammer Ring"; and the lines sung by Matt Williams
(D-text) are similar to the verses *he* sings for 38-B. "Hammer Ring." An
important difference is that Chinaman's texts usually cover a range of
emotions and subject matter, while Williams's rarely stray very far
from expressions of self-pity.

50-A   Drop 'Em Down

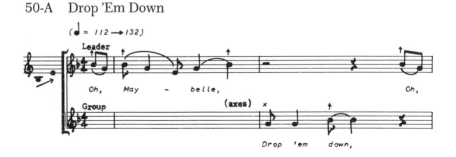

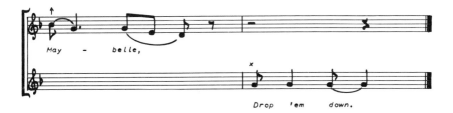

Oh Maybelle, DROP 'EM DOWN,
Oh Maybelle, DROP 'EM DOWN.

I call you, DROP 'EM DOWN,
I call you, DROP 'EM DOWN.

With my diamond . . . (*repetition
and burden continue as above*)
Oh with my four-tooth diamond . . .
Down in the bottom . . .
I call you . . .
Don't you hear me . . .
When I call you . . .
I'm in trouble . . .
On the water . . .
Won't you help me . . .
Drink a water . . .
Cool water . . .
I'm a-strikin' . . .
Strikin' fire . . .
In the timber . . .
I call you . . .
Mack Maze . . .
Cowboy . . .
Joe Willie . . .
Won't you help me . . .
Won't you help me to call 'em . . .
Norah Francelle . . .
Henry Scott . . .
Mister Bruce . . .
Won't you help me . . .
Help me call 'em . . .
Boss Duke . . .
Let me make it . . .

Driver, DROP 'EM DOWN,
You a driver, DROP 'EM DOWN.

Have mercy, DROP 'EM DOWN,
Have mercy, DROP 'EM DOWN.

On me, DROP 'EM DOWN,
Have mercy, DROP 'EM DOWN.

Spoken: "That's it."

50-B   Drop 'Em Down

Oh Maybelle, DROP 'EM DOWN,
I call you, DROP 'EM DOWN.

With my diamond, DROP 'EM DOWN,
With my diamond, DROP 'EM DOWN.

In the mornin' . . . (*repetition
    and burden continue as above*)
Down in the bottom . . .
On a liveoak log . . .
With my partner . . .
With my four-tooth diamond . . .
Oh Maybelle . . .
Won't you help me . . .
Won't you help me . . .
Please help me . . .
This morning . . .
On a liveoak . . .
My partner . . .
He got the first butt cut . . .
Oh Cowboy . . .
He's got the first butt cut . . .
Wo Tippett . . .
He got the next butt cutt . . .
Joe Willie . . .
Well he next in line . . .
Benny Richardson . . .
He's next to him . . .

50-C   Drop 'Em Down

(a) Leader (♩ = 100)

He com-ing back by old Dar-ring-ton, He com-ing

(axes)

Group

Drop 'em down,

back by old Dar-ring-ton, He gon-na

Drop 'em down.

get my part-ner, He gon-na

Drop 'em down,

get my part-ner **(b)** Well, we

Drop 'em down.

go-in' to the bot-tom, Well, we

Drop 'em down,

go-in' to the bot-tom, **(c)** Well, I'm

Drop 'em down.

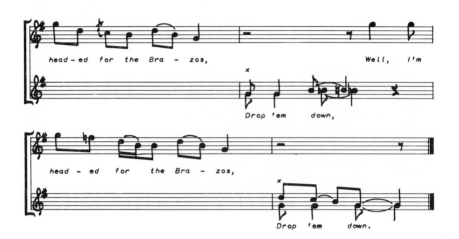

I got a lifetime to drop 'em, DROP 'EM DOWN,
I got a lifetime to drop 'em, DROP 'EM DOWN.

I'm gonna drop 'em for the rider . . . (*repetition
    and burden continue as above*)
Wo Lordy have mercy . . .
I'm gonna drop 'em for the Major . . .
I'm gonna drop it in the mornin' . . .
Well partner won't you help me . . .
I'm gonna drop 'em all day long . . .
Now partner tell my mama . . .
I gotta write away to Austin . . .
Have a talk with the gov'nor . . .
A-well to see will he pardon me . . .
What you reckon that he told her . . .
A "Just ten years longer . . .
Well-a then I might pardon him". . .
That gov'nor must be crazy . . .
You can run and tell the sergeant . . .
A that-a I've got a-worried . . .
Well, I'm headed for the Brazos . . .
A-well old Rattler can't hold me . . .
A-well I'm headed for Dallas . . .
Oh Dallas Carrie . . .
That's the girl I'm gonna marry . . .
Partner look-a look-a yonder . . .
A-well I b'lieve I spied a spirit . . .

Tell me what is the spirit . . .
"A-well it's nothing but a liveoak". . .
Wo Lordy have mercy . . .
A-well the captain gone to Houston . . .
Gonna get me a diamond . . .
He coming back by old Darrington . . .
He gonna get my partner . . .
Well we goin' to the bottom . . .
I gonna hew down the liveoak . . .
Gonna hew it for the rider . . .
I'm gonna hew it in the mornin'. . .
Oh everybody gets a-worried . . .
A-gets a-worried with this diamond . . .
I drop 'em late in the evening . . .

50-D   Drop 'Em Down

I'm gettin' worried, DROP 'EM DOWN,
I'm gettin' worried, DROP 'EM DOWN.

I want the major . . . (*repetition and*
   burden continue as above)
I'm gettin' worried . . .
I want the major . . .
Goin' tell him my troubles . . .
Oh major . . .
I done got worried . . .
About my trouble . . .
I'm gettin' worried . . .
Where's the sergeant . . .
I believe I'll leave you . . .
You better run here . . .
I'm fixin' to leave here . . .
I'm headed to the river . . .
I'm goin' home man . . .
I hear the sergeant . . .
He don't lead me . . .
What's the trouble . . .
Done got a hungry . . .
That's my trouble . . .

51   Drop 'Em Down Together

J. B. Smith, Ramsey 2, 23 August 1965, 407.3, N.C.

A simple text—one that lets a single couplet run through two four-line stanzas. All the lines are from the general repertory, which is rare for Smith.

51   Drop 'Em Down Together

Drop 'em down te - geth - er, Drop 'em down te - geth - er, Drop 'em down to - geth - er, Whoa, Lord.

Drop 'em down together,
Drop 'em down together,
Drop 'em down together,
Whoa, Lord.

Make 'em sound much a better, (3x)
When you drop 'em down together.

B'lieve I'll call my baby (4x)

Partner, help me call 'em, (2x)
Won't you help me call 'em,
Oh, Lord.

Oh Sandy Point Ida, (3x)
Whoa, Lord.

Well she used to be my rider, (3x)
Whoa, Lord.

Old Sandy Point Carrie, (3x)
Whoa, Lord.

That's the girl I'm gonna marry, (3x)
Oh, Lord.

Oh partner, help me call 'em, (2x)
Well partner, help me call 'em,
Oh Lord.

Won't you bring me a drink a water, (3x)
Whoa, Lord.

Well I don't wanna drink it, (3x)
Whoa, Lord.

Gonna pour it on my diamond, (2x)
Whoa, Lord.

Diamond strikin' fire, (2x)
Well my diamond strikin' fire,
Whoa, Lord.

Won't you raise 'em up a higher, (2x)
G'on and raise 'em up a higher,
Hold on.

Well my partner got the butt cut, (3x)
Whoa, Lord.

Buddy got the second, (2x)
Oh, yeah.

I got the wing,
I got the wing, Lord (2x)
Yes, oh, Lord.

52   Believe I'll Call the Rider

J. C. Spring and group, *logging,* Ellis, 22 March 1966, 444.3, J.M.

This song, like 56. "Early in the Morning," consists not of stanzas, but groups of lines punctuated by axe-strikes, occasionally spotted with a line like "Wo my Lordy," which is *not* a chorus, but is used as occasional punctuation or merely to give the lead singer a moment to think of another group of lines. There are three motifs in the lines: the "Believe I'll call" set, the lines about working positions on the tree (butt cut, second cut, and so on), and the lines about the axe itself—the diamond in the singer's hand.

Mrs. McCulloh discussed the three sections of the song which she transcribed: Pattern A, "Believe (sung 'b'lieve') I'll call mama," starts on the 5th or 7th above the tonic and descends (via the 3rd or 4th) to the tonic. This progression sometimes takes four measures, sometimes two. Pattern B, "Tip away and leave you," starts on the 3rd below the tonic, rises to the tonic, and sometimes descends to the 3rd below. The beginning of the song (opening pattern) is a kind of mixture of the two patterns; it's mostly pattern B. After this introductory section you get a large block of pattern A, which is broken twice by pattern B.

Although the singers often vary the melody slightly after the opening lines, the kind of melodic ambivalence that occurs here is rare in the really good leaders. No one in the prison said anything about Spring's leading style, or Cowboy's (see song 56, which has some of the same problems), but these men got to lead only when Chinaman didn't feel like it, and then only on logging and flatweeding songs—not for crosscutting. Their meter seems regular enough, but the melodic ambivalence (not the same as simple melodic variation) may be sufficiently confusing for the others so that it is troublesome with crosscutting work, where the physical situation permits no room for confusion in body movement.

---

52   Believe I'll Call the Rider

Captain, wo Lord, (*Opening pattern*)
Believe I'll call the RIDER,
HOLLERIN' WO LORD,
BELIEVE I'LL CALL THE RIDER,
Call him with my DIAMOND,
Call him WITH MY DIAMOND,
Two-way diamond,
TWO-WAY DIAMOND
Tell him 'bout MY DIAMOND
Tell him 'BOUT MY DIAMOND
Diamond's strikin' FIRE,
Diamond STRIKIN' FIRE,
DIAMOND STRIKIN' FIRE
Let me call the major
Help me call the major
Tell him I'm goin' crazy,
Crazy with MY BLADE,
CRAZY WITH MY BLADER
Believe I'll call the governor
BELIEVE I'LL CALL THE GOVERNOR
Tell him 'bout my TROUBLES (2x)
Troubles on the BRAZOS (2x)
OH MY LORD,
HELP ME TO CALL (2x)

Believe I'll CALL MAMA (2x) (*Pattern A*)
WO, MY LORDY,
MAMA CAN'T HELP ME
MAMA CAN'T HELP ME.
Believe I'll CALL MARY (2x)
Tell me who's your BABY (2x)
Sugarland MARY (2x)
Drivin' me CRAZY
Crazy with my DIAMOND (2x)
Wo MY LORDY
Diamond strikin' FIRE (2x)
Fire in the TIMBER (2x)
Won't you tell THE SERGEANT (2x)
Get me new DIAMOND (2)
OH MY LORDY
Drop 'em in TOGETHER (2x)
Make 'em all BETTER (2x)
Wo my LORD

Tip away and LEAVE YOU (2x) (*Pattern B*)
Leave you with my sergeant (2x)
Well my partner got the crown end
Well my buddy got the second (2x)
Bring me DRINK A WATER (2x)
Don't want TO DRINK IT
I DONT WANT TO DRINK IT
Put it on MY DIAMOND (3x)
'Cause my diamond's ON A FIRE (2x)
Second cut's SHADY (2x)
Butt cut is a CRAZY (3x) (might be "brave end")
Won't you help to CALL 'EM (2x)
Call a LITTLE LOUDER (2x)
Believe I'll call 'BERTHA (3x)
Tell me how you CALL HER (2)
Call her WITH MY DIAMOND (2x)
Spoken: Bertha.

---

53   Choppin' Charlie

Johnny Jackson (lead) and Frank Young, Ramsey 1, 16 August 1965,
369.5, N.C.

Speaking about "Choppin' Charlie," Jackson said:

"They haven't been singing it around here lately. I know they sung it about fifteen years ago when I first came around. They got a bunch a newer songs that they sings, they let the older stuff go.

"Somebody was supposed to have been choppin' wood, you know, a guy named Charlie. They say the warden never let him go to dinner, made him chop through supper, chopped from morning till night. Said he had a short axe, that's the reason it was called a hatchet. You know, a axe with part of the handle cut off, it was short like a hatchet."

This song was not recorded while men were actually working, but Jackson and the other two leaders who sang it (Matt Williams, Ramsey 2, 17 August 1965, 379.3; and Theo Mitchell, Wynne, 6 January 1966, 452.2) all said that it was used for logging. Lomax, 1936-A, pp. 80–82, includes several stanzas from this song in one they title "Great God-a'mighty." On *Negro Prison Camp Work Songs*, Folkways p. 475, there is a similar song, "Chopping in the New Ground."

53   Choppin' Charlie

Oh Choppin' Charlie, GREAT GODAMIGHTY,
OH CHOPPIN' CHARLIE, OH MY LORD.

Well he chopped all day long, GREAT GODAMIGHTY,
Well he chopped all day long, OH MY LORD.

He don't a eat no dinner, GREAT GODAMIGHTY
He chopped through his supper, OH MY LORD.

Oh Choppin' Charlie, GREAT GODAMIGHTY,
Oh Choppin' Charlie, OH MY LORD.

Well he chopped with a hatchet, GREAT GODAMIGHTY,
Well he choppin' with a axer, OH MY LORD.

Oh Choppin' Charlie, GREAT GODAMIGHTY,
Oh Choppin' Charlie, OH MY LORD.

Well he choppin' for the sergeant, GREAT GODAMIGHTY,
Well he choppin' for the captain, OH MY LORD.

Well he choppin' for the major, GREAT GODAMIGHTY,
Well he choppin' for the warden, OH MY LORD.

54   Godamighty

A. "I Got the Crane Wing," David Tippen, Theo Mitchell, and group, Wynne, 20 August 1965, 388.3, N.C.
B. "I Got a Record," Ebbie Veasley and group, Wynne, 20 August 1965, 388.9, N.C.
C. David Tippen and group, Wynne, 6 January 1966, 424.2

55   Texarkana Mary

A. Jesse "G.I. Jazz" Hendricks and group, Ramsey 2, 3 July 1964, 35.3, J.M.
B. "Wonder What's the Matter," Jesse "G.I. Jazz" Hendricks and group, Ramsey 2, 17 August 1965, 380.3

These may be two songs or wide variants of the same song. In either case, the C-text of "Godamighty" is a bridge between the two, somewhere between the two A-texts. The titles are those given by the lead singers, and they suggest that the notion of title is something that may be of importance to outsiders but doesn't really matter very much to the prisoners themselves. One title is simply the last line sung (55-B), two are the first line sung (54-A, 54-C), and one is specifically inconsistent with the first line of the song (55-A). (I asked for the title after the performance, and G.I. said "Texarkana *Mary*"—which suggests that the noun in the first stanza is highly variable. The two names he uses most often in songs are Ida and Mary, so for him perhaps it doesn't make much difference.) All texts are primarily concerned with women and guards; there is also some mention of the work ("the crane wing" stanzas and a few others), and the personal statement about being tried by fire and water (54-B). There is an irony there, of course: the man who survives the two traditional challenges for the virtuous hero is still locked up for life, perhaps to go crazy with his blade, controlled by a captain who shows no mercy.

The "Captain Joe Harper" mentioned in the last group of stanzas of "Wonder What's the Matter" (55-B) is a real captain in the TDC, and the song is another instance of the black man being permitted to sing what he could not say and survive.

54-A   I Got the Crane Wing

Tippen:

Well, I got the crane wing, OH, MY LORDY,

Well, I got the crane wing, GODAMIGHTY, GOD KNOWS.

Well, my partner got the same thing, OH, MY LORDY,

Well, my partner got the same thing, GODAMIGHTY GOD KNOWS.

Gonna call on my Jesus . . . (*repetition and burdens continue as above*)

I'm buckin' in the timber . . .

Well, yonder come the rider . . .

He's troublin' the water . . .

Got to beat him to the Brazos . . .
Oh, get old Ranger . . .
And saddle old Norah . . .
Gonna ride him all over . . .
Got to make it to the Brazos . . .
Wo, Captain, don't murder me . . .
"How long you servin'?". . .
Captain, I'm servin' lifetime . . .
Whatcha reckon he told me . . .
"Buddy, you got ninety-nine . . .
But it ain't no difference . . . (*second burden becomes "OH MY LORD"*
   for the remainder of the song)
Between ninety-nine and lifetime". . .
Please have mercy . . .
Have mercy on me, sir . . .
Well I'm tryin' to make it . . .
I'm tryin' to make it in a hurry . . .

Mitchell:
Partner, I got the crane wing, OH MY LORDY,
And you got the same thing, OH MY LORD.

A he can't rob her, OH MY LORDY,
A he can't rob her, OH MY LORD.

54-B   I Got a Record

Told my mama, WO, LORDY,
I wrote my mama, WO, MY LORD.

I asked her 'bout Rosie, WO, MY LORDY,
I asked her 'bout Rosie, WO MY LORDY.

"Son, Rosie done married," WO, MY LORDY,
"Son, Rosie done married," GODAMIGHTY, GOD KNOWS.

"Mama, who did she marry?" WO, MY LORDY,
"Mama, who did she marry?" WO, MY LORD.

"Well, she married Jack O Diamonds". . . (*repetition and burdens
continue as in previous stanza*)

He's a river, river ruler . . .
He's a number-one driver . . .
He's a pull-do fooler . . .
"Son, have you got a record?". . .
Captain, I been tried, sir . . .
Been tried by fire . . .
And fire wouldn't burn me . . .
Been tested by water . . .
Big Muddy wouldn't drown me . . .
I b'lieve I'll go crazy . . .
Go crazy with my blader . . .
Captain, I got life, sir . . .
Captain, won't you have mercy . . .
On a longtime man, sir . . .

54-C   Godamighty

A Godamighty, A GODAMIGHTY,
A GODAMIGHTY, A GODAMIGHTY.

You better jump in a hurry, GODAMIGHTY KNOWS,
You better jump in a hurry, GODAMIGHTY, GOD KNOWS.

Got to buckle up my shoe, sir . . . (*repetition and burdens continue as in previous stanza*)

Got to carry the news, sir . . .
Gonna take it to Marylou, sir . . .
Gonna tell her 'bout my trouble . . .
Well, hello, Lou . . .
Ain't you glad to see me? . . .
"Daddy is you free, lord?". . .
Well I broke and run, sir . . .
Well a yon' my boss man . . .
Got a Colt forty-one, sir . . .
Well he had him a pacer . . .
When I broken and run, sir . . .
Well I wake up in the mornin' . . .
Well he hear me a-groanin' . . .
"Son, what's the matter?". . .
Well, I dreamed about Carrie . . .
That's the girl I'm gonna marry . . .

55-A   Texarkana Mary

(♩ = 122)

Leader

Well, she mar-ried old Ray - mond holl'-rin' Wo, Lord,

Group

mond   Wo,   Lord,

Well, she mar-ried old Ray - mond,   God-a-might-y, God knows.

Well, she mar-ried old Ray - mond,   God-a-might-y, God knows.

Ol' Ray-mond killed Hay-mond holl'-rin' Wo, Lord, Well, Ray-mond killed

mond   Wo, Lord, Well, Ray-mond killed

Wo, Texarkana Ida, holl'rin' WO, LORD,
WO, TEXARKANA IDA, GODAMIGHTY, GOD KNOWS.

Won't you help a me to call 'em, holl'rin' WO, LORD,
WON'T YOU HELP A ME TO CALL 'EM, GODAMIGHTY, GOD KNOWS.

Won't you looka, looka yonder . . . (*repetition and burdens continue as
    above*)
Well, I b'lieve I see a spirit . . .
Man, tell me what a spirit . . .
"It's a liveoak spirit". . .
Won't you raise 'em up higher . . .
Won't you help a me to call 'em . . .
Well, I b'lieve I'm goin' crazy . . .
I'm goin' crazy in the bottom . . .
I'm goin' tell you 'bout the rider . . .
He keep a drivin' me crazy . . .
Won't you looka over yonder . . .
Black Ida's in the bottom . . .
I'm gonna cut until I find her . . .
Wo, Lord, Idabelle . . .
Won't you looka, looka yonder . . .
Oh, Mary got married . . .
Well, she married old RayMOND, holl'rin' WO, LORD
Ol' Raymond killed Haymond . . .
Wo, Lord, Mary a holl'rin' WO, LORD,
OH YOU, MARY, GODAMIGHTY, GOD KNOWS.

55-B   Wonder What's the Matter

Well don't you know me, holl'rin' WO, LORD,
Baby, don't you know me, GODAMIGHTY KNOWS.

Don't you hear me keep a callin', holl'rin' WO, LORD,
Don't you hear me keep a callin', GODAMIGHTY KNOWS.

Keep a callin' my baby, holl'rin' WO, LORD,
KEEP A CALLIN' MY BABY, GODAMIGHTY KNOWS.

Well my baby's in Dallas . . . (*repetition and burdens as in previous stanza*)
Won't you raise 'em up a higher . . .
Oh looka, looka yonder . . .
Wo, partner, quit your doggin' . . .
Well we come here to hold 'em . . .
Ol' Fort Worth Carrie . . .
That's the girl I'm gonna marry . . .
Wo, scoopin' and hamin' . . .
Won't you looka, looka yonder . . .

Well I believe I spied the devil, holl'rin' WO, LORD,
WELL I BELIEVE I SPIED THE RIDER, GODAMIGHTY KNOWS.

Tell me who is that devil . . .
It was Captain Joe Harper . . .
He's the devil in the bottom . . .
Well I wonder what's the matter . . .

56   Early in the Morning

A. Willie "Cowboy" Craig and group, *logging,* Ellis, 24 March 1966, 451.4–452.1, J.M.
B. "Godamighty Knows," Willie "Cowboy" Craig and group, *logging,* Ellis, 22 March 1966, 446.5

This song was the most difficult of all the songs to transcribe. Simple things, such as whether a stanza should be eight lines or four lines with an indicated caesura, are meaningless, perhaps, to a reader—but there is a difference between those two methods of putting a song on a page. Some songs simply *feel* as if they were four long lines, others as if they were eight short ones. The inclusive time, the metric time as well as elapsed time, might be exactly the same for the two, and the difference is intangible. It was partially reassuring to read in Mrs. McCulloh's note (see below) about the shift in phrasing from eight- to seven-beat phrases within the song itself. I have tried here, as always, to give a sense of the song with the lines and line breaks; each mid-line caesura (usually indicated by a comma) and each line-end was marked in the singing by an axe-stroke. Sometimes the second half was missing, as if the singer suddenly were perceiving his metarhythm in segments of threes rather than twos; at such points there is just a half-line typed.

The A-text begins with stanzas that are common in the worksongs, usually associated with 15. "Midnight Special" or 48. "Haming on a Live Oak Log." Then, after the second sextet the meter, melody, and chorus change. And, as Mrs. McCulloh notes, the group's involvement becomes less direct as Cowboy's singing becomes more idiosyncratic.

One of the common thematic units in the songs is a sequence of one kind or another plugged into a fairly set formulaic line; incremental repetition with slight modulation is also common. In that regard, note the sequence of prison units in the B-text.

Both A- and B-texts are related to parts of the two preceding songs, 54. "Godamighty" and 55. "Texarkana Mary," but the style of the leader and the verse sequence are so idiosyncratic that Cowboy's songs are presented here as separate items.

Mrs. McCulloh wrote about the A-text:

"Basically, you have a regular axe sound ("X") and a series of musical phrases short enough to fit between the X's.

"*First section:* The two six-line stanzas ("Well it's early in the morning," and "Well I'm down in the bottom") consist of eight-beat phrases with an axe stroke on the first beat of each phrase. Musically you could have split these six-line stanzas into two-line stanzas, but since each six-line stanza concludes with the chorus-like "Hollerin' Oh my Lordy," the textual unit should remain intact. The two-line pattern breaks down like this: the first two-measure phrase begins on the octave above and descends through the 3rd to the tonic; the second phrase hovers on the 3rd; the third phrase is similar to the first; and the fourth phrase hovers on the tonic.

"*Third section:* Axe strokes in this section fall on the first beat of seven-beat phrases. Count them: seven! (Leon [McCulloh] commented that with a rhythm like that he wouldn't want to be out in the middle of the axe-blades.) [This kind of irregularity does *not* occur in any of the tree cutting songs, where it would be really dangerous.] But the sequence of these phrases is not so predictable as in the first section. (One consequence of this is that in the first section you find strong group singing and even harmonization. Here, however, there is virtually no harmonization, and the sing-along is weak; the only place the group really sings out forte is on the "Wo Lord," which is always signaled by "Hollerin'.") The only constant sequence in this third section is the "hollerin'" on the tonic followed by "Wo Lord," which starts on the 5th, and descends through the 4th to the 3rd.

"The other phrases are also descending ones. One type starts on the 4th, 5th, or 6th, and descends through the 3rd to the tonic; the other type starts on the 4th, 5th, or 6th, and descends through the 3rd to the tonic, but ends up back on the 3rd. In general, you get one or more descents to the tonic between each descent to the tonic and return to the 3rd, and the "Hollerin' Wo Lord" phrase is usually preceded by a descent to the tonic. You get an average of maybe nine-to-ten phrases between each occurrence of the "Hollerin' Wo Lord." Incidentally, the "Waterboy" (about halfway down this section) functions like the "Wo Lord," and moves from the 5th down to the 3rd.

"Back to the *Second section:* I was curious to see how Cowboy got from one melodic phrase complex to another, from an eight-beat pattern to a seven-beat pattern. From the beginning of this section ("Partner got to hold 'em"), he uses the seven-beat pattern except for the two repetitions of "Godamighty knows," which are eight-beat. These phrases are similar to "When the ding-dong ring" and "Got the same damn thing" in the first section. He is still using the octave-down-to-tonic pattern, but here two in a row, rather than alternating with other phrases as in the first section. He still has phrases starting on the 3rd, but they wind up on the tonic. Even the "Wo Lord" in this section descends from the 3rd to the tonic rather than from the 5th to the 3rd. But at this point he moves into the 4th/5th/6th-to-tonic pattern typical of the third section."

56-A   Early in the Morning

Well, it's noth-ing on the ta - ble,   but the spoon and the pan,

ta - ble,   spoon and the pan,

Well, you say an-y-thing a-bout it,   catch the hell out the man

say an-y-thing a-bout it,   the hell out the man

Holl'r-in' Oh my   Lord - y,   Oh my Lord-y   Lord,

my   Lord - y,   my Lord-y   Lord,

Holl'r-in' Oh my   Lord - y,   Oh my Lord-y   Lord.

Holl'r-in' Oh my   Lord - y,   Oh my Lord-y   Lord.

(2nd Section)

Part-ner got to hold   'em,   hold 'em no   long - er,

long - er,

God - a - might - y   knows,   God - a - might - y   knows,

knows,   y   knows,

knows,   Holl'r-in'   wo,   Lord,   God-a-might-y   knows.

knows,   Wo,   Lord,   a-might-y   knows.

Well, it's early in the MORNING, when the DINGDONG RING,
Go a-marching to the TABLE, got the SAME DAMN THING.
Well, it's nothing on the TABLE, but the SPOON AND THE PAN,
Well, you SAY ANYTHING ABOUT IT, catch THE HELL OUT THE
   MAN
Hollerin' oh MY LORDY, OH MY LORDY, LORD,
HOLLERIN' OH MY LORDY, OH MY LORDY, LORD

Well, I'm down in the BOTTOM, on a LIVE OAK LOG,
Well, I'm down THERE ROLLIN', like a LOWDOWN DOG.
Well, the captain and the SERGEANT, come a RIDING ALONG,
Say, "You better GO TO HAMING, IF YOU WANT TO GO HOME.
Hollerin' oh MY LORDY, OH MY LORDY, LORD,
HOLLERIN' OH MY LORDY, OH MY LORDY, LORD.

Partner got to hold 'em, hold 'em no LONGER,
Godamighty KNOWS, Godamighty KNOWS
Partner who's the RIDER, partner who's THE RIDER,
GodaMIGHTY KNOWS,
Hollerin' WO LORD, GODAMIGHTY KNOWS,
GodaMIGHTY KNOWS, GODAMIGHTY KNOWS.
Partner can't HOLD ME, hold ME NO LONGER.
Partner's got the ROBBER, partner's got THE ROB'.
What you CALL THE ROBBER, CRANE WING ROBBER,
Godamighty KNOWS,
Wo Lord, GODAMIGHTY KNOWS.
Partner got TO HELP ME, help me TO CALL 'EM,
Help me TO CALL 'em, Godamighty KNOWS.
Make it dead easy, make it dead easy
GODAMIGHTY KNOWS, GODAMIGHTY KNOWS
Believe I'll call for water,
GODAMIGHTY KNOWS, GODAMIGHTY KNOWS.
Waterboy, oh waterboy,
Bring me DRINK A WATER, BRING ME DRINK A WATER,
GODAMIGHTY KNOWS.
Don't want TO DRINK IT, DON'T WANT TO DRINK IT,

GODAMIGHTY KNOWS.
POUR IT ON MY DIAMOND, POUR IT ON MY DIAMOND.
Diamond STRIKIN' FIRE, GodAMIGHTY KNOWS,
Hollerin' WO LORD, GODAMIGHTY KNOWS.

Partner's GETTIN' WORRIED, PARTNER'S GETTIN' WORRIED,
Worried 'BOUT MABEL, Mabel and the BABY,
GodaMIGHTY KNOWS,
Hollerin' WO LORD, godAMIGHTY KNOWS.
Partner I got to LEAVE, partner I got to LEAVE,
LEAVE YOU DOGGIN',
GodaMIGHTY KNOWS.
Leave YOU DOGGIN', doggin' with the CRANE,
Doggin' with THE CRANE, GodaMIGHTY KNOWS,
Hollerin' WO LORD, GodaMIGHTY KNOWS,
GODAMIGHTY KNOWS.
Partner I'm GETTIN' WORRIED, partner I'M GETTIN' WORRIED,
Worried 'bout MABEL, Mabel and THE BABY,
Mabel and THE BABY, Godamighty KNOWS,
Hollerin' WO LORD, GodaMIGHTY KNOWS.
Partner can't HOLD ME, partner can't HOLD ME,
Hold me with his—[end of tape 451]
Godamighty knows.
Believe I'll CALL THE GOVERNOR, believe I'll CALL THE GOVERNOR
"What you gonna tell him?" Tell him I'm in TROUBLE,
Tell him I'M IN TROUBLE, Godamighty KNOWS.
This the way I CALL HIM,
Hollerin' WO LORD, Wo LORD GOVERNOR,
Godamighty KNOWS, Godamighty KNOWS,
Wo MY LORD—

Spoken: Jack! Rollin' it up here boss!

56-B   Godamighty Knows

Well-a where you learn to rob her, OH MY LORDY,
Learned it on Darrington, GODAMIGHTY, GOD KNOW.

Who was the rider, GODAMIGHTY, MY LORD,
Bullin' Charlie Frazier, GODAMIGHTY, GOD KNOW.

I said who was the rider, GODAMIGHTY, MY LORD,
Godamighty knows.

Cold blood murder, GODAMIGHTY, GOD KNOW,
Cold blood murder, GODAMIGHTY, GOD KNOWS.

Murder on Darrington, GODAMIGHTY MY LORD,
Who was the rider,
Bullin' Jack O Diamonds,
BULLIN' JACK O DIAMONDS,
Cold blood murder, COLD BLOOD MURDER,
GODAMIGHTY KNOWS.

Central's on the highway, GODAMIGHTY KNOWS.
Central's on the highway, GODAMIGHTY KNOWS.
Ramsey's in the bottom, Ramsey's in the bottom,
GODAMIGHTY, GOD KNOWS, GODAMIGHTY KNOWS.
Clemens' on the water, Clemens' on the water,
GODAMIGHTY KNOW, GODAMIGHTY KNOWS.
Whoa Lord, Godamighty knows,
Central's on the prairie, GODAMIGHTY KNOWS,
CENTRAL'S ON THE PRAIRIE, GODAMIGHTY KNOWS.
Hollerin' WO LORD, GODAMIGHTY KNOWS,
GODAMIGHTY KNOWS.
Believe I'm the Devil, Believe I'm the DEVIL,
GODAMIGHTY KNOWS,
WO LORD, GODAMIGHTY KNOWS.
Partner I got to leave, partner I got to leave,
Leave you doggin', GODAMIGHTY KNOWS.
Doggin' with the crane wing, doggin' WITH THE CRANE WING,
GODAMIGHTY KNOWS,
Partner won't help me, partner won't help me,
Help me to call 'em, help me to call 'em,
GODAMIGHTY KNOWS.
Raise 'em up HIGHER, RAISE 'EM UP HIGHER.
DROP 'EM DOWN TOGETHER,
MAKE IT DEAD EASY, MAKE IT DEAD EASY,
WO LORD, MAKE IT DEAD EASY,
MAKE IT DEAD EASY, Godamighty KNOWS.

Flatweeding Songs (57–65)

---

57 Raise 'Em Up Higher

A. Johnny Jackson and group, *flatweeding*, Ramsey 1, 22 August 1965, 400.4, N.C.

B. Johnny Jackson and group, Ramsey 1, 1 July 1964, 23.2

C. "Twenty-One Hammers," David Tippett and Johnny Jackson, Ramsey 1, 2 July 1964, 26.4

D. "Forty-Four Hammers," Virgil Asbury and group, Retrieve, 5 July 1964, 46.2

E. "Alberta," Joseph "Chinaman" Johnson and group, *flatweeding*, Ellis, 21 August 1965, 398.3, N.C.

A few versions of this song appear on LP recordings. Among these are: "Old Dollar Mamie," by "22" and group, and "Old Alabama," by B.B. and group, both on *Negro Prison Songs from the Mississippi State Penitentiary*, Tradition TLP 1020; the B-text appears on *Negro Folklore from Texas State Prisons*, Elektra EKS-7296; " 'Berta," by Big Louisiana, Rev. Rogers, and Roosevelt Charles (while log cutting) on *Prison Work-songs*, Folk-Lyric LFS A-5.

The "dollar a yard" stanza in the A-text appears in "I'm Going to Leland," sung by Frank Jordan and group, Parchman, Mississippi, recorded in 1936 by John A. Lomax, on *Afro-American Spirituals, Work Songs, and Ballads*, AAFS L-3. Variants of the penultimate stanza of the D-text appear throughout the South. It is reported by Odum and Johnson, 1925, pp. 252–253 ("Well, de boat's up de river an' dey won't come down / Well, I believe, on my soul, dat dey's water boun' "), and by Newman White, p. 207 ("The boat's up the river / And she won't come down; / I believe to my soul / She must be water bound / The boat's up the river / And she won't come down; / One-long-lonesome-blow / And she's Alabama bound," from Tennessee river deckhands) and p. 280 ("The boat is up the river and she won't come down / She must be heavy loaded and water bound," from Alabama).

The D-text is more ornamented than the others, but the metrics are approximately the same; the extra words in the middle of the line were usually sung *during* the caesurae slots by someone other than the lead singer. That performance also appears on *Negro Folklore from Texas State Prisons*, Elektra EKS-7296.

57-A   Raise 'Em Up Higher

*Hoe strokes are somewhat irregular

Var.

Raise 'em up higher, higher, DROP 'EM DOWN,
RAISE 'EM UP HIGHER, HIGHER, DROP 'EM DOWN,
RAISE 'EM UP HIGHER, HIGHER, DROP 'EM DOWN,
NEVER KNOW THE DIFFERENCE WHEN THE SUN GOES DOWN.

Dollar Mary told old DOLLAR BOB, (3x. *Group sings full line on both
    repetitions.*)
THE DRESS SHE WANTED COST A DOLLAR A YARD.

Hush your mouth and DON'T YOU SAY A WORD, (3x)
YOU SHALL HAVE IT IF IT'S IN-A THIS WORLD.

Set on the cooler, let YOUR FEET HANG DOWN, (3x)
HAVE ON NOTHIN' BUT YOUR MORNIN' GOWN.

Raise 'em up HIGHER, HIGHER, DROP 'EM DOWN, (3x)
NEVER KNOW THE DIFFERENCE WHEN THE SUN GOES DOWN.

Who's that a walkin' DOWN THAT ROAD,
WHO'S THAT A WALKIN' DOWN A THAT ROAD,
WHO'S THAT WALKIN', WALKIN' DOWN THAT ROAD,
WALK JUST LIKE SHE GOT A HEAVY LOAD.

Dollar Mary told OLD DOLLAR BOB, (3x)
DRESS SHE WANTED COST A DOLLAR A YARD.

57-B   Raise 'Em Up Higher

Similar to 57-A, but with these additional stanzas:

Never been to Houston a-boy, BUT I BEEN TOLD, (3x)
WOMEN IN A HOUSTON GOT THAT GOOD JELLY ROLL.

Look mighty cloudy, boys, BUT AIN'T GONNA RAIN, (3x)
SUN DRAWIN' WATER, BOYS, FROM NO-MAN'S LAND.

57-C   Twenty-One Hammers

Sung unison. Melody is exactly the same as 57-A. Commas indicate the strong caesurae.

Twenty-one hammers fallin', in a line, (3x)
Nobody's hammer buddy, ring a like mine.

Ring like silver and it, shine like gold (3x)
Price on my hammer boys, ain't never been told.

Look at Alberta comin', down that road, (3x)
Walkin' just like she, got a heavy load.

Ain't that enough to worry, convict's mind, (3x)
See Roberta reel and, rock behind.

'Berta say she love me but I, believe she's lyin', (3x)
Ain't been to see me since, a last July.

Dollar Mary told a, Dollar Bob, (3x)
Dress she wanted cost a, dollar a yard.

Hush your mouth and don't you, say nar' a word, (3x)
You shall have it if it's, in this world.

So many dollars broke her, apron string, (3x)
Dollars were fallin' like a, shower a rain.

57-D   Forty-Four Hammers

Oh forty-four hammers ringing, RINGING IN A LINE,
FORTY-FOUR HAMMERS RINGING, Well-a, well-a, RINGING IN A
   LINE,
Nobody's hammer here will, LORDY NOW, RING LIKE MINE,
NOBODY'S HAMMER HERE WILL, Well-a, well-a, RING LIKE MINE.

Shine like silver and it, LORDY NOW, SHINE LIKE GOLD,
SHINE LIKE SILVER AND IT, well-a, well-a, SHINE LIKE GOLD,
Sound like thunder when the, my Lordy, THUNDER ROLL,
SOUND LIKE THUNDER WHEN THE, well-a, well-a, THUNDER ROLL.

Never been to Houston but a, I been told (*pattern of repetition continues as above*)
Women in a Houston got a, baby, sweet jelly roll (2x)

When they walk they reel and, Lordy now, rock behind (2x)
That's enough, partner, to worry, now, a convict's mind (2x)

Every time I see you with some, 'nother guy (2x)
I ask you how about it, [you] say you, you ain't got time (2x)

Don't want legs and don't want, don't want no thighs (2x)
All I wanna do is see your, Lordy now, natural eyes (2x)

Big boat's up river turning, Lord now, 'round and 'round (2x)
Flywheel knockin' now, 'Bama bound (2x)

Wo, Roberta where you, been so long (2x)
Had no lovin' since a, Lordy now, you been gone (2x)

57-E   Alberta

See Alberta comin' DOWN THAT ROAD,
SEE ALBERTA COMIN' DOWN THAT ROAD,
See Alberta comin' DOWN THAT ROAD,
Walkin' just like she got a HEAVY LOAD.

Wo, 'Berta, don't you HEAR ME GAL?
WO, 'BERTA, DON'T YOU HEAR ME GAL?

Twenty-one hammers fallin' IN A LINE,
TWENTY-ONE HAMMERS FALLIN' IN A LINE,
Twenty-one HAMMERS FALLIN' IN A LINE,
None a them HAMMERS, BOYS, THAT RING A LIKE MINE.

Ring like silver and it SHINE LIKE GOLD, (3x)
Price a my hammer, boys, AIN'T NEVER BEEN TOLD.

Wo, 'Berta, don't you HEAR ME GAL?
WO, 'BERTA, DON'T YOU HEAR ME GAL?

Big leg Berta, if you COME AND BE MINE, (3x)
Have to do nothin' in the SUMMERTIME.

Set in the cool 'n' let your FEET SWING DOWN, (3x)
Have on nothin' but your mornin' gown.

58   Down the Line

Houston Page and group, *flatweeding*, Ramsey 1, 22 August 1965, 401.1,
N.C.

This is similar, melodically and structurally, to a crosscutting song in
this collection—"Plumb the Line." "Down the Line" probably derives
from the same religious antecedents as "Plumb the Line"; see notes to
that song.

58   Down the Line

Oh well I b'lieve I'll roll on DOWN THE LINE,
A well I b'lieve I'll roll on DOWN THE LINE,
A well I b'lieve I'll roll on DOWN THE LINE,
IT TAKES A NUMBER ONE DRIVER DOWN THE LINE.

A well Black Betty's in the bottom now, DOWN THE LINE, (3x)
IT TAKES A NUMBER ONE DRIVER DOWN THE LINE.

A well my gal is in Houston now . . . (*repetitions and burdens continue as above*)
A well I'm callin' on you lead row . . .
A well I'm callin' on you tail row . . .
Oh well the captain is a ridin' now . . .
A well I b'lieve I'll roll on . . .
A well I b'lieve I'll move on . . .

59   Long Hot Summer Days

A. Joseph "Chinaman" Johnson and group, *flatweeding*, Ellis, 22 March 1966, 446.1, J.M.
B. David Tippen, Ebbie Veasley, and group, Wynne, 18 August 1965, 383.5, N.C.

The subject matter of this song needs no explanation for anyone who has ever experienced the Texas Gulf country in the bottomlands below Houston in the summertime, the months when heat blasts down from above, rises up from the ground, and seems to ripple horizontally across the fields all at once, the long summer when almost no rain falls but the air stays so humid that nothing dries except when hung in direct sunlight. The sun rises hot and red and goes down hot and red, and tempers and temperatures rise at about the same pace.

Mrs. McCulloh noted, about her transcription of the A-text: "I transcribed two stanzas, the main melodic difference being in the opening phrases. The first part of the song uses the 'Make you want to see your mama' form; the last part, beginning with 'Everybody gets worried,' uses the other form of the tune. They stick to a hoe-strike every six beats, even when they get involved in a couple of 5/4 measures."

See Lomax, 1936-B, pp. 120–122 for a version with different stanzas; Leadbelly sings a mixture of this song and "Rattler" (62 in this collection) on *Rock Island Line*, Folkways FA-2014. A version recorded by John A. and Ruby T. Lomax from the singing of Clyde Hill and group, Brazoria, Texas, in 1939 appears on *Afro-American Spirituals, Work Songs, and Ballads*, AAFS L-3.

59-A   Long Hot Summer Days

When old Hannah go to beaming,
WHEN OLD HANNAH GO TO BEAMING,
WHEN OLD HANNAH GO TO BEAMING,
LORD GODAMIGHTY,
WHEN OLD HANNAH GO TO BEAMING,
WHEN OLD HANNAH GO TO BEAMING,
WHEN OLD HANNAH GO TO BEAMING,
IN THE LONG HOT SUMMER DAYS.

Make you want to see your mama . . . (*repetitions and burdens con-*
   tinue as above)
Everybody gets worried . . .
When old Rattler go to howling . . .
Well the bosses go to squabbling . . .
Make you want to walk the water . . .

59-B   Long Hot Summer Days

Sung in unison:
Godamighty look-a yonder, (3x)
Lord, Godamighty,
Godamighty look-a yonder, (3x)
In them long hot summer days.

Old Hannah go to beamin'. . . (*repetitions and burden continue as above*)
Well the bullies go to screamin'. . .
Well the bosses go squabblin'. . .
And you better go to rollin'. . .

---

60   Yellow Gal

Johnny Jackson, Houston Page, and group, *flatweeding*, Ramsey 1, 22 August 1965, 401.3, N.C.

An adequate discussion of the folklore of skin color would require far more space than is available here. We might note that there has been an enormous variation in the value accorded skin color—by blacks *and* whites—during the past two centuries. In the first part of this century, there were a number of songs and verses about light-skinned Negro women. See White, pp. 311–324, for examples and discussion of this song motif. Stanza 64 of J. B. Smith's song describes a yellow woman with golden teeth. For notes and texts of blues dealing with women of different coloration, see Oliver, pp. 76–85.

Almost every good group leader I met in the TDC led this song on at least one occasion (performances by J. B. Smith, Matt Williams, Jesse "G.I. Jazz" Hendricks, and Joseph "Chinaman" Johnson are at tape locations 37.6, 39.3, 63.7, 380.1, 389.1, and 447.6; one of Chinaman's versions [447.6] was done while crosscutting). Leadbelly sings it on *Take This Hammer,* Folkways FA-2004 (verses printed in Asch and Lomax, p. 54), and on *Last Sessions,* Folkways FP-2942. Another version, recorded from the singing of Harold Burton and group on Ramsey in 1951, appears on *Treasury of Field Recordings, I,* Candid 8026. Lomax, 1936-A, pp. 243–245, prints a version from a "Texas prison," which may be the same as the text in the *Lomax MS.* (A/9–144) noted as "from singing of James (Iron Head) Baker."

60   Yellow Gal

Jackson:
Oh my yella, my yellow, YELLOW, YELLOW GAL,
Oh my yella, my yellow, YELLOW, YELLOW GAL.

Oh my big-leg, bow-leg YELLOW, YELLOW GAL,
Oh my big-leg, bow-leg YELLOW, YELLOW GAL.

Oh my knock-kneed, pigeon-toed, YELLOW, YELLOW GAL,
Oh my knock-kneeded, pigeon-toed, YELLOW, YELLOW GAL.

Oh my yellow, my yellow . . . (*repetition and burden continue as above*)
Oh my bow-legged, knock-kneeded . . .
Oh my yellow, my yellow . . .
Well I'll die and go to Hell about my . . .
Well my yellow, my yellow . . .
Well my papa slapped my mama 'bout my . . .
Wo my yellow, my yellow . . .
Well my bow-legged, knock-kneeded . . .
Well I'm doin' lifetime about my . . .
Wo my yellow, my yellow . . .
Well I'll die and go to Hell about my . . .
Oh my yellow, my yellow . . .

Page:
Well I'm hamin' on the Brazos 'about my . . .
Well I'm doin' ninety-nine 'bout my . . .
Wo my yellow, my yellow . . .
Well my mama slapped my papa 'bout a . . .
Well my knock-kneeded, bow-leg . . .
Well my yellow, my yellow . . .

61   I Shall Not Be Moved

A. Joseph "Chinaman" Johnson and group, *flatweeding*, Ellis, 21 August 1965, 398.2, N.C.

B. Jesse "G.I. Jazz" Hendricks and group, Ramsey 2, 4 July 1964, 36.6

Charlie Patton, in the early twenties one of the two most influential bluesmen in the Mississippi Delta, recorded a very nice version of this song; it has been republished on *The Immortal Charlie Patton*, Origin Jazz Library OJL-1. The Archive of American Folk Song *Check List* lists two performances: a group of Negro convicts, Parchman, Mississippi, recorded by John A. Lomax in 1936 (615A), and the Rev. J. R. Gipson, of Jasper, Texas, recorded by John A. and Ruby T. Lomax in 1940 (3980 A7). Chinaman leads the song (not at work) on *Negro Folk Lore from Texas State Prisons*, Elektra EKS-7296. A more modern version is on *We Shall Not Be Moved: Songs of the "Freedom Riders" and the "Sit-Ins,"* Folkways FH-5591. I have not found any early published texts, but the lyrics do have about them a mid-nineteenth-century *feel*.

61-A   I Shall Not Be Moved

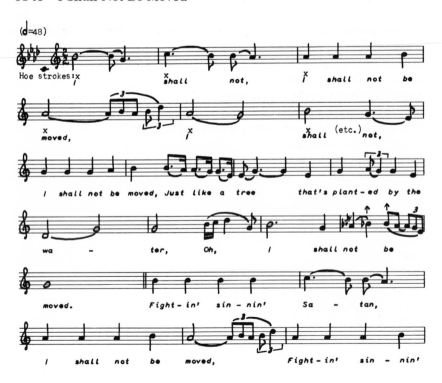

Sa - tan, I shall not be moved, Just like a
tree that's plant - ed by the wa - ter, Oh,
I shall not be moved.

I shall not, I SHALL NOT BE MOVED,
I SHALL NOT, I SHALL NOT BE MOVED.
Just like a tree THAT'S PLANTED BY THE WATER,
OH, I SHALL NOT BE MOVED.

Fightin' sinnin' Satan, I SHALL NOT BE MOVED,
Fightin' sinnin' Satan, I SHALL NOT BE MOVED.
JUST LIKE A TREE THAT'S PLANTED BY THE WATER,
OH, I SHALL NOT BE MOVED.

Oh my way to Heaven . . . (*repetitions and burdens continue as in
    previous stanza*)
Jesus is my captain . . .
On my way to Heaven . . .
I shall not . . .
Sanctified and holy . . .
I shall not . . .

61-B   I Shall Not Be Moved

The church of God is marchin', I SHALL NOT BE MOVED,
Oh Lord, the church of God is marchin', I SHALL NOT BE MOVED,
JUST LIKE A TREE THAT'S PLANTED BY THE WATER,
I SHALL NOT BE MOVED.

Oh I shall not . . . (*repetition and burdens continue as above*)
I'm on my way to Heaven . . .
Come and join this army . . .
The preacher died a shouting . . .
Wo, I shall not . . .

62   Rattler

A. Joseph "Chinaman" Johnson and group, *flatweeding*, Ellis, 21 August 1965, 397.5, N.C.

B. Houston Page and group, *flatweeding*, Ramsey 1, 22 August 1965, 401.2, N.C.

C. Jesse "G.I. Jazz" Hendricks, Matt Williams, and group, Ramsey 2, 4 July 1964, 37.4

D. Johnny Jackson, Houston Page, and group, Ramsey 1, 16 August 1965, 372.3

Rattler is the superhound; he can do all the things that any dog sergeant would want his best dogs to enjoy doing if they were smart enough to know what their master really wanted of them: he prefers tracking convicts to chewing on a bone, he'll walk across a log (*you* try, sometime, putting your dog on a wobbly surface), he can swim the treacherous water. He is so good, in fact, that the convicts admire his skill. (Think about Bruno Bettelheim's many comments about how captives tend to take on the value system of their captors.)

In any event, "Rattler" is one of the most frequently heard flatweeding songs in Texas prisons, and even now, years after the song was first introduced to the system, there is always at least one dog on every farm that bears the name "Rattler."

The song seems to go back quite a while. Talley, p. 46, reports a hunting song version in which Rattler not only drives cattle and hunts rabbit, hog, and possum, but occasionally brings home a chicken. The last stanza of that song has a rhyme set "dew/too," like the third stanza of the B-text. Newman White, p. 232, reports a version from North Carolina:

> I carried old Raddler out,
> Thought I'd catch a coon.
> Every time old Raddler barked,
> I found he'd treed the moon.

And B. A. Botkin reprints in *Treasury of American Folklore* (1944, p. 19) a story in which Davy Crockett's dog is named "Ratler" (the story is taken from *Sketches and Eccentricities of Col. David Crockett, of West Tennessee*, New York, 1833, pp. 125–127).

There are several recorded versions: Leadbelly, *Rock Island Line*, Folkways FA-2014, the song "Old Riley," (printed in Asch and Lomax, p. 38) which is a mixture of "Rattler" and "Long Hot Summer Days" (song 59 in this collection); *Negro Prison Camp Worksongs*, Folkways P-475 (printed in Courlander, 1963-B, pp. 103–105); Doc Reese on *The Blues at Newport, I, 1964*, Vanguard VRS-9180. There are several performances in the Archive of American Folk Song: Marie Womble, Banner, Mississippi, recorded by Herbert Halpert, 1939 (3034 A3); Skyline Farms group, Washington, D.C., recorded by Alan Lomax, 1938 (1630 A2); Moses (Clear Rock) Platt and James (Iron Head) Baker, Central at Sugarland, recorded by John A. and Alan Lomax, 1934 (this appears on *Negro Work Songs and Calls*, AAFS L-8). The Lomaxes published two texts: 1936-B, pp. 106–108, and 1936-A, pp. 66–67. A version by Harry Belafonte and group is on *Swing Dat Hammer*, RCA LPS-2194.

Note that when Chinaman has a rhyme he uses it over two stanzas, but Houston sings a straight couplet. Chinaman is a better group leader, and knows how to conserve his repertory. (A version led by Chinaman, not at work, is on *Negro Folklore from Texas State Prisons*, Elektra EKS-7296.) "Number One" and "Number Two" in the D-text refer to work squads.

62-A   Rattler

Won't you here, here, Rattler,
HERE, RATTLER, HERE,
A-won't you here, here, Rattler,
HERE, RATTLER, HERE!

Won't you seek him old Rattler, won't you bite him old Ring,
HERE, RATTLER, HERE,
Won't you seek him old Rattler, won't you bite him old Ring,
HERE, RATTLER, HERE!

Well old Rattler he was a Walker dog . . . (*repetition and burden continue as above*)
He could swim big Brazos, he could walk a log . . .
Well it's here, here, Rattler . . .
Well I b'lieve I've got three trustys gone . . .
Well ole Eatem, ole Beatem, ole Cheatem done gone . . .
Well ole Rattler here's a marrow bone . . .
You can eat that meat, you can leave it alone . . .
"I don't want no marrowbone . . .
Well I want that bully that's long gone". . .
Well it's soon one mornin'. . . .
When I heard that sergeant blow his horn . . .

62-B   Rattler

* Disregarding irregularities of meter, hoe strokes come invariably at intervals of a whole note.

Whoa, Rattler was a mighty dog,
HERE, RATTLER, HERE,
Ole Rattler was the sergeant's dog,
HERE, RATTLER, HERE!
I said, HERE, OLE RATTLER,
HERE, RATTLER, HERE!

Ole Rattler was a great big dog,
HERE, RATTLER, HERE,
He could swim that Braz', he could walk that log,
HERE, RATTLER, HERE!
I said, HERE, OLD RATTLER,
HERE, RATTLER, HERE!

Ole Rattler was a tippin' through the morning dew,
HERE, RATTLER, HERE!
You know the captain was mad and the niggers was too . . . (*three-line burden continues as above*)

Ole Rattler was a great big dog,
HERE, RATTLER, HERE!
You better count your niggers, 'cause I believe one's gone . . .

Ole Rattler was a tipping through the morning dew,
HERE, RATTLER, HERE!
You know the captain was mad and the niggers was too . . .

Ole Rattler was a big old dog,
HERE, RATTLER, HERE!
Well he could swim that Braz', he could walk that log . . .

62-C   Rattler

G.I.:
Well old Rattler was a nigger dog,
HERE, RATTLER, HERE,
Well old Rattler was a nigger dog,
HERE, RATTLER, HERE.

Well old Rattler there's a nigger gone . . . (2x, *burden continues as above*)
You got to ride, ride, dog man . . . (2x)
Says, Old Rattler, here's a marrowbone . . . (2x)
You can eat it or you can leave it alone . . . (2x)
"I don't want no marrowbone . . . (2x)
I just want to know how long he's gone". . . (2x)
Well old Rattler's on the nigger's trail . . . (2x)
Well old Rattler caught him by the tail . . . (2x)
You got to ride, ride, sergeant . . . (2x)

Williams:
For that nigger he is a long gone . . . (2x)
Well a tell me who's that long gone . . .
'At's old Eatem, old Beatem, old Cheatem done gone . . .
Won't you here, here, Rattler . . . (2x)
Won't you come and get this marrowbone . . . (2x)
"Well I don't want no marrowbone . . .
"I want the nigger they say is long gone". . .
Won't you here, here, Rattler . . . (2x)

[They] tell me old Rattler jumped a cottontail . . .
Well he run him up through that new way trail . . .
Won't you here, Rattler . . . (2x)
"Well I want that nigger's a long gone". . . (2x)
Well they say old Rattler was a Walker's hound . . . (2x)
He could swim big Brazos, walk a liveoak log . . .

Well they say old Rattler was a nigger's dog . . .
Won't you here, here, Rattler . . . (2x)
Well I seed the sergeant when he shot the gun . . .
Well I heared that sergeant when he shot his gun . . .
Well I knowed by that there was a nigger gone . . .
So I said, "Here, here, Rattler". . .
Well I, here, here, Rattler . . .

Spoken: "Woof, woof, woof; That's got it. Treed him."

62-D   Rattler

Jackson:
When I first come down on the Brazos line,
HERE, RATTLER, HERE,
Number One was jumpin', Number Two was flyin',
HERE, RATTLER, HERE.

Well old Rattler he was the sergeant's dog . . . (*burden continues as above*)
Well old Rattler he will get you for his marrowbone . . .

You better here, old Rattler . . . (2x)

Page:
Old Rattler was a mighty dog . . .
Well he could swim that Braz', he could walk that log . . .

Old Rattler was a tipping through that morning dew . . .
You know the captain was mad and the niggers was too . . .

You better here, old Rattler . . . (2x)

Jackson:
You better sic him old Rattler, better bite him old Ring . . .
You better eat him old Rattler till you hear his name . . .

You better here, old Rattler . . . (2x)

Old Rattler was a mighty dog . . .
Old Rattler could swim that Braz', he would walk that log . . .

I say here, old Rattler . . . (2x)

Better sic him old Rattler, bite him old dog . . .
You better count your niggers, 'cause I believe one gone . . .

I say here, old Rattler . . . (2x)

---

63   Black Gal

A. Joseph "Chinaman" Johnson and group, *flatweeding*, Ellis, 21 August 1965, 398.1, N.C.
B. J. B. Smith and Louis "Bacon and Porkchop" Houston, Ramsey 2, 17 August 1965, 375.5

64   Tampa

A. Ebbie Veasley and group, Wynne, 18 August 1965, 383.4, J.M.
B. Jesse "G.I. Jazz" Hendricks, J. B. Smith, Matt Williams, Louis "Bacon and Porkchop" Houston, and group, Ramsey 2, 4 July 1964, 38.3

65   On My Way to Mexico

Jesse Lee Warren and group, Ellis, 11 July 1964, 62.7, J.M.

These three songs have several common melodic and thematic elements, but they are separate songs nevertheless. They all are related to a number of other songs recorded in earlier years, and in many regards they are more directly related to one another *through* those songs than they are to one another directly. See, for example, the composite text in Lomax, 1960, pp. 546–547 (taken from Lomax, 1936-A, pp. 13–14); White, p. 267. A number of recordings are of interest: B.B. and others, "Old Alabama," on *Negro Prison Songs from the Mississippi State Penitentiary*, Tradition TLP-1020, and a variety of discs in the Archive of American Folk Song at the Library of Congress: Augustus (Track Horse) Haggerty and group, Huntsville, recorded by John A. and Alan Lomax, 1934 (218A1 and 219A2); group, Bellwood Prison Camp, Atlanta, Georgia, recorded by John A. Lomax, 1934 (253 A2); group, State Farm, Virginia, recorded by John A. Lomax, 1936 (750 A1); group, State Penitentiary, Parchman, Mississippi, recorded by John A. Lomax, 1933 (1858-B1-10 in.); "Tamp 'em Up Solid," recorded in Livingston, Alabama, by John A. and Ruby T. Lomax, 1940 (4059 B1); and Zora Neale Hurston, "Tampa," Jayville, Florida, recorded by Herbert Halpert, 1939 (3139-A1).
Buffalo Bayou is east of Houston. The import of the "mouth full a

gold" in the 63-B-text is an older Negro status symbol of having front teeth replaced with gold teeth when possible, for gold teeth were a sign of demonstrable affluence (see Faulkner, 1962, for an amusing account of the adventures of one such tooth in and out of a whorehouse in Memphis). Note stanza 64 in J. B. Smith's song.

Both "Tampa" texts seem related more to railroad work than to prison. Note that the 64-B-text mentions the "T.P." (Texas Pacific Railroad), and towns across the Gulf of Mexico: Tampa, Mobile Bay, New Iberia (Louisiana). That text is also distinctive because it is one of the rare work songs in which another leader takes over every two verses or so, and it is obvious that some of these verses are responses to what has just been sung. So not only are they describing their situation, but they are also interacting with one another—for example, Smith asserts his capability after Williams has asserted his. Although it obviously originated as a railroad text, none of the inmates who sang it admitted to any knowledge of or experience on railroad section gangs.

The text of "On My Way to Mexico" shares some lines with 63-B, but it differs structurally and melodically. In structure, it is similar to "Stewball" (song 20 in this collection). Sometimes inmates start "On My Way to Mexico," "Black Gal," or "Tampa" and drift, within a stanza or two, into "Stewball." (This happened with Houston and a group, Ramsey 2, 4 July 1964, 43.13; Johnny Jackson and group, *logging*, Ramsey 1, 22 August 1965, 400.2; and David Tippett and group, *flatweeding*, Ellis, 22 March 1966, 445.4.)

63-A   Black Gal

Did you hear 'bout Ada gettin' drownded,
In the Buffalo Baw [Bayou], buddy,
IN THE BUFFALO BAW?
DID YOU HEAR 'BOUT ADA GETTIN' DROWNDED,
IN THE BUFFALO BAW, BUDDY,
IN THE BUFFALO BAW?

That old black gal keeps on a squabblin',
Wanta buy her some shoes, buddy . . . (*repetition
    by group continues as above*)

Well I gave her a hundred silver dollars,
Just to buy her some shoes, buddy . . .

Well she come back drunk and staggerin',
With her belly full a booze, buddy . . .

Well I doubled up both a my fistes,
And I blackened her eyes, buddy . . .

Oughta heard that black gal hollerin',
"Don't you murder me, buddy". . .

Did you hear 'bout Ada gettin' drownded,
In the Buffalo Baw, buddy . . .

Got a bulldog weigh five hunderd,
In a my back yard, buddy . . .

When he bark he roar like thunder,
All under the ground, buddy . . .

When you hear my bulldog barkin',
There's a burglar 'round, buddy . . .

Did you hear 'bout the waterworks in Georgia,
Just a burnin' down, buddy . . .

63-B   Black Gal

In each stanza, Smith sings the first line, then both sing the rest, in
unison.

Well that black gal, she keep on a hollerin',
'Bout a new pair a shoes, buddy, 'bout a new pair a shoes.
Well I gave her five silver dollars,
Just to buy some shoes, buddy, just to buy some shoes.

But she came back whoopin' and hollerin',
With her belly full a booze, buddy, with her belly full a booze.
Well she came back whoopin' and hollerin',
With her belly full a booze, buddy, with her belly full a booze.

Well the black gal she keep on a-hollerin',
'Bout she want some clothes, buddy, says she want some clothes.
Till I give her fifty silver dollars,
Just to buy her some clothes, buddy, just to buy her some clothes.

But she came back a whoopin' and hollerin',
With her mouth full a gold, buddy, with her mouth full a gold.
Yes, she came back whoopin' and hollerin',
With her mouth full of gold, buddy, with her mouth full a gold.

Well I doubled up my fists and I hit her,
And I blackened her eyes, buddy, and I blackened her eyes.
Yeah, I doubled up my fists and I hit her,
And I blackened her eye, buddy, and I blackened her eye.

Well I went down to her mama,
And I knocked on the door, buddy, and I knocked on the door.
Well she came through the house a-tippin',
Like a black cat on the floor, buddy, like a black cat 'cross the floor.

She said, "Get away from my window,
Quit knockin' on my doors, buddy, quit knockin' on my door.
'Cause you dirty down mistreater,
My daughter don't want you no more, buddy, don't want you no more."

64-A   Tampa

I got a long tall YELLOW GAL IN GEORGIA,
 KEEP A WRITIN' TO ME, BUDDY, KEEP A WRITIN' TO ME.
I GOT A LONG TALL YELLOW GAL IN GEORGIA,
 KEEP A WRITIN' TO ME, BUDDY, KEEP A WRITIN' TO ME.

When I roll my long time, Mama,
 BACK EAST I'M GOIN', BACK EAST I'M GOIN'.
WHEN I ROLL MY LONG TIME, MAMA,
 BACK EAST I'M GOIN', BACK EAST I'M GOIN'.

Well I tamped all the way FROM TAMPA, FLORIDA,
 IN TWENTY-ONE DAYS, BUDDY, IN TWENTY-ONE DAYS . . .
  (*group repeats both lines, as above*)

But I broke my BRAND NEW HAMMER,
TAMPIN' ON MY WAY BUDDY, TAMPIN' ON MY WAY . . .

You gonna kill YOUR FOOL SELF DRIVIN',
TRYIN' TO TAMP LIKE ME, BUDDY, TRYIN' TO TAMP LIKE ME . . .

64-B   Tampa

G.I.:
Well I tamped all the way from TAMPA, FLORIDA,
In forty-one days, buddy, IN FORTY-ONE DAYS.
YES, I TAMPED ALL THE WAY FROM TAMPA, FLORIDA,
IN FORTY-ONE DAYS, BUDDY, IN FORTY-ONE DAYS.

If you want to be a T.P. Tamper,
You got to tamp like me, buddy, YOU GOT TO TAMP LIKE ME.
IF YOU WANT TO BE A T.P. TAMPER,
YOU GOT TO TAMP LIKE ME, BUDDY, YOU GOT TO TAMP LIKE ME.

Smith:
You got to raise your tamper higher,
Up above your knees, buddy . . . (*group continues with repetition, as above*)

Did you hear about ADA gettin' drownded,
In the Mobile Bay, buddy . . .

Well that poor girl she got drownded,
Tryin' to follow me, buddy . . .

Williams:
Did you hear about the waterworks in Georgia,
Just a burnin' down, buddy . . .

Well I tamped all the way from New Ibery,
In forty-one days, buddy . . .

Houston:
Did you hear 'bout Ada shootin' Shorty,
In the Mobile Bay, buddy . . .

Smith:
If I don't be a number one tamper,
I'd a died on the way, buddy . . .

Williams:
Raise your tamper up higher,
Up above your knee, buddy . . .

You can make a day dead easy,
If you tamp like me, buddy . . .

Well I tamped all the way from New Ibery,
In forty-one days, buddy . . .

Smith:
If I don't be a number one tamper,
I'd a died on the way, buddy . . .

---

65   On My Way to Mexico

Well I woke up EARLY THIS MORNIN',
I WAS A FEELIN' MIGHTY WRONG,
WELL I RANG UP THIRTY-TWO-TWENTY,
BUT THAT BLACK GAL, SHE HAD A DONE GONE.

SHE'S GONE TO HER MAMA, JUST TO STAY ALL DAY,
SHE'S GONE TO HER MAMA, JUST TO STAY ALL DAY.

Well I went down, mighty TO HER MAMA,
AND I KNOCKED ON, MAMA'S DOOR.
SHE COME A SLIPPIN', MIGHTY TO THE WINDOW,
LIKE A BLACK CAT SLIPPIN' ACROSS THE FLOOR.

She said, "Who's that, BANGIN' ON MY WINDOW?"
She said, "WHO'S THAT KNOCKIN' ON MY DOOR."
SHE SAID, SHE SAID, "GET AWAY YOU MISTREATER,
'CAUSE MY DAUGHTER DON'T WANT YOU NO MORE."

STARTED KICKIN' OUT WINDOWS, WOOO, AND A KNOCKIN'
    DOWN DOORS,
STARTED KICKIN' OUT WINDOWS, HUH! AND A KNOCKIN' DOWN
    DOORS.

Well I was ON MY WAY TO CALIFORNIA,
AND I STOPPED BY MEXICO.

I GOT ARRESTED FOUR MILES FROM MEMPHIS,
AND I WON'T GO THERE NO MORE.

HAD TO SLEEP IN THE JAILHOUSE, PARTNER, ALL NIGHT LONG,
    OH LORD,
HAD TO SLEEP IN THE JAILHOUSE, PARTNER, ALL NIGHT LONG.

Appendix 1: A Note on Nicknames

I have observed that while inmates in the Northern systems tend to keep the names they had when they came to prison, inmates in Southern prisons tend to develop nicknames for one another.

In Texas prisons there are racial differences in the way nicknames are applied. Many white inmates' nicknames are nothing more than word-plays on their real names (Lumpkin becomes "Lump-Lump"), while the Negroes' nicknames reflect anything from a personality conflict to a sentence length ("Slick-Jesus," "Ninety-Nine," "For-Life," and so forth). Some of the black inmates have *two* nicknames, one favorable and one unfavorable; the whites never have more than one. In general, the white nicknames are less favorable than the black nicknames. Often, I was told, the blacks will ignore an option to attack a defect—"I know one that's pretty fat and his nickname is not 'Fatty' but 'Solid.'"

In the free world we think sometimes that people fit their names, but that is usually an illusion—there *are* large, tough, hairy Elmers—but the name bestowed in the informal rechristening of a totally enclosed folk community such as a Southern prison is often painfully appropriate. In many instances tales accompany the names to explain the genesis or justify their usage (see Jackson, 1967-A, for some of these). This is the case especially with guard nicknames (see, for example, "The Original Jack O Diamonds"). Inmate nicknames are used all the time and one not infrequently encounters men whose free world names are unknown in the prison population; guard nicknames are never used when addressing guards, but are almost always used in inmate conversations about them.

Several of the inmates named here have nicknames. I doubt that very many inmates at Ellis would know who Joseph Johnson was, but almost anyone in the TDC knows all about "Chinaman." He got the nickname because he has prominent high cheekbones and slightly tilted eyes, a result of some Indian genetic admixture. Willie Craig got his nickname, "Cowboy," because he has done a lot of rodeo riding (he competes, and usually places well, every year in the prison rodeo), not the sort of thing that would get a white man such a nickname but distinctive enough in the Southwest where no black bronc rider—no matter how good—has ever been named champion. Marshall Phillips' nickname was "Ten-Four," which he says he got because he was arrested in a stolen police car after he tried to shut up its radio by hollering "Ten four! ten four!" into the microphone as he had seen policemen do when they had arrested him on other occasions. "Bacon and Porkchop" got his nickname because, he says, he used to steal them whenever he could.

I think the inmates' nicknames for guards are particularly important. There is a certain power people feel when they can *name* something. (Think how comfortable people are when they have a psychological name for a friend's aberration, and how spooked they act when all they know is their friend is acting "oddly"; think how important it is for Americans to hang political labels on people who present dissenting political views—the label emasculates the potentially dangerous arguments.) The motif of the power of the name is quite old, and there are still tribes in the world where a person is given two names at birth, one his real name, the other a name that people can use; the real name is kept secret so no one can curse him with it. In prison it is of course the other way around: the second name is the one that is used to bring the guard into the convicts' mental economy; the nickname is always hung on a single characteristic, and it limits the kind of worrying done about that person or tags him in a slightly belittling way.

Appendix 2: Responsorial Patterns

There are dozens of different patterns for the relationship between the lines sung by the leader and the lines sung by the group. These are *not* antiphonal relationships (which implies a back-and-forth between *groups*) but rather call-and-response relationships. The following are some of the patterns found in the Texas convicts' songs. (See Courlander, 1963-B, pp. 92–94, for structures he found in his examinations of Southern Negro materials.)

	Leader	Group	
	Leader	Group	
1.	A	b	Leader sings line, group sings burden; leader repeats the line, group sings burden; leader sings new line, group sings burden, and so forth. See 25. "Jolly" and 36. "I Need Another Witness."
	A	b	
	C	b	
	C	b	
2.	A	b	Leader sings line, group sings burden; group sings the repeat of the leader's line and second burden; leader sings new line, group sings first burden, and so forth. See 40-A. "I'm in the Bottom."
		a	
		c	
	D	b	
		d	
		c	
3.	A	b	Leader sings half-line, group finishes the line with burden; group repeats the whole line with burden twice, then sings chorus line. See 41-C. "Plumb the Line."
		ab	
		ab	
		c	
	D	b	
		db	
		db	
		c	

4.	A	b	Leader sings line, group sings first burden; leader sings second line, group sings second burden; leader sings first line, group sings second line. See 21-C. "Go Down Old Hannah."
	C	d	
	A	c	

5.	AB	b	Leader sings two-phrase line, group repeats second phrase; leader repeats the first two-phrase line; leader sings second two-phrase line, group repeats second phrase of that line. See 22-A. "Shorty George."
	AB		
	CD	d	

6.	A,A	b	Leader sings line of one phrase and repeats, group sings burden; leader sings new line of one phrase and repeats, group sings burden, and so forth. See 24. "Old Aunt Dinah."
	C,C,	b	
	D,D,	b	

7.	A	b	Leader sings first half line, group finishes the line; group repeats the whole line twice; group sings new fourth line. See 57-A. "Raise 'em up Higher."
		ab	
		ab	
		c	

8.	A	a	Leader sings line and group repeats line; leader sings new line, group repeats new line, and so forth. After a number of these there may be a chorus. See 20-A. "Stewball" or 39-B. "Lost John."
	B	b	
	C	c	

9.	A	b	Group sings same burden, leader sings different lead line each time. See 17. "Grey Goose," 35-A. "Jody," 62-A. "Rattler."
	C	b	

10.	A	b	Leader sings line, group sings first burden; leader repeats line, group sings second burden; leader sings new line, group sings first burden; leader repeats new line, group sings second burden. See 19. "Pick a Bale a Cotton," 54-A. "I Got the Crane Wing."
	A	c	
	D	b	
	D	c	

11.	A	b	Leader sings half line, group completes it; leader sings second half-line, group completes it. No repetition, no burden. See 48-C. "Haming on a Live Oak Log."
	C	d	
	E	f	

12.	A		Leader sings first line; group sings next three lines. (They may be repeats or new lines.) See 65. "On My Way to Mexico."
		b	
		c	
		d	

13.   A   Leader sings full two-line stanza; group re-
       B   peats the two lines. See 63-A. "Black Gal."
                a
                b

There are other patterns, but the above should give some idea of the range of involvement, the variety of structure. In all the above the leader has the option of whether or not to join the group in its parts, especially when there is a direct repeat or chorus.

Glossary

A number of the terms and persons defined or identified in this list are discussed by the inmates in "One Lost Valley."

Aggie. Hoe.

Backgrounders. All singers in a group *except* the leader.

Bat. Strip of leather, twenty-four inches long and four inches wide, used in the old days for whipping inmates. Also called the *red heifer*.

Beartracks, The Track. Nickname of Carl Luther McAdams, presently warden of Wynne Unit, previously warden of Retrieve, Ramsey, and Ellis. See 37. "Grizzly Bear."

Beto, George. Director of the TDC since the death of O. B. Ellis in 1961.

Big bell. Bell rung to signal the men out to work in the morning and after the noon meal; still used on some of the farms.

Black Annie. One name for the truck driven by Bud Russel (see below) to take men from the county jail to prison after trial.

Black Betty. Another name for Bud Russel's truck; more frequently used for the truck that takes inmates from one prison unit to another.

Boss. Prison guard.

Bottom. Rich, alluvial farm land near the rivers.

Brazos River. Begins at the intersection of the White and Double Mountain Fork rivers, about sixty miles north of Abilene; it runs north a little bit, then turns south, passes about thirty-five miles west of Fort Worth, goes through Waco, Navasota, and Brenham, passes a few miles west of Houston, and reaches the sea at Freeport. The river winds through all the southern units of the prison system (Ramsey, Retrieve, Darrington, Sugarland, Central, and Jester) and it serves as an important image in many of the songs. In fact, the contiguity of the Brazos is why the work songs are called *river songs* by the convicts.

Bring. Force someone to do something.

Bud. See *Russel, Bud.*

Build a cholley. Call for someone to make a small fire in a work area.

Building tender. Inmates who are in charge of the prison wings.

Bull Durham. Rolling tobacco issued to inmates.

Bullin'. Hardworking; bullying.

Bully. Inmate working in the line.

Calling them. Singing lead.

Captain. One of the ranks in the guard hierarchy, usually the man in charge of half the work force in the field. In the old days a captain was in charge

311

of each camp. (See entry for *rider.*) The term was used extensively in the South in the free world (meaning the white boss) and may derive from that.

Carry. Be in charge of, take on the work of. "The boss carrying the squad" is the boss in charge of the squad; "I can't carry you" means "I can't do your work for you."

Catch the hall. When a man commits an infraction of the rules in the field, he is told to "catch the hall" when he returns to the building that night, that is, wait to see the major for a summary trial.

Chain. A group of prisoners being transferred from one institution to another. When someone says "I'm going to catch the chain" without indicating a new institutional assignment, he usually means he is going home.

Chock. Beer brewed by inmates in a variety of unused cavities (boots, jars, toilet bowls, etc.).

Crane wing. If one's axe doesn't hit straight down when cutting up logs it sometimes lifts a long splinter out of the surface of the log. That splinter is the *crane wing.*

Cunningham. J. B. Cunningham was transfer agent for the Texas Prison System for a short time around 1910 (see entry for *Russel, Bud*). An A. J. Cunningham was the first man to lease convicts from the TPS, in the early 1870's, but it is unlikely that the songs refer to him.

Diamond. Axe.

Dobie. Dumpling.

Dog boy, dog sergeant. See *rider.*

Dozens. Formulaic insults in oral tradition of black youths, mainly in urban areas. The insults focus on sexual excesses and perversions of female members of the opponent's family.

Eating on the Johnny. Having a meal in the fields. See *John Henry.*

Ellis, O. B. Director of Texas Department of Corrections, 1948–1961; generally credited with bringing the Texas prisons into the twentieth century.

Flatweeding. Working with hoes.

Go down. Work to exhaustion.

Go my bail. Speak up on my behalf.

Haming. Working, probably derives from an elision of *hammering.*

Hammer. Axe.

Hammering. Working with an axe; sometimes the word means working in the fields.

Hang. When the axe sticks in the tree.

High rider. The one guard in any large work area who is armed with a rifle; he positions himself a distance from the work force and the other guards, so he can have a view of the whole area and have a shot at anyone moving out of that area.

Jack. Call for a pause in working, name for a rest break. "As you cut, chips pile up under there. You jack and brush the chips away where you can see what you doing. Those chips pile up in there, they liable to pile up and hit somebody in the eye. Sometimes you holler, 'Way, Jack!' And that means you're gonna rest. You do like that and take two or three minutes' rest, then you start back to singing again. And if there ain't no Jack, the man say, 'There ain't no jackin' till the timber start to crackin'.' That means keep on till the tree falls."

Jack O Diamonds. Guard in the 1940's who carried a Luger and was reputed to have killed more inmates than anyone else. (See "One Lost Valley" for extensive inmate comments about him.)

Jesse James. See *Seefus, Jesse James.*

John Henry. The wagon that brings food to the men when they eat in the fields. Known also as the *Johnny Wagon.* A note in the TDC *Newsletter,* July 1, 1964, says: "Mr. J. B. Floyd of the Print Shop found this version of the way 'John Henry' originated in a book entitled *25 Years Behind Prison Bars.* 'I was told by an old guard who began guarding prisoners in 1864 that the first dinner wagon was driven by an old man called John Henry and since that time meals carried to men working have been called 'John Henrys.' According to Mr. Floyd, Bill Mills, author of the book, is an ex-convict who started serving time in the Texas Prison System in 1910." No inmate I questioned connects this term with the protagonist of the well-known song.

Lead row. First man in a squad, usually the best worker; the *tail row,* usually the next best worker, is located at the far end of the squad from the lead row, and the men between are expected to keep up with the two end men. The man working next to the lead row is called the *push row.* "They carry most of the slower men in the squad about in the center. Put their fastest mens on the outside where they keep 'em in a swing. Then the guard usualy rides about center of the squad, that to kind of keep the others pushed up. They have lead rows in each squad."

Levee camp. A settlement around a landing place on a river.

Line. The groups of men working in the fields on any particular day.

Major. See entry for *rider.*

Middle. Planted areas between turnrows.

Mojo. A mojo in black folk magic is supposed to give the individual possessing it superior powers, often sexual. J. B. Smith defined his use of the term in song: "Mojo hands: that's a boy gone to them witch doctors, hoodoo people, that believe in them. We use the term mojo hand for a guy that seems to have something extraordinary or can do something the other fellas can't hardly do, or he holds out longer. The lead row fellas here, the lead row bullies, is usually got long wind and they can work, work, and work. And it's hard for the pull-dos to keep up with them."

Peckerwood Hill. The name given the prison graveyard for inmates whose bodies are not claimed by a family member. When I first saw Ramsey's Peckerwood Hill most of the graves had no marker (it's been straightened up some since), and there was no way of telling how many men were buried there, how they died, or how long they had been interred. I asked a guard why it was called Peckerwood Hill, and he said, "I don't know. It's always been called that." I later asked some inmates the same question, and one said, "What kinda bird don't fly? A bird what's on Peckerwood Hill." The men around him laughed, and he acted as if he had answered my question; I guess he did.

Picket. Guard towers surrounding the dormitory compounds; also the small control room in the central hallway of each prison.

Pull-do. An incompetent worker, someone who shirks or makes too many mistakes, someone who can't pull his own weight in a squad.

Punch it. Escape.

Rattler. The original tracking hound, the one who can follow any trail, walk a log, swim the treacherous Brazos river. There is a well known song about him (62), and he is sometimes mentioned in other songs. I've been told that it is traditional to name at least one dog on each farm "Rattler." See the note for song 62 for more about the name.

Red heifer. Another name for the *bat* (see above).

Rice Hotel. A hotel in Houston, at one time rather posh.

Ride. Give someone a hard time.

Rider. When the men work in the fields they are watched by at least one, and usually several, guards on horseback, all of whom are called riders. The *high rider* (see above) is the only rider armed with a rifle; he is positioned away from the workforce so he can have a better view of the area (and so no one can get the jump on him). A captain will be in charge of a large work area; there are usually two majors, one in charge of the building and the other in charge of the entire field force (in the old days, before shifting to the warden system, the prisons were each in the charge of a major, the individual camps under a captain). Accompanying the men to the fields is a pack of tracking dogs handled by the inmate *dog boy,* supervised by the guard *dog sergeant.*

River. The Brazos, mostly, since all the southern TDC farms are touched by it. (The farms around Huntsville—Ellis and Eastham—are on the Trinity, but Ellis is a relatively new prison and Eastham's population was never large enough or interested enough to get the Trinity into the song repertory). There are many images of making it to the river and crossing over (song 7 ends, after a statement about going to the river, "Sergeant, sergeant, you can blow your horn, /I'll be long gone to the promised land.") In the old days, the river was as much an obstacle to the guards as it was to the escaping convicts: the Brazos is too treacherous to trust a good horse in, and a man who swam it had a good chance of staying loose for a little while. Before radio communication, it was hard for the pursuers to catch up if an inmate crossed over, and the dogs would have to be relocated to pick up his trail again (walkie-talkies, as is pointed out in the inmate comments, have changed that). But there is also something of the spirituals' tradition of the function of a river, the folkloristic motif of the transmogrifying capability of a body of dangerous water.

River song. The Texas convicts' name for the songs they do at work. Called "river song" because it was down on the river bottoms where the work was done.

Rock. Sing while working.

Rollin'. Working.

Russel, Uncle Bud. Bud Russel, was for years the prison's transfer agent, the man who would travel around the state to bring prisoners from the county jails to Huntsville. Russel joined the system in 1908 as assistant to John Luther, then transfer agent of the Texas Penitentiary; Luther was succeded by J. B. Cunningham and Russel continued as assistant. In 1912 he became transfer agent himself and held the job for forty years. He handled 115,000 prisoners (summarized from Simmons, p. 180).

J. B. Smith said of him:

"He's the first man that brought me to the penitentiary. In nineteen and thirty-eight. He's the first man that rode me down from Dallas County Jail. Two years. Bud Russel. Put a chain on your neck and a lock—little Yale lock. Turn your collar up and say, 'All right, boys, get ready to put on this necktie.' A Yale lock and a chain and you had a throw chain he'd run through the whole line. If one guy run, he got to carry the whole bunch with him. You can't do it, he had you. Bud Russel, he worked here for quite a few years. I thought it was just talk when I first heard of Bud Russel, but there actually was one. Don't know what the Bud means, but he was rustle."

Another inmate, listening, said, "The name is still used throughout the system: 'Well, let's go get Uncle Bud's Cotton,' or 'Let's get some a Uncle Bud's cows.' Whatever it might be, it's still used."

"Just like 'Uncle Sam,' Smith said.

Seefus, Jesse James. Has the reputation of being the fastest cotton picker ever to be an inmate in the TDC. I had heard about him for several years, and when I was told he was a participant at a prison rodeo I attended one year, I asked one of the inmates to point him out to me. The inmate said he would, but asked a favor: Seefus had for years told everyone he had been arrested by Sky King and had been brought in after his capture in Sky King's airplane; the inmate would introduce me to Seefus, but would it be all right if he said I was Sky King? I agreed and after one of the events he brought Seefus over to where I was sitting by the chutes and said, "Jesse James, here's the fella that wanted to see you. You remember him, don't you? It's Sky King."

Seefus looked at me, nodded, stuck out his hand, said, "Hiya, Mr. Sky King, nice to see you again," and walked away. The other inmate muttered and did the same.

Seefus's name appears in a number of the songs. J. B. Smith sang one stanza about him (song 31, stanza 55), about which he said, "Jesse James Seefus, he claims himself a walkin' electric chair in the cotton patch. He say, 'I'll 'lexecute anybody that keeps up with me. Picks as much cotton as I do.' "

"He'll get them or picking that much cotton will?"

"Working. If you try to stay with him. He's a eight or nine hundred pound picker. I saw him in a two-man squad. Sergeant carried him and another boy from my home town, Johnny Thomas, he's in the free world now. He picked like Jesse James. Sometimes they'd take three rows together, sometimes they'd take one apiece, sometimes they take two, depending how they catch them and the condition the cotton is in."

"How much cotton does a regular man pick?"

"The high squads, they pick 350 or 400. They don't have to pick that much now. You can get in on a couple of hundred pounds now."

Sergeant. See *rider*.

Shake it, Jake! Call for rain; inmates will sometimes shout this just as it starts to rain. The image is slightly scatalogical.

Simmons, Lee. General Manager of the Texas Prison System 1930–1935; advocate of the *bat* and other forms of corporal punishment; man who set up the killing of Bonnie and Clyde.

Singletree. Beam used for hitching mule to cart.

Skinner. Man who handles muleteams.

Strain. Work area.

Stuck out. Away from one's group.

Tail row. See *lead row*.

Tamp. Work; probably derives from railroad usage of "tie-tamping," but in prison it means work with any instrument.

Tighten up. Work more closely together, work faster.

Timber gettin' limber. Call indicating that a tree is getting ready to fall, it has begun swaying back and forth.

Turnrow. Road around a large planted area.

Uncle Bud. See *Bud Russel*.

Walls, The. The main unit of the prison system in Huntsville, the only unit with walls (all the others have cyclone fences topped with barbed-wire and guard towers surrounding the building compound), the only one without a farm.

Wing. The top of the tree, the part with the branches; a section of the buildings. (Not the same as *crane wing,* see above *q.v.*)

Yella dent corn. Over ripe corn.

Works Cited

A. BOOKS AND ARTICLES

Abrahams, Roger D. 1964. *Deep Down in the Jungle . . . Negro Narrative Folklore from the Streets of Philadelphia.* Hatboro, Pa., Folkore Associates.

Allen, William F., C. P. Ware, and L. M. Garrison. 1867. *Slave Songs of the United States.* New York (Reprinted, New York, Peter Smith 1951).

Asch, Moses, and Alan Lomax, eds. 1962. *The Leadbelly Songbook.* New York, Oak Publications.

Bate, Walter Jackson. 1952. *Criticism: The Major Texts.* New York, Harcourt, Brace.

Botkin, Benjamin A. 1944. *Treasury of American Folklore.* New York, Crown.

Brakeley, Theresa C. 1950. "Work Song." In Maria Leach, 1950, 1181–1184.

Brandel, Rose. 1961. *The Music of Central Africa.* The Hague, M. Nijoff.

Brown, John Mason. 1868. "Songs of the Slave." In *Lippincott's Magazine,* 2 (December), 617–623. (Reprinted in Jackson, 1967-B, 109–118).

Buckley, Bruce. 1953. " 'Uncle' Ira Cephas—A Negro Folk Singer in Ohio." *Midwest Folklore,* 3:5–18.

Burke, Kenneth. 1966. *Language as Symbolic Action.* Berkely, University of California Press.

Carey, George C. 1965. "A Collection of Airborne Cadence Chants." *Journal of American Folklore,* 77:52–61.

Chappell, Louis W. 1933. *John Henry: A Folk Lore Study.* Jena, Frommann-sche Verlag, Walter Biedermann.

Charters, Samuel B. 1955. *The Country Blues.* New York, Rinehart.

Check-List of Recorded Songs in the English Language in the Archive of American Folk Songs to July, 1940. 1942. 2 vols. Library of Congress, Music Division. Washington, D.C.

Colcord, Joanna C. 1964. *Songs of American Sailormen.* New York, Oak Publications. (Reprint of *Roll and Go, Songs of American Sailormen.* 1924. Indianapolis.)

Courlander, Harold. 1963-A. *Negro Songs from Alabama.* 2nd. ed. New York, Oak Publications.

—— 1963-B. *Negro Folk Music, U.S.A.* New York, Columbia University Press.

Dorson, Richard M. 1965. "The Career of John Henry." *Western Folklore,* 24:155–168.

—— 1967. *American Negro Folktales.* New York, Fawcett.

Faulkner, William. 1962. *The Reivers.* New York, Random House.

Gordon, Robert Winslow. 1938. *Folk-Songs of America.* National Service Bureau publication 73-S, mimeo. Sponsored by the Joint Committee on Folk Arts, WPA, Federal Theatre Project. (Original versions of fifteen articles that appeared in edited form in the *New York Times,* between January 2, 1927 and January 22, 1928.)

317

Guthrie, Woody. 1966. *Born to Win*. New York, Macmillan.

Harlow, Frederick Pease. 1962. *Chanteying Abroad American Ships*. Barre, Mass., Barre Gazette.

Hugill, Stan. 1961. *Shanties from the Seven Seas*. London, Routledge and Kegan Paul, and New York, Dutton.

Huntington, Gale. 1964. *Songs the Whalemen Sang*. Barre, Mass., Barre.

Jackson, Bruce. 1966-A. "Who Goes to Prison: Caste and Careerism in Crime." *Atlantic Monthly*, 217 (January), 52–57.

———— ed. 1966-B. *Folklore and Society*. Hatboro, Folklore Associates.

———— 1967-A. "Prison Nicknames." *Western Folklore* 26 (January), 48–54.

————1967-B. *The Negro and His Folklore in Nineteenth Century Periodicals*. Publications of the American Folklore Society, *Bibliographical and Special Series*, 18. Austin.

———— 1967-C. "Prison Worksongs: The Composer in Negatives." *Western Folklore* 26 (October), 245–268.

———— 1967-D. "What Happened to Jody." *Journal of American Folklore*, 80 (October–December), 387–396.

Johnson, Guy B. 1927. *John Henry: Tracking Down a Negro Legend*. Chapel Hill, University of North Carolina Press.

Johnson, James Weldon, and J. Rosamond Johnson. 1962. *The Books of American Negro Spirituals*. New York, Viking.

Laws, G. Malcom, Jr. 1964. *Native American Balladry*. Rev. ed. Publications of the American Folklore Society, *Bibliographical and Special Series*, 1. Philadelphia.

Leach, MacEdward. 1966. "John Henry." In Jackson, 1966-B, 93–106.

Leach, Maria. 1950. 2 vols. *Standard Dictionary of Folklore, Mythology and Legend*. New York, Funk and Wagnalls.

Lomax MS. Collected Papers of John A. Lomax in the Texas Archives at the University of Texas. Boxes A/9–142 and A/9–143 ("Ms. Negro religious and miscellaneous ballads"), A/9–144 ("Miscellaneous Ballads"), A/9–152 ("Bawdy"), and A/9–154 ("Iron Head, Prison Ballads").

Lomax Notes. "Notes by John A. and Ruby T. Lomax, for 'Southern Recording Trip,' March 31–June 14, 1939." Archive of Folk Song, Library of Congress, AFS 2589–2728.

Lomax, Alan. 1960. *The Folksongs of North America*. Garden City, Doubleday.

Lomax, John. 1946. *The Adventures of a Ballad Hunter*. New York, Macmillan.

Lomax, John A., and Alan Lomax. 1936-A. *American Ballads and Folk Songs*. New York, Macmillan.

———— 1936-B. *Negro Folk Songs as Sung by Lead Belly*. New York, Macmillan.

———— 1941. *Our Singing Country*. New York, Macmillan.

Lord, Albert. 1960. *The Singer of Tales*. Cambridge, Mass., Harvard University Press.

Merriam, Alan P. 1962. "The African Idiom in Music." *Journal of American Folklore*, 75, 120–130.

Merriam, Alan P. 1964. *The Anthropology of Music*. Evanston, Northwestern University Press.

Nketia, J. H. Kwabena. 1963. *African Music in Ghana*. Legon, Ghana University Press.

Odum, Howard W., and Guy B. Johnson. 1925. *The Negro and His Songs*. Chapel Hill. University of North Carolina Press.

———— 1926. *Negro Workaday Songs*. Chapel Hill, University of North Carolina Press.

Oliver, Paul. 1960. *Blues Fell This Morning*. London, Cassell.

Parrish, Lydia. 1942. *Slave Songs of the Georgia Sea Islands*. New York, Farrar, Straus.

Puckett, Newbell N. 1926. *Folk Beliefs of the Southern Negro*. Chapel Hill, University of North Carolina Press.

Scarborough, Dorothy. 1925. *On the Trail of Negro Folk-Songs.* Cambridge, Mass., Harvard University Press.

Simmons, Lee. 1957. *Assignment Huntsville: Memoirs of a Texas Prison Official.* Austin, University of Texas Press.

Talley, Thomas W. 1922. *Negro Folk Rhymes.* New York, Macmillan.

Thanet, Octave. 1892. "Folk-Lore in Arkansas." *Journal of American Folklore,* 5: 120–125.

Texas Department of Corrections. 1968. *A Brief History.* Huntsville, Texas.

Texas Department of Corrections. 1967. *20-Year Progress Report.* Huntsville, Texas.

Texas Department of Corrections Newsletter. July 1, 1964. Huntsville, Texas.

Van Deusen, John G. 1944. The *Black Man in White America.* Washington, D.C., Associated Publishers.

Waterman, Richard. 1948. "Hot Rhythm in Negro Music." *Journal of the American Musicological Society,* 1: 24–37. (Reprinted in *Acculturation in the Americas,* edited by Sol Tax. Proceedings of the 29th International Congress of Americanists, vol. 2, 1952, pp. 207–218.)

Webb, Walter Prescott, ed. 1952. *The Handbook of Texas.* 2 vols. Austin, Texas State Historical Association.

White, Newman I. 1928. *American Negro Folk-Songs,* Cambridge, Mass., Harvard University Press.

Work, John W., ed. 1940. *American Negro Songs and Spirituals.* New York, Bonanza.

B. RECORDINGS

Anthology LPs are listed by album title; titles in italics are LP albums, titles in quotation marks are 78 or 45 rpm singles. These are discs cited in this book only; for a more ranging discography of Afro-American folk music, see Courlander, 1963-B, pp. 302–308.

Afro-American Blues and Game Songs. Archive of American Folk Song L-4. Edited by Alan Lomax.

Afro-American Spirituals, Work Songs, and Ballads. Archive of American Folk Song L-3. Edited by Alan Lomax.

Alexander, Texas. "Levee Camp Moan." On *The Country Blues,* RBF-9.

American Folk Music III. Folkways FA-2953. Edited by Harry Smith.

Anglo-American Ballads. Archive of American Folk Song L-1. Edited by Alan Lomax.

Angola Prison Spirituals. Folk-Lyric LFS A-6. Collected and edited by Harry Oster.

Angola Prisoners' Blues. Folk-Lyric LFS A-3. Collected and edited by Harry Oster.

Belafonte, Harry. *Swing Dat Hammer.* RCA LPS-2194.

Bibb, Leon. *Tol' My Captain.* Vanguard VRS-9058.

The Blues at Newport, I, 1964. Vanguard VRS-9180.

Boyd, Eddie. "Third Degree." Chess V-4374.

Broonzy, Big Bill. *Last Sessions: Part Three.* Verve V-3003.

Country Blues, The. RBF-9. Edited by Samuel Charters.

Hopkins, Lightnin'. *Fast Life Woman.* Verve V-8453.

Hurt, John. "Spike Driver Blues." Okeh 8692. (Repub. on *American Folk Music III*)

James, Skip. *Devil Got My Woman.* Vanguard VSD-79723.

Jazz: The South. Folkways FJ-2801. Edited by Frederick Ramsey, Jr.

Ledbetter, Huddie. *Last Sessions.* Folkways FA-2941 and FA-2942. Edited by Frederick Ramsey, Jr.

—— *Leadbelly Legacy:* four ten-inch Folkways LPs—FA-2004 (*Take This Hammer*), FA-2014 (*Rock Island Line*), FA-2024 (*Leadbelly Legacy 3*), and FA-2034 (*Easy Rider*). Republished as two twelve-inch LPs: *Leadbelly Legacy 1*, FA-2941, and *Leadbelly Legacy 2*, FA-2942.

———— *Leadbelly: The Library of Congress Recordings*. Elektra EKL 301/2. Edited by Lawrence Cohn from original recordings made by John A. Lomax.

———— *Leadbelly Memorial*. Stinson 17, 19, 48, 51. Four LPs.

———— *Play Party Songs*. Stinson SLPX-39.

———— *Leadbelly Sings Folksongs*. (With Woody Guthrie, et al.) Folkways FA-2488.

———— *Ledbetter's Best*. Capitol F-1821.

Negro Folklore from Texas State Prisons. Elektra EKS-7296. Collected and edited by Bruce Jackson.

Negro Folk Music of Alabama. Folkways FE-4417, FE-4418, FE-4471, FE-4472, FE-4473, FE-4474. Collected and edited by Harold Courlander.

Negro Prison Camp Work Songs. Folkways P-475. (Republished as FE-4475.) Recorded by Toshi and Peter Seeger, John Lomax, Jr., Chester Bowes, and Fred Hellerman.

Negro Prison Songs from the Mississippi State Penitentiary. Tradition TLP-1020. Collected and edited by Alan Lomax.

Negro Religious Songs and Services. Archive of American Folk Song L-10. Edited by Benjamin A. Botkin.

Negro Work Songs and Calls. Archive of American Folk Song L-8. Edited by Benjamin A. Botkin.

Niles, John Jacob. *John Jacob Niles*. Folkways FA-2373.

Patton, Charlie. *The Immortal Charlie Patton*. Origin Jazz Library OJL-1.

Prison Worksongs. Folk-Lyric LFS A-5. Collected and edited by Harry Oster.

Rhodes, Eugene. *"Talkin' About My Time."* Folk Legacy FSA-12. Recorded and edited by Bruce Jackson.

Shelton, B. F. "Cold Penitentiary Blues." Victor 40107.

Smith, J. B. *Ever Since I Have Been a Man Full Grown*. Takoma B-1009. Collected and edited by Bruce Jackson.

Thomas, Henry. *Henry Thomas Sings the Texas Blues*. Origin Jazz Library OJL-3.

Treasury of Field Recording, I. Candid 8026. Edited by Mack McCormick.

Treasury of Field Recording, II. 77 Records 77LA-12/3. Edited by Mack McCormick.

Unexpurgated Folk Songs of Men. (No recording company or record number given on album or disc.) Collected and edited by Mack McCormick.

We Shall Not be Moved: Songs of the "Freedom Riders" and the "Sit-Ins." Folkways FH-5591.

Yazoo Delta . . . Blues and Spirituals. Prestige 25010. Collected and edited by Alan Lomax.

Alphabetical List of Songs

Index of Names